Emerging Systems for Managing Workplace Conflict

David B. Lipsky

Ronald L. Seeber

Richard D. Fincher

Emerging Systems for Managing Workplace Conflict

Lessons from American Corporations
for Managers and Dispute
Resolution Professionals

JOSSEY-BASS
A Wiley Imprint
www.josseybass.com

Published by Jossey-Bass
A Wiley Imprint
989 Market Street, San Francisco, CA 94103–1741   www.josseybass.com

Jossey-Bass books and products are available through most bookstores. To contact Jossey-Bass
directly call our Customer Care Department within the U.S. at (800) 956–7739, outside the
U.S. at (317) 572–3986 or fax (317) 572–4002.

Jossey-Bass also publishes its books in a variety of electronic formats. Some content that
appears in print may not be available in electronic books.

Library of Congress Cataloging-in-Publication Data

Lipsky, David B., date.
    Emerging systems for managing workplace conflict: lessons from American corporations
for managers and dispute resolution professionals/David B. Lipsky, Ronald L. Seeber,
Richard D. Fincher.
      p. cm.
    Includes bibliographical references and index.
    ISBN 0-7879-6434-4 (alk. paper)
    1. Conflict management. 2. Dispute resolution (Law) I. Seeber, Ronald Leroy.
II. Fincher, Richard D., date. III. Title.
HD42.L566 2002
658.4'053—dc21   2003002025

Printed in the United States of America
FIRST EDITION
HB Printing   10 9 8 7 6 5 4 3 2 1

Contents

Figures, Exhibits, and Tables

Figures

Exhibits

Tables

Preface

Managing conflict effectively has become a nearly universal concern. In this book, we discuss the ongoing search for better methods of managing and resolving workplace conflict. In Part One, we describe how dissatisfaction with traditional methods of resolving workplace disputes, such as litigation, has caused many U.S. employers to use alternative dispute resolution (ADR), especially mediation and arbitration. We discuss why the use of workplace ADR led some employers to develop workplace conflict management systems—to move beyond ADR to a more holistic, proactive approach. Analyzing the forces and factors at work in this move away from traditional techniques and toward a systems approach is the central concern of Part One.

In Part Two, we move from the "what" and "why" of conflict management systems to the "how." We describe how corporations and other organizations design, implement, and evaluate workplace conflict management systems. We describe the advantages and disadvantages of the options that organizations need to consider and, using material we have gathered from almost sixty corporations, explain how some organizations designed the systems they are using.

In Part Three, we consider the future of workplace conflict resolution. We focus first on the barriers to the growth of these systems and then on why we think these barriers will be overcome and the growth of systems will continue to occur.

THE BROADER CONTEXT FOR CONFLICT MANAGEMENT

Although our basic concern in this book is conflict management in the workplace, we recognize that almost everyone in the United States is affected by the efforts of our society, through both its governing bodies and private organizations, to manage and control conflict. Thus, we think it might be useful here to provide a broader context for the content of our book. Not only employers and employees but also sellers and buyers, lenders and borrowers, doctors and patients, parents and children, teachers and students, and the parties in almost any relationship are seeking new ways of reducing, if not eliminating, the disruptive effects of conflict.

Whenever the parties in a relationship do not share common values, objectives, and interests, conflict is likely to occur. In other words, conflict is inevitable in most relationships. That is not necessarily bad because constructive conflict can lead to innovative and durable solutions to problems that might not have been contemplated had the parties in that relationship fully shared the same values and objectives.

Conflict cannot always be channeled in a positive direction, however, and its costs frequently outweigh its benefits. The costs of conflict fall into at least four categories. First, there are the direct costs of conflict borne by the parties in a relationship—the money and time they devote to dealing with conflict. In employment litigation, for example, the most obvious direct costs are the costs to the parties of hiring attorneys, as well as the consultants and experts needed in many cases. In labor relations, when conflict results in a strike, the direct costs include the wages lost by the employees on strike and the revenues and profits lost by an employer forced to shut down his or her operation.

Second, there are the indirect costs borne by parties who are not directly involved in the relationship—what might be referred to as the innocent bystanders. This collateral damage caused by conflicts may be very grave indeed. The damages of wars, labor disputes, and the breakup of families are difficult to confine to the parties directly involved in the conflicts. Often civilians pay a heavier price than soldiers, customers lose more than employers and unions, and children are hurt more than parents in these disputes.

Third are opportunity costs associated with conflict. The resources and energy devoted to resolving conflicts could have been devoted to other productive endeavors. Fourth are costs associated with the damage that conflict does to interpersonal and interorganizational relationships. These relational costs have a financial dimension but are usually observed first as a toll on the emotional and psychological well-being of the parties affected by the conflict. Conflicts often permanently impair relationships, and this impairment can outlast any of the financial costs of the conflict. Serious conflicts are frequently associated with attitudes of distrust and hostility that color all future interactions between the parties. Often conflicts lead to the termination of relationships.

In the United States and other civil societies, the traditional means of managing and resolving conflict were based on several sources of authority. Agreement on common values and norms of behavior placed boundaries on the nature and extent of conflict. In the past, these values and norms usually had their roots in the religious beliefs and customs shared by the members of a society. Conflict was also controlled through the enactment of laws and their enforcement. Respect for the sanctity of law served as a significant constraint on overt forms of conflict. The court system provided forums in which disputes over the application and interpretation of laws could be resolved.

A shared recognition by members of society of the authority of private institutions also created limits on the incidence and intensity of conflict. Societies have always depended on the family to control and resolve conflicts (although family is often a source of many conflicts too). Religious institutions provided another important means of managing and resolving conflicts. Still other private sector organizations—corporations, unions, colleges, hospitals, and the like—had the authority to resolve, if not prevent, conflicts in the realms in which they operated. Many of these organizations either tried to avoid or ignore conflict, or they used their authority to punish those responsible for it.

For most of U.S. history, these various sources of authority were effective in managing and resolving conflict. There were periods in our history that were conspicuous exceptions to this generalization, of course—the Civil War, the depression of the 1930s, and the turbulent 1960s, to name three. In this book, we contend that the concept of the social contract is useful for understanding how methods of managing and resolving conflict change from one period to another. Ken Binmore provided one useful definition of the social contract:

> We are all players in the game of life, with divergent aims and aspirations that make conflict inevitable. In a healthy society, a balance between these differing aims and aspirations is achieved so that the benefits of cooperation are not entirely lost in internecine strife. Game theorists call such a balance an *equilibrium*. Sustaining such equilibria requires the existence of commonly understood conventions about how behavior is to be coordinated. It is such a system of coordinating conventions that I shall identify with a social contract.[1]

We maintain that the social contract that prevailed through most of the twentieth century in the United States was destabilized first by the social protests of the 1960s and the challenge those protests presented to traditional sources of authority and then by the forces of globalization, competition, and technological change that affected all aspects of U.S. society in the last quarter of the twentieth century. The decline in the authority of traditional institutions combined with the economic imperatives of globalization caused the traditional social contract to come unstuck and brought about the need for new approaches to conflict management and resolution. As the twentieth century drew to a close, it became increasingly apparent that a new social contract—a new "system of coordinating conventions"—was emerging. The traditional sources of authority, on which effective conflict resolution had depended in the past, were undergoing significant changes, and there was growing recognition of the need for new approaches to managing conflict.

It was in this context that ADR emerged in about the mid-1970s as a reaction to growing dissatisfaction with the U.S. court system. The perception that litigation was becoming increasingly costly, slow, and unresponsive to the needs of disputants led to a search for more efficient means of resolving conflict. One possible strategy was to reform the court system itself, and the push for tort reform in the 1980s and 1990s was one manifestation of this strategy. Reforming the court system, however, has had limited success and, in the view of most U.S. businesses, has not resulted in significant reductions in the time and cost of litigation. The research we report in this book demonstrates that U.S. corporations, especially, saw the use of ADR principally as a strategy of controlling the costs of disputes. As we show in Chapter Three, major U.S. corporations adopted ADR not only for employment disputes but also for a variety of other types of disputes, including commercial, product liability, intellectual property, and environmental disputes.

As an example, the purchase of a computer produced by any well-known manufacturer is accompanied by a warranty that requires that a purchaser who has a complaint about the product waive the right to sue the manufacturer in court and agree instead to have the dispute settled by arbitration under an arbitration scheme maintained by the manufacturer. The use of arbitration instead of the court system to resolve product liability claims is now a widespread practice in the sale of consumer durable goods. To cite another example, an organization we studied, Kaufman and Broad, one of the largest residential construction companies in the nation, includes in its contracts with buyers of its homes a clause that calls for the use of mediation and, in some cases, arbitration if the buyer has a complaint about the quality of the house he or she has purchased. (See the Glossary for definitions of *mediation* and *arbitration*.)

Another organization we studied, Kaiser Permanente, the largest health maintenance organization in the nation, requires patients to sign agreements under which they waive their right to sue Kaiser and its medical staff and instead mandates the use of arbitration to resolve allegations of medical malpractice and similar claims. One of the authors of this book recently leased a new Toyota and was not at all surprised to discover that the lease agreement required the use of arbitration to resolve product liability complaints the lessee might have against the auto manufacturer. He brought the provision to the attention of the dealer, who had no idea it was in the lease.

ADR has been called a quiet revolution in the administration of justice, and even today many people are unaware of how widespread its use is in our society. As a consequence of its use, a significant shift in the resolution of many types of disputes from the court system to private forums has taken place. Some observers have claimed that this shift represents the de facto privatization of our system of justice. An index of privatization is the declining trend in the use of trials to resolve disputes. Hope Viner Samborn reports a significant drop in federal trials over the past thirty years. In 1970, of the 127,280 civil and criminal cases filed in the federal courts, 10 percent were resolved after a jury or a bench trial; in 2001, of the 313,615 cases filed, only 2.2 percent were resolved by a jury or a bench trial. Evidence suggests similar trends in state courts. As Samborn notes, the growth of private dispute resolution "makes some jurists uneasy." Concerned jurists, Samborn reports, believe that private dispute resolution "shields lawsuits from the imposition of public values about important concerns, such as discrimination in the workplace, price fixing or unsafe products."[2] Nevertheless, most jurists acknowledge that private dispute resolution reduces costs, minimizes the use of scarce judicial resources, and produces reasonable results for the parties.[3]

At the heart of many of these debates about the merits of ADR is the question of whether it truly provides a level playing field for the disputants. Ironically, perhaps, resolving many of these debates will fall within the province of the court system. To date, the courts have generally supported the use of private dispute resolution to resolve public claims, but many legal questions remain unanswered. The courts are unlikely to reverse their support for ADR generally, but they will need to deal with questions of due process and procedural fairness in the use of private dispute resolution—for example, the right of the parties to have counsel, the concern about conflicts of interest and the need for disclosure, and the nature and limits of confidentiality in ADR procedures. In the end, we believe, the debate over the merits of ADR is not so much one over legal issues as it is one over values. What does our society believe about the various means of controlling and resolving conflict? What is the right balance between private and public methods of resolving conflict? In our collective striving to achieve a more just and humane society, does it matter whether the vehicle we use is a public or a private forum?

Indisputably, these are legitimate questions, and they need to be addressed. But our research strongly suggests that ADR is now firmly institutionalized in a majority of U.S. corporations, at least for employment and commercial disputes. We believe our society passed the tipping point in the use of ADR at some point in the 1990s. In the last chapter of the book, we discuss the fact that few, if any, organizations that adopt the use of ADR ever go back to older methods of resolving disputes. Indeed, we argue throughout the book that when organizations begin to use ADR, they tend to go forward rather than back. They move beyond the procedures and techniques of ADR and toward the use of a system, at least in the workplace. They begin their journey by attempting to manage litigation, then expand their concern to the management of disputes, and ultimately reach the point of systematically managing conflict. In our view, the question, at least for major employers in the United States, is not whether the journey will be undertaken but how long it will take to complete it.

OUR PERSONAL JOURNEY

We would like to add a word about our personal journey through this topic. Each of us has his professional roots in labor relations and human resource management. We have spent between twenty-five and thirty-five years apiece as teachers, researchers, and practitioners in our field. We have served as mediators, fact finders, and arbitrators in countless labor disputes, and we have served as consultants to numerous public and private sector organizations. But we acknowledge that we are relative newcomers in the realm of ADR and conflict management. Like many of our colleagues, we began to move from labor relations to ADR about a decade ago. When we made the transition, we had the naive view that what we needed to know about ADR we had largely learned through our experience with mediation, arbitration, and dispute resolution more generally in labor relations.

Before long, we discovered that the lessons we had learned in labor relations were not necessarily useful in ADR, even in workplace ADR. Although some of the lessons were indeed transferable, many others were not. We learned that many of the issues that have long been settled in labor relations have barely been formulated in ADR. Many of the practices that were well established—institutionalized—in labor relations either could not possibly be used in workplace ADR or were still being tested. Many of the differences between labor relations and workplace ADR stem from the fact that in the former, employees are represented, and often by strong and powerful organizations, and in the latter, they are not.

Representation or the absence of it, however, is not the only factor that distinguishes labor relations and workplace ADR. Arguably, it may not even be the major factor. Another obvious factor is the significant difference in the statutory framework supporting each form. The law of labor relations is largely federal in nature and has evolved over several decades to a point at which most major issues have been settled. Critical issues do occasionally arise, but their resolution usually has only marginal effects on practice. The law of workplace ADR, by contrast, is only partly based in federal statute (primarily the Federal Arbitration Act) and is largely a matter for state control. It has mainly emerged only within the past twenty-five years, and there are still critical issues that need to be decided that can be expected to have significant effects on practice.

There are obvious differences also between traditional labor relations practitioners and workplace ADR practitioners. One needs only to attend the meetings of professional societies in the two fields to understand these differences. They are related to age, race, gender, and experience; in labor relations, there is less diversity among practitioners than there is in ADR. There also seem to be cultural differences between the two fields, partly the result of differences in the degree of diversity but also partly because of other factors. In labor relations, institutions (and most of the practitioners) have reached maturity and, some believe, may be in decline. Opportunities to enter the practice of labor relations are limited. Some believe the future of labor relations is bleak, and one sometimes encounters a sense of hopelessness in the field. In workplace ADR, institutions are only now being established, and there are a growing number of opportunities, particularly for young people, to embark on a career in the field. There is the expectation that ADR will continue to expand in the future, leading to an attitude of hope rather than despair among practitioners. The feeling we had when we moved from labor relations to ADR was not unlike the feeling immigrants must have had a century ago when they left the traditional and often rigid societies of the Old World for the opportunities they expected to find in the growing and dynamic United States.

Our intellectual journey into ADR and beyond to conflict management systems has been an exciting one. Along the way, we have encountered many new ideas, many new problems that need solutions, and many challenges. We view this book, the culmination of over six years of intensive research, as a personal milestone in our intellectual travels through uncharted domains.

ACKNOWLEDGMENTS

A six-year project like this one could not have been completed without the cooperation and assistance of numerous individuals and organizations. The origins of this project date to the spring of

1996, when Cornell president Hunter Rawlings and provost Don Randel approved the establishment of the Institute on Conflict Resolution at the School of Industrial and Labor Relations (ILR). We are indebted to them and also to Edward J. Lawler, dean of the ILR School, for their support of our efforts down through the years. It was the support and counsel of Ted Kheel, president of the Foundation for Prevention and Early Resolution of Conflict and one of the nation's most renowned mediators and arbitrators, that made the establishment of the institute possible. The idea of undertaking a study of the use of ADR by U.S. corporations grew out of discussions that we had with Ted and also with William Lurie, past president of the Business Roundtable, and Tom Donahue, past president of the AFL-CIO. We are indebted to them for their encouragement and guidance. We also acknowledge the help and support of PriceWaterhouseCoopers in the early stages of this project and especially thank Fred Roffman, who served as director of marketing during the first phase of the study.

We are grateful for the funding that we received from several organizations. Part of our research was funded by a grant provided by the William and Flora Hewlett Foundation. We thank Stephen Toben and other officers of the foundation for their support of our efforts. We also thank the Research and Education Foundation of the National Academy of Arbitrators for its financial support and are grateful for funding provided by the School of Industrial and Labor Relations.

This book is based primarily on the results of a survey we conducted of the general counsel of the Fortune 1000 and on-site interviews with executives, managers, and attorneys in approximately sixty organizations. We are deeply indebted to the more than seven hundred individuals who participated in our survey and interviews. We acknowledge our reliance on the pioneering work of the Society of Professionals in Dispute Resolution (now the Association for Conflict Resolution) and the members of its ADR in the Workplace Initiative who drafted *Designing Integrated Conflict Management Systems: Guidelines for Practitioners and Decision*

Makers in Organizations. Our definition of a conflict management system is drawn directly from this report.

We have benefited greatly from conversations we have had over the years with a distinguished group of people who share our interests: Myrna Adams, Reginald Alleyne, John Bickerman, Lisa Bingham, Norm Brand, Joan Dolan, John Dunlop, Sharon Henderson Ellis, David Feller, Joe Gentile, Walter Gershenfeld, Alvin Goldman, Ann Gosline, Cynthia Hallberlin, Ralph Hasson, James Henry, Carole Houk, Homer LaRue, Randy Lowry, Jennifer Lynch, Susan Mackenzie, Bernard Mayer, Robert McKersie, Nancy Peace, Peter Phillips, Michel Picher, Chris Sickles Merchant, Peter Robinson, Mary Rowe, Anthony Sinicropi, Carl Slaikeu, Lamont Stallworth, Tom Stipanowich, Anne Thomas, William J. Usery, and Ellen Wolf.

We owe a very special debt to Lavinia Hall, who served as deputy director of the Institute on Conflict Resolution from 1997 to 2000 and continues to serve as a consultant to the institute. Lavinia played a key role in shaping the research project on which this book is based. She conducted many of the interviews at the corporations included in our study and is the coauthor, with Lipsky and Seeber, of a paper, "An Uncertain Destination: On the Development of Conflict Management Systems in U.S. Corporations," which is an earlier version of Chapter Four of this book. Her intellectual influence was essential in the development of the thinking that undergirds this book.

We offer special thanks to Arnold Zack, a distinguished neutral and past president of the National Academy of Arbitrators. He has worked closely with the Institute on Conflict Resolution virtually since its inception and is the source of many of our insights about conflict resolution. He played the key role in the establishment of the Alliance for Education in Dispute Resolution, which is headquartered at the institute and serves as chair of the executive committee of the Alliance. We also thank our friend and colleague Thomas Kochan, who served as the coprincipal investigator under our grant from the Hewlett Foundation and has consulted with us on all aspects of this project.

We have made presentations on various aspects of our research at numerous conferences and symposia. The list of our presentations includes annual meetings or conferences of the Association for Conflict Resolution, the Dispute Resolution Section of the American Bar Association, and the Industrial Relations Research Association. We also made presentations at the International Industrial Relations Association's World Congress in Bologna in 1998 and in Oslo in 2001 and at the Center for Advanced Human Resource Studies' Berlin conference in 2002. Presentations were also made at meetings of the New York State Bar Association, the Wisconsin Bar Association, the CPR Institute for Dispute Resolution, and the Forbes Magazine "Superconference" on ADR in both 1997 and 1998. In addition, we gave talks at conferences sponsored by the U.S. Embassy, the U.S. Chamber of Commerce, and other organizations in Germany. We also presented versions of our research at seminars sponsored by the Cornell Institute for Workplace Studies, the ILR School, and the Massachusetts Institute of Technology. We are grateful for all the important comments we received from participants at these events.

The Computer-Assisted Survey Team (CAST) at Cornell University conducted the survey of the Fortune 1000. Yasamin DiCiccio Miller, director of CAST, provided invaluable assistance not only on that survey but also on other projects conducted by the institute. We also thank Lisa Horn for her assistance in our survey work. We are grateful to several Cornell colleagues who offered us advice and guidance, including Sam Bacharach, Dennis Campagna, Phil Dankert, Maralyn Edid, Ted Eisenberg, John Forrester, Tom Germano, James Gross, Harry Katz, Michael Kimberly, Sally Klingel, Stephen LaLonde, Gordon Law, Ann Martin, Patricia McClary, James Mingle, Stuart Schwab, David Sherwyn, and Katherine Stone.

We have been fortunate to work with a superb group of graduate research assistants at Cornell. We especially acknowledge the invaluable assistance provided by Barbara Prescott. We also thank Rick Tallarigo, Zachary Henige, and Kate Mrozak for their contribution to this work. Alexander Colvin, a doctoral student at the ILR School from 1995 to 1999, wrote an excellent doctoral dissertation on dispute resolution systems. Included in his research are some of the same corporations we have studied. We benefited greatly from our interactions with Alex when he was conducting his dissertation research.

Over the years, several editors have worked with us, significantly improving the quality of our prose. We especially thank Elaine Goldberg, who expertly edited the first draft of this book. We also thank Elizabeth Holmes and Erica Fox for their editorial help. We owe a great debt to Alan Rinzler, who suggested to us that Jossey-Bass would be interested in publishing a book based on our research. We deeply appreciate Alan's assistance throughout the writing of the book. We also thank Amy Scott, Seth Schwartz, and Rachel Anderson for their expert editorial assistance.

Our colleagues at the Institute on Conflict Resolution play a critical role in assisting us in all stages of our work. We thank Rocco Scanza, deputy director of the institute, for his advice and guidance. We also owe special thanks to Chris Colosi, the institute's program coordinator, for his outstanding assistance. Theresa Woodhouse has provided outstanding logistical and other administrative assistance at many stages of the project. We are especially grateful to Missy Harrington. Without her day-to-day assistance, this book would not have been possible. Words are not adequate to express our indebtedness to Missy for her willingness to offer service above and beyond the call of duty.

Last, but not least, we thank our families for their love and support and their willingness to tolerate our very peculiar work habits. We owe a very special thanks to Mary-Jeanne, Julia, and Laura Fincher; and Ellen Wilson, Brent, Zachary, and Keith Seeber; and Sandy Lipsky.

February 2003

David B. Lipsky
Ithaca, New York
Ronald L. Seeber
Ithaca, New York
Richard D. Fincher
Phoenix, Arizona

Emerging Systems for Managing Workplace Conflict

Part One

The Evolution of Conflict Management Systems

Chapter One

Introduction

The Emergence of Conflict Management

In 1999, Coca-Cola Enterprises found itself in a difficult situation. The costs of employment conflict were already escalating when it lost a large class-action lawsuit brought by its African American employees. In response, Coca-Cola began a series of pilot programs designed to resolve employment disputes within the company rather than wait to settle them through the courts or administrative agencies. These programs were the beginning of a strategic move toward a different approach to the management of conflict.

Through a gradual but sustained effort, the company created the Diversity Council, which then endorsed the development of a conflict management system for Coca-Cola. A team created to design that system, under the leadership of Melanie Lewis, corporate manager of conflict management, ultimately chose to develop and implement what they described as an integrated, comprehensive, and strategic approach to conflict management. This system used an ombudsperson office, mediation, and arbitration; training in the use of the system; and a strong set of internal support structures. By 2002, Coca-Cola had put into place a system designed to revolutionize the way it handled employee conflict and employee disputes.[1]

PECO Energy came to the conflict management fold in a more graduated fashion. Long the most visible nonunion electric utility in the United States, it faced an International Brotherhood of Electrical Workers organizing campaign in the mid-1990s. Although the employees did not choose representation in the subsequent election, that experience revealed the employees' conflicts

and their unmet needs. Thus, PECO tried to improve conflict resolution within the organization.[2]

That the expression of unmet employee needs came through a
union organizing campaign was not acceptable to the company's
leadership. PECO had put a peer review program for employment
disputes in place in 1993, and it had worked well, but senior managers believed not well enough. They felt that opportunities for
early resolution of conflicts and disputes were being lost. In 1996,
they began to evaluate alternatives and additions to their peer
review process. Ultimately, through benchmarking, internal focus
groups, and other data gathering, PECO chose to institute a full-
blown alternative dispute resolution (ADR) system, including the
use of mediation and arbitration.

Schering-Plough had a completely different experience. A significant loss from damages in a sexual harassment case in the mid-
1990s caused the pharmaceutical company's executives to wonder
if that case might have been prevented, or the damage minimized,
through a more effective conflict resolution system. They assembled a team to consider whether the company should move toward
an ADR system of some kind.

Following an extensive benchmarking effort and a data-based
simulation of potential costs and benefits that might accrue from
such a program change, company leaders rejected the adoption of
any part of an ADR system. Two significant factors in that decision
were the speculative nature of the system's supposed benefits and
resistance from line management. Thus, Schering-Plough chose to
continue the procedures already in place for the resolution of
employee conflicts and disputes with the corporation.[3]

These three cases—Coca-Cola Enterprises, PECO, and Schering-
Plough—are similar not for the outcome they produced when they
examined dispute resolution in their companies but for what they
considered. Each of the companies was dissatisfied with the current means by which employee disputes were resolved, each
engaged in a comprehensive analysis of the situation, and each
reached a conclusion—all three different. But each of them was

considering a question newly significant to U.S. corporations in the 1990s: Is the system in use to manage and resolve disputes with employees adequately serving our needs?

These three cases are broadly representative of an important trend in organizations: a substantial dissatisfaction with conventional approaches to dispute resolution and an attempt to stem that dissatisfaction by replacing old approaches with newly minted dispute resolution systems. The trend of dissatisfaction with current systems, the adoption of new systems, and the impact of this shift in dispute resolution are the major concerns of this book.

Having investigated ADR and conflict management systems for the past six years, we are convinced that there is a sea of change in U.S. organizations that reflects an emergence of systems of conflict management and a new paradigm for organizations. This change is diffuse in origin, young enough to be thought of as largely experimental, and without adequate evidence to evaluate its impact fully. Yet the vast majority of private corporations and a large number of public and nonprofit organizations are midstream in a change process in which they are reevaluating their approach to conflict.

Why has this occurred? What precipitating incidents cause organizations to seek to change their dispute resolution systems? What do organizations expect to gain from changing? Are there detectable differences in the approaches that different organizations are using to implement these changes? Why do some organizations—Schering-Plough, for example—reject this change in approach? And, finally, what does this systemic change mean for organizations, employees, and public institutions? These questions drive our inquiry, and our goal in this book is to provide answers to them.

INCLINATION TO CHANGE

Organizations do not set in motion a process of wholesale shift to new systems unless there is substantial dissatisfaction with the old. That is the case with dispute resolution. A number of trends have converged to produce motivation for change.

Dissatisfaction with Conventional Approaches to Dispute Resolution

The traditional approaches of organizations to disputes have been largely reactive, reflecting compliance with systems imposed on the organizations by outside institutions. Disputes with consumers, governmental agencies, and other organizations have generally been resolved in the courts and other public forums established for that purpose. The dissatisfaction with these public forums, which has been growing for some time, reached a crisis point in the past ten years.[4] Litigation is seen as time-consuming, often going to ludicrous lengths, and costly. It is also often viewed as producing results unacceptable to either party to the dispute. Organizations view compliance with court-ordered settlements with barely concealed hostility, and at a minimum, judicial and administrative agency decisions are seen as less than perfect. In sum, the courts and administrative agencies set up to resolve disputes are viewed with antipathy, if not hostility, by nearly all except members of the legal profession, which is an integral part of the system.

A second trend in U.S. corporate life has been the long-term decline in the labor movement and thus in the use of collective bargaining and its attendant processes to resolve employee complaints. Collective bargaining as an institution reached its high-water mark covering about a third of the U.S. private sector in the 1950s.[5] Since that time, the labor movement has been on a steady decline to its current point, with less than 10 percent now represented by unions.

Collective bargaining provided explicit channels for the resolution of employee-employer disputes. Strikes were the means by which collective interest disputes were resolved, and, while never viewed as positive, they were effective for that purpose. Collective bargaining nearly always established elaborate grievance systems, usually culminating in a binding arbitration procedure for the final resolution of disputes over rights.

U.S. corporations never embraced collective bargaining and tried to limit its influence by fighting the existence of unions wherever they emerged. Some corporate leaders held the naive view that when unions did not exist, conflict would disappear. More sophisticated corporations recognized that workplaces produce conflict and that if unions and collective bargaining were not the vehicle for dispute resolution, another means would have to be substituted. Elaborate human resource systems designed to surface and channel employee dissatisfaction generally did not produce an effective substitute for this important function of unionism. Minor conflicts with employees often did not surface at all, and those that did came through unwanted, expensive litigation under the ever-growing system of individual legal rights in the workplace. Thus, employers in the 1990s found themselves facing the Hobson's choice of unions they did not want or alternative but ineffective means of dealing with employee conflict.

A third source of dissatisfaction came from the changes made by organizations to deal with the increased competition from globalization and deregulation in the latter part of the twentieth century. Especially at a time when organizations were being forced to reinvent themselves, organizational effectiveness was critically dependent on a committed, well-trained, well-organized workforce. Efficient workforces offered a potential competitive advantage. Conflicts that remained unresolved or did not surface in a productive fashion severely compromised organizational effectiveness and the quality of the good or service produced.

Although conflict was seen as a natural outgrowth of contemporary organizational life, turnover of employees due to conflicts was viewed as an unproductive waste of talent and organizational resources. The fact was that a smooth-functioning organization demanded a smooth-functioning system of dispute resolution. Yet many businesses found themselves without such a system even after they had made the other organizational adjustments necessary for survival.

The total effect of these forces of dissatisfaction was a powerful motivation for organizational change. Faced with the realization that conflict is inevitable, and without effective means of dealing with that conflict, one business after another attempted to create a new system of dispute resolution. Many went well beyond that into a new realm of conflict management.

Litigation, Dispute, and Conflict Management

Up to this point, we have used the terms *dispute management* and *conflict management* interchangeably, without a concrete distinction between them. However, although we do not wish to dwell on this topic, it is important to reflect on the differences between the two. Lawyers sometimes say that they engage in ADR routinely by trying to negotiate rather than litigate in appropriate cases. This happens after filing, however, and rarely involves trying to resolve disputes before they become litigation, much less trying to prevent conflicts from even becoming disputes

It is our belief that conflict management is much more comprehensive than dispute management. At the root of this conclusion is a distinction between conflicts and disputes. Conflicts can be seen as nearly any organizational friction that produces a mismatch in expectations of the proper course of action for an employee or a group of employees. Conflicts do not always lead to disputes; sometimes they are ignored, sometimes suppressed, and sometimes deemed unimportant enough to be left alone. Disputes are a subset of the conflicts that require resolution, activated by the filing of a grievance, a lawsuit against an organization, or even a simple written complaint.

Accepting this distinction between conflicts and disputes allows the argument naturally to progress to a divergence in the attempt to manage them. The management of disputes, which represent only the tip of the iceberg of conflict, is a significantly less complex problem. To manage disputes successfully, the organization need only maneuver the dispute into a forum most to its advantage to attain lower costs (transactional and outcome), a quicker speed of resolution, or simply a higher probability of a better outcome. Such activities would be seen as effective management of disputes. Thus, much of what we see of dispute management looks like forum shopping.

Organizations that desire to manage conflict must go well beyond this smaller set of processes and into more facets of organizational life, encompassing a much wider range of questions, the involvement of more parts of the organization, and a more complex system. The goals of a conflict management system are broader and more numerous. Conflict management systems attempt to channel conflict in productive directions, for example, not just to manage its resolution. They spread the responsibility for conflict and its resolution to the lowest levels of the organization. Thus, they require training to be widespread. They seek to transform the organization, not just a set of processes. These and other distinctions and requirements of a conflict management system will be explored fully in this book. It is sufficient at this point to say that because of their complexity and the potential rewards they offer an organization, conflict management systems are a much more fruitful arena for inquiry and exploration. This distinction among dispute and conflict management systems, and litigation, is graphically depicted in Figure 1.1. These three systems differ in terms of the depth of their

Figure 1.1. The Conflict Pyramid

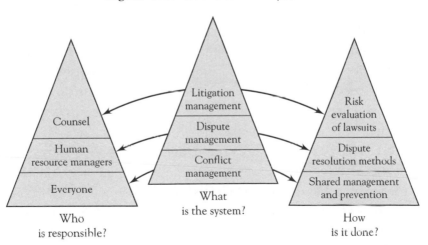

involvement in the organization, the people responsible for the management of the system, and the functions involved in the creation and maintenance of the system. Dispute management is always more complex than litigation management, and conflict management more complicated than both. We will elaborate on these distinctions later in the book.

Conflict Management Systems

We believe that the study of conflict management systems requires a comparison of multiple features. Systems differ on many important dimensions, each containing the potential to lead to unique outcomes. There are variations in the process of the design of a system—for example: Who is involved? How is the system created? How is the system implemented? These design features are not trivial because, as we will show, the values implicit in the design process are often reflected eventually in the system itself. Next, conflict management systems vary in the way they are structured: Who controls the system? Is the system centralized or decentralized? What are the goals of the system? Who is responsible?

Systems also vary in the procedures they employ for conflict resolution. We have investigated systems that include ombudspersons, peer review panels, facilitated discussions, mediation, arbitration, and multiple variations on these basic procedures. The choice of procedures can reflect on the values underlying the system itself. Some conflict management systems place value on participation in the conflict resolution process, some on having any disputes that occur be resolved as quickly as possible, and some value simply surfacing conflict. The solutions created to reach these fundamental goals will be reflected in the procedures used within the system.

We believe it is also important to identify and analyze the participants in the conflict management system. One simple distinction is the amount that the system relies on outsiders—neutrals and consultants, for example—to feed and maintain it. But it is important to go beyond the use of outsiders and into the organization itself. The extent to which line managers are involved and responsible for resolving conflict is an important distinction between systems.

Finally, since (as one of our colleagues has repeatedly told us) we are what we measure, it is important to analyze what is judged by an organization to be critically important by looking at the features of the system they choose to measure and evaluate. Therefore, this is another important feature of a well-functioning system and one on which we will make comparisons.

THE CONCEPT OF A CONFLICT MANAGEMENT SYSTEM

In our development of the concept of a conflict management system, we have intentionally concentrated on decision making at the management level for two principal reasons. First, although considerable research on the operation of various ADR procedures exists, very little has been done on the formation of organizational strategies.[6] It appears obvious to us that understanding the growth and diffusion of ADR policies throughout business in the United States, and the barriers to that diffusion, requires a clear delineation of how top managers make decisions on the management of disputes. Second, a survey of the use of ADR by the Fortune 1000, conducted by two of us in 1997, revealed that some corporations were moving beyond the use of individual ADR policies to the adoption of a system to deal with their organization's conflict management. We were especially interested in understanding the transition to a systems approach undertaken by that vanguard of U.S. organizations. We therefore have been conducting on-site interviews at a number of U.S. enterprises and collecting publicly available information on the use of ADR by other businesses and large corporations.

There is no general agreement on the precise definition of a conflict management system, even among experts.[7] Clearly, though, an authentic system is not merely a practice, a procedure, or a policy. It is something more encompassing, which may incorporate all three—practice, procedure, and policy. Our understanding of systems is rooted in the classic works on the system concept.[8] We prefer the definition contained in a report prepared for the Society for Professionals in Dispute Resolution (SPIDR) by an ad hoc committee and published under the title, *Designing Integrated Conflict Management Systems: Guidelines for Practitioners and Decision Makers in Organizations*, by the Institute on Conflict Resolution at Cornell. David Lipsky was a member of that ad hoc committee.[9] It should be noted that in 2001, SPIDR, the Academy of Family Mediators, and CRENet (Conflict Resolution Education Network) merged to become the Association for Conflict Resolution (ACR). We will use ACR when referring to this report.

The ACR committee elaborated on the five essential characteristics of an integrated conflict management system in its report, which we quote at length with the permission of ACR (we summarize these characteristics in Exhibit 1.1):

1. Scope

An effective integrated conflict management system provides options for preventing, identifying, and resolving all types of problems, including those disputes that do not fall into a category protected by statute, contract, or specific policy (such as interpersonal disputes). Its purview includes "non-hierarchical" disputes between employees or between managers. Such an integrated system is available to all persons in the workplace—workers, managers, professionals, groups, teams involved in disputes, and those close by ("bystanders") who are affected.

This broad scope is important for several reasons. First, it allows employees and managers to raise concerns without framing them as violations of legal rights. This encourages employees and managers to raise concerns early and in a manner that is more likely to be conducive to problem solving. Second, a broad scope encourages employees and managers to address conflict between peers and problems that are not associated with a known individual. These conflicts can become destructive of organizational goals when there

Exhibit 1.1. The Five Characteristics of an
Integrated Conflict Management System

- Scope: A system should have the broadest feasible scope, providing options for all people in the workplace, including employees, supervisors, professionals, and managers, to have all types of problems considered.

- Culture: A system should welcome dissent (or tolerate disagreement) and encourage resolution of conflict at the lowest possible level through direct negotiation.

- Multiple access points: Users of a system should be able to identify and have access to the person, department, or entity most capable (in terms of authority, knowledge, and experience) of advising the individual about the conflict management system and managing the problem in question.

- Multiple options: A system should allow users the choice of more than one option for resolving a problem or dispute; more specifically, a system should contain both rights-based and interest-based options for addressing conflict.

- Support structures: A system requires support structures that are capable of coordinating and managing the multiple access points and multiple options; the structure should integrate effective conflict management into the organization's daily operations.

is no avenue for their constructive resolution. Third, while integrated conflict management systems are often introduced because of intra-workplace concerns, very frequently organizations expand the use of these systems to external complaints, as a means for receiving, preventing, and resolving concerns of customers, clients, and members of the public.

2. Culture

To manage conflict effectively, an organization must accept conflict as inevitable. Many organizations discourage the constructive management of conflict by sending the message that those who raise concerns are themselves the problem. Effective integrated conflict management systems communicate the propriety of raising concerns and encourage employees and managers to address these concerns as early as possible and at the lowest possible level. An integrated conflict management system provides an environment in which people can voice a concern or dispute without fear of retaliation. Employees, supervisors, and leaders are all trained to address conflict constructively, are supported in their efforts to do so, and are held accountable for results. Persons who are access points for the system may also serve as coaches for the disputants, helping them to resolve their dispute without proceeding to other options within the system. For example, Polaroid Corporation's policy stresses a commitment to create an environment that recognizes disputes as a natural cultural process and communicates to employees that they can expect to air their issues with full assurance of "safe harbor" and without adverse repercussions.

3. Multiple Access Points

An integrated conflict management system allows employees to enter the system through many access points, such as supervisors, union stewards, workplace leaders, employee assistance practitioners, human resources officers, ethics officers, conflict management coordinators, ombudspersons, internal legal counsel, health care providers, religious counselors, and equal employment opportunity personnel. Employees are not bounced from one department to another. The availability of multiple access points significantly reduces barriers to entering the system and encourages employees to address problems early and constructively.

4. Multiple Options

An integrated conflict management system gives employees the opportunity to choose a problem-solving approach to conflict resolution, to seek determination and enforcement of rights, or to do both. Employees have the opportunity in appropriate cases to move between rights-based grievance procedures and interest-based processes; within existing statutory and contractual restraints, they are not required to choose prematurely between the two. For example, an employee who files a grievance may also be able to pursue mediation if all disputants agree. Effective systems minimize red tape so that employees may access multiple options and resources.

Why Are Multiple Options Necessary?

Rights-based processes, such as grievance procedures, arbitration, adjudication, and appellate processes, provide the opportunity to seek a determination of whether legal or contractual rights have been violated. These rights may arise from employer policy, individual or collective bargaining contracts, statute, or common law. Rights-based processes are essential to an effective integrated conflict management system because:

- They provide the opportunity to seek redress for unfair treatment or violations of statutory rights, such as the right to work free of discrimination, harassment, or unsafe working conditions.
- A small percentage of disputants in any organization very strongly prefer a rights-based approach.
- For some issues, a rights-based approach is more appropriate.

Interest-based options, such as direct negotiation and mediation, use problem-solving techniques to address the perceived needs of the complainant or other parties. Interest-based options are essential to an effective integrated conflict management system because:

- They are flexible, enabling disputants to maintain more control over the process and the outcome, which results in greater satisfaction.
- They can be used at the lowest level and when the conflict first surfaces, resulting in faster, more cost-effective solutions, often with less damage to workplace relationships.
- They can boost morale by providing the potential for healing and strengthening workplace relationships between employees,

and for helping bystanders whose morale or working conditions may have been damaged by the dispute.

- They allow for creative solutions not available through rights-based processes.

- Disputants may be more satisfied with the result and the process, which leads to more voluntary compliance with the settlement.

- They can be used by disputants who are unwilling to use rights-based processes.

- They provide redress for issues that do not fit into a "grievable" or actionable category. Traditional grievance procedures require an employee to label a concern as a violation of some right. Some employees turn to rights-based processes for lack of another option, when their issue is not actionable under a statute or grievance mechanism. In such cases, a quick and direct interest-based process may be the ideal mechanism both to bring a "non-actionable" dispute to the surface and to resolve it.

- They reduce the burden on the rights-based processes by deflecting many disputes to a more appropriate process. This allows rights-based systems to function more effectively for those who seek resolution through them.

- They provide ways for employees to come forward with information about problems such as safety hazards, drug and alcohol use, threats to national security, conflict of interest, waste, fraud, theft, harassment, potential violence, or even equipment repair needs, without fear that they will be swept, against their will, into an investigation or adversarial process.

- They provide a mechanism for employees who simply wish to suggest a change of policy, procedure, or structure in the organization, to recommend re-orientation of a team project, or to start an orderly process for dealing with a policy, group, or department that is seen to be a problem.

- They foster skills that enhance teamwork and other effective workplace interactions, and reinforce positive organizational values.

- They help reduce turf battles, accommodate the many different philosophies that operate in an organizational setting, and promote respect for diversity.

Critically, multiple options provide avenues for bringing to the surface underground issues that destroy morale and reduce productivity. Some employees will not come forward with a problem because they fear they will be thought disloyal, will be considered a complainer, will become involved in a confrontation, will lose their privacy and dignity, or will face reprisal. Others will not use rights-based processes because of the psychological—and, potentially, economic—costs of seeking redress. Others do not trust those in the supervisory chain of command. The way persons address conflict is affected by ethnic and cultural background, educational level, gender dynamics, and individual temperament. Multiple options provide the greatest opportunity to resolve concerns early and easily, before they escalate into more destructive, time-consuming, and costly disputes.

5. Support Structures

To develop an effective integrated system, an organization must provide necessary systemic support and structures that coordinate access to multiple options and promote competence in dealing with conflict throughout the organization. These structures nurture systemic change. They make interest-based language and behavior an everyday practice and change the way employees deal with both dissent and conflict. By integrating these structures and options, the organization moves toward "conflict competency."[10]

To successfully implement an integrated conflict management system, an organization must develop support throughout its infrastructure. People at all levels of the organization must believe and communicate the same message: that conflict can and should be actively managed through one of the many channels of the integrated conflict management system.

Designers of systems need to pay particular attention to questions of fairness, an issue we address in detail in Chapter Five. Here, it is sufficient to say that the ACR committee, after considerable debate, reached agreement on eight essential elements of a fair conflict management system:

1. To the extent possible, participation in a system should be voluntary.
2. The privacy and confidentiality of the processes should be protected to the fullest extent allowed by law.
3. Neutrals (mediators, arbitrators, ombudspersons, and so forth) should be truly neutral and impartial.
4. Neutrals should be adequately trained and qualified.
5. The legitimacy of a system will be enhanced to the extent that it is "characterized by diversity in [its] core of neutrals, including mediators and arbitrators."
6. A system should have policies that specifically prohibit any form of reprisal or retaliation.
7. A system must be consistent with an organization's existing contracts, including collective bargaining agreements.
8. A system must not undermine the statutory or constitutional rights of the disputants.

Our own research has shown that some organizations that claim to have conflict management systems could not meet all the criteria prescribed by the ACR committee. In fact, in U.S. organizations today, a system as prescribed by ACR is more the ideal than the reality. Our studies of organizations that we believe have systems, even though they may fall short of the ideal recommended by ACR, reveal several other characteristics these organizations share:

A *proactive approach*. The organization's approach to conflict management is proactive rather than reactive. The organi-

zation has moved from waiting for disputes to occur to preventing (if possible) or anticipating them before they arise.[11]

Shared responsibility. The responsibility for conflict (or litigation) management is not confined to the counsel's office or
an outside law firm, but is shared by all levels of management.

Delegation of authority. The authority for preventing and
resolving conflict is delegated to the lowest feasible level
of the organization.

Accountability. Managers are held accountable for the successful prevention or resolution of conflict; the reward and performance review systems in the organization reflect this
managerial duty.

Ongoing training. Education and training in relevant conflict
management skills are an ongoing activity of the organization.

Feedback loop. Managers use the experience they have gained
in preventing or resolving conflict to improve the policies
and performance of the organization.

WHY STUDY CONFLICT MANAGEMENT IN THE WORKPLACE?

This book is about new systems of managing workplace conflict.
Obviously, organizations also face other types of conflict: conflicts
with their customers, conflicts with other organizations, and perhaps conflicts with regulators. Although all these sources of conflict are worthy of study, we focus primarily on the workplace, for
four reasons.

First, the management of conflict with consumers and other
businesses is more often than not done by a simple, mundane
approach. Organizations try to manage predictably occurring disputes. Many credit card firms and other organizations providing services to consumers expect a certain number of disputes with their
own customers to arise. These organizations wish primarily to

resolve these disputes in as cheap and quick a fashion as possible. AT&T, for example, adopted a well-publicized arbitration scheme for the resolution of disputes with its long-distance telephone customers. Although this particular scheme has been successfully challenged in the courts,[12] it is reflective of a larger attempt to remove customer disputes from the court system and put them into forums more easily managed by the corporation.

Second, business conflict management is more opaque and the study of it more problematic than the examination of the workplace. Both the process and the results of private conflict management are shielded from public scrutiny. The same is true in business-to-business conflict. Indeed, one strong motivation for the use of arbitration in business-to-business disputes is that the evidence, the process, and the outcome are not matters of public record, as would be the case in most disputes in the court system. Thus, gathering data on business-to-business disputes is difficult, if not impossible, in most situations. This kind of conflict also seems to be most subject to instrumental motivations. Organizations seek to manage business-to-business disputes once they arise, not conflicts that can be productively channeled. For these reasons, we chose not to study business conflict management.

Third, our own background, experiences, and expertise are in the workplace. In addition, our case studies have revealed that two, or even more, philosophies and approaches to conflict can exist across dispute areas even within a single organization. That makes the topic rich and interesting. An organization might be completely dissatisfied with existing systems of dispute resolution for employment matters, for example, and at the same time be completely satisfied with the courts as a forum for resolving all of its business-to-business disputes. Such an organization could be proactive in employment matters, seeking to surface conflicts before they become full-blown disputes, and completely reactive to other kinds of conflict, preferring to resolve them only when forced. We have found few, if any, corporations that have a consistent strategic approach to the management of different types of disputes.

Finally, we focus on the workplace and systems of employment conflict management because that area is the most controversial and potentially the most beneficial to business. Several significant Supreme Court decisions made in the past decade relate to employment conflict management systems.[13] These decisions allowed employers to require employees to sign "predispute waivers," which are discussed thoroughly in Chapter Seven. Although these legal challenges have focused primarily on predispute waivers of statutory rights in favor of arbitration forums, the attendant controversy has caused wide-ranging discussion and examination of these systems.

Critics have charged that employee rights and access to justice are being compromised in the name of business efficiency. Advocates adamantly argue that organizations with effectively functioning systems of conflict management will gain significant advantages over their competitors as they minimize the costs of unnecessary, expensive disputes with their own employees, without diminishing the rights of those employees. How can these competing claims of sacrificed justice and organizational expediency be reconciled? We believe that this is an important and significant question for employers, employees, and the public.

The employment milieu also offers a significant opportunity for study. This is a time, as we will show in this book, of vast change and even of an acceleration of change in organizations. There is widespread experimentation in the development and implementation of conflict management systems. At this point, enough knowledge about these systems and case studies exists to begin to evaluate this change. Many organizations have sufficient experience to be able to reach conclusions about the effect of these changes. Thus, we have an opportunity to compare practices across organizations and integrate those comparisons into some conclusions.

This is particularly true as we study and report on the motivation of organizations to change their approach to employment conflict management and on how the systems are designed and implemented. There are not sufficient data for the effective evaluation of the long-term functioning of these systems and their indirect effect on other organizational goals. Corporations are still searching for best practices; there is no accepted model of the best way to go. Our examination of system development at this time can contribute to that search for the dominant model.

OUR METHODOLOGY AND DATA

In this book, we combine the data we have gathered over the past five years from four separate but interrelated research efforts. We also rely on the wide-ranging published literature on conflict management, dispute resolution, and the evaluation of dispute resolution systems and their components.

In the spring of 1997, Lipsky and Seeber surveyed the general counsel or chief litigators of the Fortune 1000 on topics related to ADR. We were interested in whether the trend toward ADR and away from the courts was as widespread as we thought by observation. This survey and one other[14] remain the only widespread empirical data on ADR usage by U.S. corporations. The detailed results of our survey have been published elsewhere.[15]

The empirical results from that survey were the springboard that led to this book. In asking questions in that survey related to the overall corporate strategic approach to dispute resolution, we uncovered significant differences based on corporate size, industry, and competitive pressures. Other significant differences in corporate behavior were based on such individual characteristics as the history of the company and the preferences of those responsible for determining the company's strategic direction. The results were informative, but we found ourselves with as many new questions as ones we had answered.

Although we do not rely heavily on that data in this book (we do report some of the findings in Chapter Three), that survey served as the jumping-off point for the hypotheses about organizational behavior that we present here. The data on individual corporations piqued our interest in learning more about some of the companies, so two of us, Lipsky and Seeber (assisted in large part by Lavinia Hall), chose approximately forty companies for further examination. Coincidentally, at about the same time, Fincher began to survey and conduct case studies of workplace dispute and conflict management in a large sample of organizations. It became apparent that Lipsky and Seeber, on the one hand, and Fincher, on the other, were studying the same organizational phenomena using virtually the same methodology, and so we decided to join forces to write this book. In combination, the organizations we studied number more than fifty. They cover a broad spectrum of industries and represent a cross section of approaches and philosophies to ADR and conflict management.

These firms do not represent a random sample of the Fortune 1000 research and are not all from that group. The sample consists not only of large private sector corporations but also of several public sector and nonprofit organizations. We provide examples of organizations that range across a spectrum, from those that have fully developed conflict management systems to those that rely completely on litigation to resolve their disputes. All of the organizations we have studied, however, are large by almost any standard, and accordingly their experience with conflict management systems does not necessarily represent that of medium-size and small employers.

We also chose our sample of cases on pragmatic grounds. Each of these organizations has a very public posture toward conflict management in that they have gathered and shared information—through conferences or other presentations or publications—and each was either willing to talk to us about their experience or had published enough information to allow us to report on those efforts. In Appendix A, we list all the organizations that are mentioned in the book at which we conducted interviews. For each of the firms personally accessed, we attempted to schedule interviews with corporate chief executive officers, chief financial officers, general counsel, human resource executives, and managers at some of their specific sites. We were seldom able to interview all of these corporate officials, however. Usually we did succeed in conducting intensive interviews with top human resource executives and general counsel or other lawyers in the counsel's office. Occasionally, we were able to interview other managers in the corporation. These interviews were conducted throughout the period 1999 through 2001. We also gathered substantial material on those companies and others from publicly available conventional sources. All this has allowed us to build a rich understanding of the strategic approach to conflict management, as well the implementation strategies and processes, for approximately fifty large organizations.

A third body of data on which we rely is one of the very few comprehensive surveys of the neutral profession. In 1999, two of us, Lipsky and Seeber, were permitted to survey the active membership of the National Academy of Arbitrators (NAA), the premier professional society of labor-management arbitrators. Although that survey had multiple purposes, a significant portion of the data collection focused on the switch within the profession from union-management arbitration to employment arbitration and mediation. We collected demographic, caseload, and attitudinal information on over six hundred neutrals. This information allows us another important lens through which to view the development of conflict management systems.[16]

We also rely on the use of research, case studies, and secondary material gathered and published by many other academics and professionals in the field of conflict and dispute resolution. In the end, we have built a detailed understanding of the experiences of well over fifty large organizations and cite throughout the book from that knowledge.

Although the data we have are rich and extensive, the usual limitations of the case study approach are applicable here. We do not have statistically reliable measures of many of the subjects on which we comment. Widespread survey data are just not available, and there are important difficulties in gathering such information. Of no small significance is a general reluctance by large organizations to put the effort into data gathering on system experience.

The organizations that do collect a lot of information on their system have a natural reluctance to share it. Nonetheless, in spite of the data limitations, we can comfortably claim this book to be the most comprehensive effort in this arena to date.

THE DESIGN AND OUTLINE OF THE BOOK

We seek to accomplish two objectives in this book and to appeal to two audiences. Our first goal is to explain the rise of conflict management systems in the United States. To that end, we have built an organizational model in the tradition of the social sciences that seeks to explain corporate motivation and differences among corporations. We hope this model will allow others to do further research to explain why this rise has occurred and why organizations choose different paths.

We then turn to our second goal, which is to give readers an understanding of how organizations build conflict management systems. Here, we rely heavily on a synthesis of our knowledge of corporate practice. In the end, it is our hope that this book will be of use to scholars and teachers of conflict management and dispute resolution, as well as to the community of professionals who make these systems work.

The book is organized toward the fulfillment of these goals. In Part One, we devote three chapters to the understanding of why conflict management has become such an important subject in organizations. Chapter Two examines the traditional means by which conflicts and disputes were handled in the workplace. This is done in the context of the contemporary debate over the social contract. We present the principal methods of conflict resolution and the root causes that have undercut their contemporary usefulness. Our goal here is to explain the dissatisfaction with the old and to set the stage for the creation of the new. In Chapter Three, we present evidence on the creation and use of alternatives to the traditional means of dispute resolution. We make the argument that ADR is primarily a stop on the way to the creation of more complete and integrated conflict management approaches that followed closely on the heels of the ADR movement. We argue that ADR is more properly aligned with dispute management than with conflict management. Chapter Four, which closes Part One, discusses the creation of what we believe to be an important component of an emerging social contract in the workplace, the management of conflict. We focus here not only on external environmental forces for change but also on the process of change within the organization—the dynamics of strategic choice.

Part Two focuses primarily on the second goal we have set for ourselves. In these four chapters, we use our case studies of organizations to explain how conflict management systems are created and implemented. We look at what we consider to be the important design questions and options that confront the decision makers within organizations. Chapter Five focuses on the fundamental design questions and principles. It starts with the question of who designs the system, examines the uses of the systems in terms of people and conflict eligibility for participation, and concludes with the specifics of the internal features of dispute resolution that are incorporated in the conflict management system.

In Chapter Six, we present a discussion of the critical factors that have influenced system design to this point in its development. Certainly, the legal environment for arbitration has been evolving over the past decade, and we present the major points in a series of court decisions that influence design choices and outline the principles the system creators should consider. In addition, we look at other external features not affected by the legal environment, but that provide significant choices in system design. We discuss the sources for and qualifications of neutrals, a significant set of information for designers in organizations that choose to use external mediators or arbitrators.

Chapter Seven considers the second principal stage of the creation of a system: the start-up and implementation phase. In this chapter, we look at how organizations have handled everything from pilot programs to training to communication of systems change. In Chapter Eight, we describe the final design phase in the creation of conflict management systems. We not only look at the questions of what to measure and how to measure it, but we also present some of the early evidence on the performance of conflict management systems gathered by large organizations and independent researchers.

In Part Three, we return to more universal questions about the future of conflict management systems. Any talk about change in organizations must confront the flavor-of-the-day problem. If one looks back just ten years, and certainly twenty years, at the significant trends affecting management, it is easy to find examples of trends that were expected to affect every organization and the way in which they conducted their business. The literature is full of examples of such universalities that in retrospect were simply wrong or were discovered not to solve a problem as effectively as predicted.

In Chapter Nine, we attempt to deal with these questions as they apply to our topics. We recognize that despite the evidence we have marshaled, conflict management systems may be another passing fad. We recognize that there are very real barriers to the universal adoption of this strategic approach to the management of conflict. We have identified six key factors and questions that we believe predict whether conflict management systems will be a blip in the history of organizational management or a feature common to all successful organizations in the future. Chapter Ten, which ends the book, discusses what we believe to be the critical issues and dilemmas affecting this field of study and practice. In addition, we have provided two appendixes that we believe will assist some readers. Appendix A is a list of all the organizations to which we refer in this book. Appendix B lists many of the most common ADR terms and definitions. This glossary is not intended to be complete. There are many other glossaries available on the Internet and through the publications of significant neutral organizations.

Chapter Two

Forces of Change

The Transformation of the
Social Contract in the Workplace

In their recent book, *Updating America's Social Contract: Economic Growth and Opportunity in the New Century*, Penner, Sawhill, and Taylor suggest that the term *social contract* "describes the explicit and implicit agreements among the members of a political community that define the rights and responsibilities of people vis-à-vis their government."[1] They note that determining the correct balance between individual freedoms and community needs is the primary function of a social contract. "Renegotiating the social contract is always difficult," the authors say. "Such renegotiations involve intertwined questions about who will bear the costs and who will receive the benefits, about the appropriate balance between individuals and their government and about fundamental social values."[2]

Calls for a new social contract were heard increasingly as the new millennium approached. The appeal of a social contract, out of fashion for a time, made a startling comeback. Republicans and Democrats, conservatives and liberals, radicals and libertarians—representatives of seemingly every political hue—came to believe that the old social contract had been undermined by a variety of social and economic forces.

At a White House summit on jobs and the economy in 1998, for example, the participants focused on creating new employer-employee relationships. The MIT Task Force on Reconstructing America's Labor Market Institutions reported to the summit participants that it is "necessary to craft a new social contract between employer and employee," incorporating the concept of employability fostered through skills training and lifelong learning. Conferees agreed that many companies and their unions had succeeded in doing so, "often with stunning results."

At the World Conference on Science, held in Budapest, Hungary, during the summer of 1999, conference participants agreed that there was a need for a new social contract between science and society. They pointed to the dramatic effects of the Internet on intellectual property, the decline of public funding for scientific research, and the need for science to address the world's critical social problems as the reasons underlying this need.

New York City mayor Rudolph Giuliani declared in his January 2000 State of the City address, "We've worked at every level to restore the social contract in New York City, which says that for every right a person has, there is a corresponding obligation; and for every benefit received there is a corresponding duty. . . . For years, the social contract had been allowed to dissolve in New York City, or was even encouraged to dissolve. Instead, we glorified dependency. . . . Whatever was the case then, now we're moving in the direction of re-establishing the work ethic in New York City."

There have been calls for new social contracts to cover food production and agriculture, the operation of the Internet and the World Wide Web, medicine and the health care sector, child care and social welfare, and nearly every other facet of contemporary life. Apparently, however, most of the commentary has focused on the need for a new social contract to govern the workplace and employment relations. Scholars and commentators of every political stripe have joined the chorus. On the left, Jeremy Rifkin, in *The End of Work*, predicts that technological change (especially in the realm of biotechnology) and "hypercapitalism"—the spread of capitalism to all parts of the globe, including Russia and China—will necessitate a new social contract that incorporates a radical reordering of workplace relationships.[3]

Paradoxically, perhaps, the concept has been no less popular among many business executives. In a cover story, "Writing a New

Social Contract," *Business Week* discussed the longstanding division within the business community on the question of corporate social responsibility. On the one hand, according to the article, there were "liberals," who believed in a "stakeholder economy" that balanced the interests of managers, employees, customers, and communities. On the other hand were conservatives, who maintained "a faith in the restorative powers of the marketplace" and denied that corporations had the obligation to be socially responsible. This debate on corporate social responsibility gained a new urgency in the wake of Enron, Tyco, WorldCom, and other corporate scandals.

Business Week described how certain elements of the business community were attempting to define a new position regarding the social responsibility of corporations: "In isolated pockets of Corporate America, a middle path is slowly emerging, one that reflects a new paradigm for business and society in a global market. It recognizes that job security died with the 1980s—but concedes, too, that employers bear an obligation to help workers through transitions, and it attempts to align the interests of investors, managers, and employees, aiming to share both the risks and rewards of doing business."[4]

The dramatic rise in alternative dispute resolution and conflict management systems in U.S. organizations, we believe, is the consequence of forces that are giving rise to a new social contract at the workplace. In this chapter, we consider the origins of the concept of the social contract, perceptions of the old New Deal social contract that prevailed in the United States through most of the post–World War II period, and the forces that brought about the breakdown and transformation of the old social contract into a new one that is still forming.

It is the premise of this book that the rise of ADR, not only in employment relations but more broadly through all society in the United States, needs to be understood as a phenomenon that is part of a new and emerging social contract. The need for a new social contract arose out of an array of economic and societal changes that became particularly pronounced during the last couple of decades of the twentieth century—globalization and increasing market competition, technological change, urbanization, the growth of statutory regulation in business, and social relationships—and was accompanied by the deregulation of several important industries and significant alterations in the U.S. legal system.

THE EVOLUTION OF SOCIAL CONTRACT THEORY

It is not at all clear that the interest groups, policymakers, and pundits who have called for a new social contract are aware of the origins of the concept in political philosophy. The theory of the social contract had its origins in the work of seventeenth- and eighteenth-century philosophers, most notably Thomas Hobbes, John Locke, and Jean-Jacques Rousseau. The Protestant Reformation and the decline in the authority of the Catholic church had served to weaken the divine authority of the monarchical form of government. Europe had been ravaged by the wars of the Reformation, and philosophers recognized that the authority of the king, and more generally civil government, needed a new justification. "In their search, political theorists—and especially the Protestants among them—turned to the old biblical concept of a *covenant* or contract, such as the one between God and Abraham and the Israelites of the Old Testament."[5]

In classical philosophy, a social contract can be embodied in an actual document (such as the Magna Carta or a constitution) but is more likely to be implicit or hypothetical. It is a compact between rulers and their people that defines their respective rights and duties. What distinguished the theories of Hobbes, Locke, and Rousseau was their attempt "to justify political authority on grounds of individual self interest and rational consent" rather than on divine authority. These theories "attempted to demonstrate the value and purposes of organized government by comparing the advantages of civil society with the disadvantages of the state of nature, a hypothetical condition characterized by a complete absence of governmental authority."[6]

By the nineteenth century, social contract theory had fallen out of favor, while other schools of philosophy (such as Kantian idealism, logical positivism, and Marxism) had gained dominance. But in the twentieth century, social contract theory made a comeback, primarily because of the work of John Rawls. In common with his intellectual predecessors, Rawls attempted to justify governmental authority on the basis of ethical principles. In Rawls's view, a social contract codifies the legitimate and reasonable obligations of all citizens in a civil society. Rawls, in contrast to Hobbes, viewed social contract theory not as an explanation for the origins of civil government, but rather as a means of analyzing the legitimacy of political obligations.[7]

The ethical roots of Rawls's theory of the social contract have been developed by several contemporary scholars, most notably Donaldson and Dunfee, into a model called *integrative social contracts theory* (ISCT). The principal purpose of ISCT is to provide a framework for analyzing ethical dilemmas that decision makers, especially business leaders, face. ISCT is therefore taught in business ethics courses in most U.S. schools of management. "In business ethics . . . the challenge is for business communities to shape *their ethical worlds* in such a way that they are not only fair but relevant. The challenge is to shape their worlds so that they are [not only] faithful to timeless intuitions, but also are reflective of their members' more local values, including ones that are cultural or religious."[8]

The trail that connects the classical concept of the social contract with the contemporary and popular use of the term is a long and winding one. It is, to say the least, a stretch to use a term that was first meant to describe efforts to justify the sovereign authority of government and is now more popularly used to justify the special interests of various stakeholder groups.

What are the implications of these alternative concepts of the social contract for conflict resolution? In classical theory, a social contract was in the first instance a means of preventing conflicts from arising. As Hobbes wrote, there were no rules distinguishing right from wrong in the state of nature. Each person tried to obtain as much as he or she could with no regard for the welfare of others. Human life, as Hobbes famously wrote, was "solitary, poor, nasty, brutish and short." Under a social contract, individuals exchanged their unlimited liberty for the safety and security provided by sovereign power. Conflicts that arose would be resolved by the sovereign.[9]

Neither Locke nor Rousseau shared Hobbes's view that the state of nature was a state of war. Locke believed that in the state of nature, humans are bounded by divinely inspired natural law. They entered into a social contract when they recognized the practical difficulties of enforcing their rights under natural law.[10] Rousseau maintained that in a state of nature, humans, although unwarlike, had an underdeveloped sense of reason, morality, and responsibility. "Man is born free," Rousseau wrote in *The Social Contract*, "and everywhere he is in chains." A social contract, Rousseau postulated, permits humans to gain security and some measure of freedom of action in exchange for the surrender of rights and property to "the general will." Rousseau believed the general will can never be wrong since it represents the impartial and nonsectarian interests of all individual citizens. The sovereign, according to Rousseau, must have total power to guarantee the enforcement of the general will.[11]

The classic view of the social contract, in sum, justified the need for citizens to obey the law of the sovereign. Conflict could not be tolerated if it was directed against the sovereign, who represented the will of the people. Some scholars see in Rousseau's emphasis on an all-powerful sovereign the roots of totalitarianism. Locke, in contrast, maintained that if the laws of the state conflicted with natural law, natural law had to prevail. In the United States, Locke's view provided a rationale for the supremacy of the judicial branch of government. The power of the judiciary to overturn acts of the legislature is based on the view that a statute should not be allowed to violate the natural rights of citizens.[12]

Classical social contract theory provides authority for the traditional approach to the administration of justice and conflict resolution with which most of us are familiar in the United States. Contemporary theorists of the social contract, such as Rawls, Nozick, and Dworkin, have analyzed the relationship between the individual and the state, with a view to prescribing how much authority must be vested in government to bring about a just society. The level of abstraction in contemporary theory, however, precludes consideration of techniques of conflict resolution. Contemporary theorists debate conceptions of justice but do not deal with the administration of justice.[13]

Only in discussions of the "new" social contract is there more explicit consideration of alternative means of conflict resolution. Globalization, technological change, and other forces that have brought about the transformation of the old social contract bring in their wake a realization that traditional means of resolving conflict may no longer be adequate. All of the premises of the old social contract—the principle of state sovereignty and the view that the system of justice ultimately should represent the will of the people—have come under scrutiny. The transformation of the social contract, partly by design and partly by happenstance, has resulted in the adoption of new forms of conflict resolution never contemplated by classic or contemporary political philosophers.

THE TRADITIONAL SOCIAL CONTRACT
AT THE WORKPLACE

The social contract that governed the workplace for most of the twentieth century—certainly from the 1920s to the 1980s—was a compact fashioned out of the imperatives of industrialization. The unprecedented rise of unionism and collective bargaining in the 1930s caused some modification in the social contract governing the workplace, but did not fundamentally alter its shape. One can see, with hindsight, that a considerable period of stability characterized the social contract governing employment relations. For several decades, the values ascribed to by both employers and employees did not change substantially. Under the compact governing employment

relations, managers gained a relatively free hand in controlling production and the workforce and employees gained access to good
jobs at good wages.

Industrialization and the Web of Rules

In every industrial society, there needs to be a complex web of rules
governing the relationship between employers and employees.
Rules are needed for every facet of the workplace: the level of pay;
the method of payment; the scheduling, assignment, and pace of
work; standards of performance; and numerous other matters.
There also need to be rules governing the management and resolution of conflict at the workplace.

Every society needs to decide who will write these workplace
rules and who will implement them. Conceptually, three parties
could write and enforce such rules: managers, employees (and their
representatives), and the state. In the United States until the
1930s, workplace rules were almost exclusively under the domain of
the owners and managers of the enterprise. After the 1930s, unions
and managers in unionized establishments became the coauthors
of many of the rules of the workplace; in nonunion establishments,
owners and managers continued to have the authority to determine
such rules.

For most of the twentieth century, the state (elected representatives, courts, regulatory agencies, and the like) played a minimal
role in determining the web of workplace rules. Employment relationships in the United States remained largely unregulated until
the latter part of the century, when the state played an increasingly
significant role in writing and enforcing workplace rules.[14]

An understanding of the social contract at the workplace rests
on an appreciation of the concept of the web of rules. First, the
concept allows one to distinguish the *process* of establishing workplace rules, the methods of *implementing* those rules, and the *substance* of those rules. In principle, a social contract needs to govern
all three of these dimensions, implicitly or explicitly. Second, it

helps us to understand that the party or parties that determine the substantive rules need not be identical to the party or parties that control the process and implementation of those rules. Third, it prompts us to realize that conflicts can arise over each dimension—process, implementation, and substance—of the web of rules.

In the first part of the twentieth century, one party, management, more or less controlled all dimensions of the web of rules at the workplace. Management had the authority not only to write and implement the rules but also to resolve any conflicts that arose. Unions were weak or nonexistent, legislators were reluctant to intervene, and courts only rarely served as a check on management prerogatives, and then usually at the state, rather than the federal, level.

Later in the century, the spread of unionism to some significant degree modified the social contract. Collective bargaining, as a *process*, allowed unions to participate in workplace rule making. It forced managers to allow unions to write some, but not all, of the *substantive* rules of the workplace. Collective bargaining contracts explicitly incorporated at least some rules that had been largely implicit under the old prevailing social contract. The *implementation* of those rules remained largely the preserve of management, however. Through the grievance procedure, unions could challenge management's implementation of the rules, but almost never did they seek to control that dimension.

Collective bargaining thus served to legitimize some forms of conflict, but it also had the effect of controlling and limiting conflict. The use of economic weapons (strikes and lockouts) by the parties was permitted under certain conditions, for example, but the state increasingly controlled other forms of conflict (such as picketing and secondary boycotts). Most significant, collective bargaining introduced the use of mediation and arbitration as techniques of resolving conflict, a development that foreshadowed the rise of ADR in the last part of the century.

In sum, the traditional social contract at the workplace came in two forms: one for nonunion establishments and the other for unionized ones. The version that applied in union settings modified

the version that applied in nonunion settings but did not fundamentally alter it. Both versions were the result of the industrialization of the U.S. economy, both accepted the legitimacy of
capitalism and free markets, both recognized management's fundamental prerogatives, and both called for the state to play a limited
role in governing employment relations. As the century drew to a
close, however, these conditions were undermined by economic,
technological, and societal changes, and there was an increasing
recognition that a new social contract was emerging.

Scientific Management and the Standardization of Employment Practices

The growth of prosperity and power in the United States in the
first part of the twentieth century was the consequence of technological innovations that made the development of mass production and mass consumption possible. Henry Ford's perfecting of
assembly-line production in the automobile industry helped to
demonstrate the benefits of the standardization of products and
production technologies and was emulated in industries such as
electrical appliances, apparel, and textiles. The standardization of
production techniques in turn led to the standardization of
employment practices, if not across then certainly within many
key industries.

The long wave of industrialization that began in the United
States in the nineteenth century continued until after World War
II. It brought producers high profits and, in several key industries,
dominance in world markets. It also held out the promise, if not
always fulfilled, of good jobs at decent wages for a majority of
employees. Industrialization had its costs, however. One was the
periodic recessions that plagued the economy, beginning with the
"panics" of the nineteenth century and continuing through and
beyond the Great Depression of the 1930s. During these economic
downturns, producers lost profits and struggled to survive, and
employees suffered periods of unemployment often accompanied

by great hardship. Economic insecurity seemed to be the inevitable consequence of a free-market industrialized society.

Even in the best of economic times, employees had to endure the rigors and discipline of the industrial workplace. One consequence of mass production was the transfer of the control of the pace of production from skilled craftsmen to office and factory managers. As Sanford Jacoby has written, "By tying skilled workers to the firm, employers hoped to weaken craft traditions, speed the pace of work, and hasten the introduction of new technologies."[15]

At the turn of the twentieth century, the ideas of Frederick W. Taylor, the leading exponent of scientific management, were spreading through industry. Taylorism maintained that improvements in the productivity and performance of employees depended largely on increasing the specialization of the work they performed. Breaking down an individual's work into a few simple tasks, Taylor believed, would result in significant gains in worker efficiency. Specialization and standardization were two sides of the same coin: there had to be one best way to perform a job, and industrial engineers needed only to use their techniques of time-and-motion study to discover the "best way." Taylor believed that workers were motivated primarily by money, and therefore he recommended linking the amount they produced to the pay they received in order to obtain maximum productivity from them. Thus, Taylorism helped popularize the use of piece rates and incentive pay.[16]

Management Authority

Industrialization strengthened the authority of management to make decisions regarding the products to be produced, the prices charged, the business location, the investments needed in new technologies, and the deployment and supervision of the workforce. Almost all organizations had a hierarchical authority structure featuring top-down management. At the workplace, managers and supervisors had the authority to direct employees. In the absence of unions, that authority could not be questioned unless management violated the law. But even in unionized enterprises, unions for the most part did not question management's decision-making authority. They sought the right in collective bargaining agreements to appeal decisions made by managers through the grievance procedure, but did not seek to participate in the management of the enterprise.

Under the hierarchical authority structure that prevailed in U.S. enterprises through most of the twentieth century, conflict was considered dysfunctional. Managers never thought of conflict strategically; if they considered it at all, it was usually a phenomenon they did their best to avoid, suppress, or ignore. If, despite their best efforts, they were forced to deal with conflicts with their employees, the remedy was to punish those responsible. There was little tolerance for dissent at the workplace. Certainly before the passage of the National Labor Relations Act (NLRA) in 1935, it was common for managers to deal with union-organizing drives by firing the employees who led them. Even after the NLRA made this type of behavior unlawful, many employers—because of the inadequate sanctions in the law—continued to discharge union organizers.

THE "NEW DEAL" SOCIAL CONTRACT

After World War II, the United States was indisputably the leading economy in the world. It had about 5 percent of the world's population but produced nearly one-third of the world's goods and services. The core of its economic strength was in the smokestack industries: autos, steel, chemicals, electrical machinery, mining, and others. These industries were protected by restrictions on international trade, including high tariff walls, which had been heightened by depression-era legislation designed to safeguard jobs and profits. In 1960, only about 5 percent of the goods and services consumed in the United States were imported from abroad.

Product market competition was also limited by the existence of oligopolies—industries dominated by a handful of major companies. In the automobile industry, for example, a series of mergers during the postwar period dramatically reduced the number of manufacturers: Packard merged with Studebaker, Kaiser with Willys, and Hudson with Nash (to form American Motors). Mergers, however, did not save two of these companies; by the mid-1960s, the domestic auto industry became the preserve of only four manufacturers: General Motors, Ford, Chrysler, and American Motors. In 1960, GM produced nearly half the cars purchased in the United States; the number of cars imported from Europe amounted to a mere trickle, and none were imported from Japan.[17] The first imported Japanese cars, Datsuns, did not arrive in the United States until 1963.[18]

In several major industries, government regulation seriously constrained, or in fact prevented, product market competition. In the telephone industry, AT&T had a virtual monopoly over the provision of both local and long-distance service. Regulation also limited competition in airlines, railroads, over-the-highway trucking, intercity bus service, gas and electric utilities, and other industries.[19]

The protections and privileges enjoyed by many U.S. corporations gave them considerable discretion, if not total control, over price and wage setting. In protected and regulated markets, wage increases could be passed on to customers through higher prices, and prices could be raised without fear of losing too many customers. Of course, not all industries were insulated from the forces of the marketplace. Companies in industries such as textiles and apparel, wholesale and retail trade, and auto supply and repair attempted to survive in a dog-eat-dog world. The garment-producing sweatshop, the mom-and-pop grocery store, and the corner gasoline station were outside the scope of the New Deal social contract.

The workforce in the 1950s and 1960s was dominantly blue collar. At the turn of the twentieth century, about 38 percent of the workforce was employed in agriculture and about 31 percent in goods-producing industries such as mining, manufacturing, and construction. But by 1950, the proportion of the workforce in agriculture had dropped to about 23 percent, while the proportion in goods-producing industries remained about 31 percent.[20]

The Rise of Unionism

Beginning in the depths of the Great Depression, unionism had swept through the ranks of blue-collar workers. When Franklin Roosevelt became president in 1933, the union representation rate was about 5 percent. When Dwight Eisenhower became president in 1954, it was nearly 35 percent. In the great urban industrial centers of the Northeast and the Midwest, it had spread like a prairie fire in the years just before and during World War II: autoworkers in Detroit and Flint, steelworkers in Pittsburgh and Buffalo, rubber workers in Akron and Canton, and electrical workers in Schenectady and Syracuse all joined the ranks of the newly established Congress of Industrial Organizations (CIO) unions. The dramatic surge of unionism in the 1930s was often accompanied by strikes and picketing. Occasionally, the tug of war between employers and unions became violent. In the realm of industrial relations, the social contract was severely tested by conflicts between unions and employers in the 1930s.

The turmoil and tumult of the 1930s motivated the U.S. public and its elected representatives to search for policy measures that would foster fairness and equity in employment relations and remove the sources of disruption and violence. In labor-management relations, New York senator Robert Wagner sponsored the NLRA, which was passed by Congress and signed into law by President Roosevelt in 1935. This law guaranteed the right of workers to organize and be represented by unions in collective bargaining, prohibited employers from discriminating against their employees on the basis of their union activity, and gave workers the right to vote in secret ballot elections as a means of resolving union representation questions.

Also called the Wagner Act, the NLRA was significant on several dimensions. Not only did it deter violence in labor relations and encourage workers to join unions, it also represented a symbolic codification of the collective rights of workers in American jurisprudence. Under the Wagner Act, collective rights took precedence over individual rights to an extent that would never again be matched.

The New Deal era was also marked by an unprecedented emphasis on protecting the working class from the perils of death, old age, unemployment, and insecurity in general. In 1935, Congress passed the Social Security Act, which established a social insurance scheme for retired workers and their survivors, enabled the states to construct an unemployment system, and federalized the existing welfare program. Three years later, Congress acted again, passing the Fair Labor Standards Act (FLSA), which mandated a minimum wage for covered employees and premium payments for overtime work. The NLRA and the FLSA became twin keystones in the edifice of the modern welfare state.

By the end of World War II, both labor and management in the United States were anxious to rationalize and bring order to a chaotic workplace. Both sides were willing to develop processes and procedures that would serve to regulate employment relationships. The New Deal version of the social contract was the consequence of these shared objectives.

At many work sites, a broad, if fragile, consensus developed that would last for nearly thirty years. Managers would recognize the legitimacy of unions, unions would restrict their concerns to well-defined workplace issues, and government would be the impartial arbiter, helping to ensure a level playing field. The foundation had been laid for the union version of the social contract in employment relations.

Characteristics of the New Deal Social Contract

Conceptually, the New Deal social contract promised significant, tangible benefits to most (but not all) individuals, groups, and institutions in U.S. society in exchange for their accepting certain responsibilities and obligations. The scope of this social contract was very broad—broader than the social contract had ever been in the past—but clearly it did not include everyone. Its most novel feature was probably its implicit inclusion of unions. The legitimacy of unions in U.S. society had not been firmly established before the New Deal. The Great Depression and the New Deal brought about the recognition, however tenuous, that the union movement was an authentic participant in civil society in the United States.

The New Deal social contract, one can infer, also covered all major corporations and all major employers, significant segments of the nonunion workforce, most U.S. families (especially those in the middle class), and all major institutions—schools, universities, churches, the military, state and local governments, nonprofit foundations, and charities. But although this version of the social contract was broader in coverage than any previous one had ever been, it still excluded significant segments of the population, including most members of minority groups, almost all of the disabled, many of the poor and destitute, all homosexuals, significant segments of the immigrant population, and many small businesses. African Americans, for example, were relegated to second-class citizenship, in the North subjected to discrimination and in the South to Jim Crow laws, which mandated segregation. The disabled were virtually invisible, the absolutely last persons to be hired. Not until the 1960s and the 1970s was the social contract expanded to cover these members of society. Even today, it is debatable whether some of these groups—homosexuals, for example—are truly encompassed by the social contract.

For most workers, union and nonunion alike, the New Deal social contract promised a comfortable middle-class standard of living—provided the worker was a law-abiding, English-speaking, white male. After World War II, middle-class Americans were able to enjoy a level of material well-being that was unparalleled in world history. This was an era of suburbanization and mass retailing—of Levittowns and shopping malls. Home buying was fueled by federally subsidized home mortgages and vast improvements in the nation's transportation system. The construction of the interstate highway system, begun during the Eisenhower administration, became the largest public works project in the history of the nation. Before congestion became commonplace, the nation's modern new highway system allowed suburbanites easy access to jobs in central city areas and helped spur urban sprawl.

The quid pro quo for the middle-class lifestyle, which became the norm for a majority of Americans in the post–World War II period, was a set of fairly rigid obligations and responsibilities both on the job and off. Under the New Deal social contract, standardization of the terms and conditions of employment was the norm for middle-income wage earners, and conformity to accepted standards was the expectation. For the upwardly mobile middle-class worker, the imperative of conformity was famously described in nonfiction by William H. Whyte's *Organization Man* and in fiction by Sloan Wilson's *The Man in the Grey Flannel Suit*.

The implicit terms of the New Deal social contract provided corporations with many benefits, including special tax advantages, subsidies, and an array of protections from the competitive pressures of the marketplace. In exchange, corporations were expected to provide the goods and services that would guarantee prosperity, avoid a resumption of the Great Depression, and (as symbolized by the Full Employment Act of 1946) maintain only a tolerable rate of unemployment. Also, the cold war, by implication, had brought about the addition of a noteworthy clause to the social contract: one that called for corporations to protect the United States against the threat of the Communist bloc by focusing their research, investment, and manufacturing capacities on defense production. The corporations were handsomely rewarded for these efforts by U.S. taxpayers. By 1960, the tightening bond between U.S. corporations and the government caused President Eisenhower, in his farewell address, to warn the nation of the dangers of the military-industrial complex.

In large part, the corporate obligation centered on the provision of good jobs, adequate pay, and sufficient (but not perfect) job security. Until the 1970s, however, the corporate obligation did not include the provision of safe jobs, a guarantee of pensions, or the requirement to provide equal opportunity for minorities and women. Nor did the New Deal social contract prevent corporations from polluting the environment.

Labor-Management Relations Under the New Deal Social Contract

Under the New Deal social contract, unions enjoyed protections and privileges that had never previously existed, and to a degree that may never again be duplicated. Indeed, with hindsight, the status of unions under the New Deal social contract increasingly appears to be an aberration in U.S. history. Union influence expanded not only in the workplace but also in the political arena. After twenty years of jurisdictional rivalry and bitter feuding, the American Federation of Labor (AFL) and the CIO merged in 1955. George Meany became the president of the merged federation and soon made plans for the construction of new headquarters for the AFL-CIO in Washington, D.C., only a stone's throw away from the White House. The location of the building symbolically represented labor's expanding role in the inner councils of government.

Amending the Social Contract: Truman's White House Conference, 1945. The rise of unionism in the United States required the addition of some amendments to the old social contract, which were negotiated by the parties from time to time. A prime example of an effort by labor and management representatives to revise the old social contract was President Truman's National Labor-Management Conference, convened at the White House in November 1945. The thirty-six delegates who gathered for the Washington conference included the highest-ranking business executives and labor leaders in the nation. Many feared that conversion to a peacetime economy would bring about the resumption of the Great Depression. There was widespread fear that the strife and turmoil that had characterized U.S. labor relations before the war would resume in full force.

It was in this context that President Truman asked Secretary of Labor Lewis B. Schwellenbach and Secretary of Commerce Henry A. Wallace to mount a conference that would, the president hoped, set the ground rules for industrial relations in the postwar era. In his opening address, Truman implored the leaders at the conference to work out machinery that would serve to resolve collective bargaining disputes peacefully. He linked the peaceful settlement of labor disputes to the nation's prospects for postwar prosperity. In the president's view, labor-management cooperation was a necessary condition for economic expansion.[21]

Many commentators have considered President Truman's White House conference an important stepping-stone in the development of the postwar social contract governing employment relations. The conference participants considered virtually every substantive and procedural issue in labor relations. Interestingly, however, the conferees reached agreement on only two, both pertaining to dispute resolution: they supported the use of conciliation (that is, mediation) rather than compulsory arbitration or fact finding to resolve new contract disputes, and they strongly endorsed voluntary arbitration to resolve grievance disputes. The conferees' consensus on these points is widely considered to have had a significant influence on the postwar growth of the use of mediation in new contract disputes and voluntary arbitration in grievance disputes.[22]

In fact, the use of arbitration and mediation to resolve labor-management disputes in the United States dates to the second half of the nineteenth century. But it became an integral part of the U.S. industrial relations system only after World War II and Truman's White House conference. The conferees' distinction between new contract disputes and grievance disputes is one that came to permeate U.S. industrial relations in the postwar era. New contract disputes are considered disputes over "interests," and grievance disputes are considered disputes over "rights." The sharp distinction made between interest disputes and rights disputes is virtually unique to U.S. industrial relations and remains the foundation on which dispute resolution in U.S. collective bargaining has been built.[23]

President Truman's White House conference was remarkable in at least two additional respects. First, the notion that thirty-six labor, management, and public officials could shape the direction of the postwar industrial relations system—if they reached agreement—now seems to be particularly antiquated. Truman's notion that an elite tripartite group could "furnish a broad and permanent foundation for industrial peace and progress" apparently was widely shared by the press and the general public.[24] Opposition to the conference came primarily from independent and left-wing unions, which were excluded from the conference.

The Truman conference was an example of "limited corporatism," as Heckscher has noted, and has had many counterparts, including the effort by the Clinton administration, through the Commission on the Future of Worker-Management Relations, known as the Dunlop Commission (after its chair, John Dunlop), to deal with labor law reform. The Truman conference, the Dunlop Commission, and related efforts to negotiate a social contract to govern employment relations illustrate the potential and the pitfalls of the corporatist approach to policymaking.[25]

The second remarkable feature of the Truman conference is the evident consensus that existed among the conferees on the legitimacy and value of collective bargaining in U.S. society. In a key speech at the conference, Eric Johnston, president of the U.S. Chamber of Commerce, said, "Labor unions are woven into our economic pattern of American life, and collective bargaining is a part of the democratic process. The nation and management must recognize this fact. I say recognize this fact not only with our lips but with our hearts."[26] It is impossible to imagine any recent president of the Chamber of Commerce offering a similar endorsement of unions and collective bargaining. It is difficult now to recall that until the 1970s, management's acceptance of collective bargaining was routinely expressed by business executives, especially those heading large corporations. Daniel Bell, reflecting a viewpoint that was common around 1960, thought such expressions to be emblematic of "the end of ideology."[27]

The White House conferees, it needs to be noted, considered but failed to reach agreement on the other critical issues they examined. Secretary of Labor Wallace urged the conference to deal with larger macroeconomic issues, such as the relationship between wage bargains and national income, for example. Steelworker president Philip Murray pushed consideration of a national wage standard. But AFL president William Green, as well as the business leaders, did not support either Murray's or Wallace's proposals. The deadlock that developed on most issues frustrated many of the participants.

Other Features of the New Deal Social Contract. The implicit social contract that governed employers and unions for three decades following World War II contained many noteworthy features, several unique to the system of industrial relations in the United States. A number of the most innovative features were developed by Walter Reuther, president of the United Autoworkers, in negotiations with the major auto producers in 1948 and 1950. Reuther stressed the importance of longer-term collective bargaining agreements with fixed expiration dates, for example. In 1948, he negotiated a two-year agreement in the industry, and in 1950 he persuaded the auto companies to accept a path-breaking five-year agreement.

But the outbreak of the Korean War resulted in a new wave of price inflation, which undermined the wages Reuther had negotiated in the five-year contract. Pressured by rank-and-file dissatisfaction, Reuther persuaded the automakers to reopen and renegotiate their contracts in 1953. The experience chastised Reuther, who concluded in Goldilocks fashion that if one-year deals were too short, five-year deals were too long. Thus was born the three-year collective bargaining agreement, which subsequently became the norm in industrial relations in the United States.

Long-term contracts had obvious advantages for both unions and employers. For both parties, such contracts helped ensure stability and predictability in employment relations. Also, the parties' growing reliance on grievance procedures and binding arbitration to resolve grievance disputes made sense only if unions agreed not to strike for the term of the agreement and employers agreed not to lock out their workers. The development of long-term contracts containing grievance arbitration and no-strike, no-lockout clauses virtually guaranteed the parties that they would enjoy extended periods of industrial peace. This combination of features in collective bargaining agreements is nearly unique to the United States and has dramatically reduced, although not totally eliminated, the occurrence of work stoppages during the term of a contract. The use of grievance procedures and arbitration to resolve rights disputes also provides an important check on unwarranted actions by managements that seek to alter employment terms during the course of the agreement. These procedures thereby limit autocratic actions by management or labor and create orderly procedures for resolving disputes during the life of the agreement.

Perhaps the most important right that unions obtained under the New Deal social contract was the right to strike. This right had not been firmly established in law or practice before the Great Depression era. The right to strike, however, was not unfettered. The Wagner Act, as interpreted by the National Labor Relations Board and the courts, provided no guarantee that a striker would necessarily retain his or her job. The law permitted employers who were otherwise law abiding to replace strikers permanently, although employers seldom engaged in this practice under the New Deal social contract. Then the Taft-Hartley Act, enacted into law in 1947, put other restrictions on the right to strike. It essentially banned secondary strikes, picketing, and strikes over union representation issues. These restrictions had the effect of further reducing strikes and conflict and promoting workplace stability.

Still another feature of the New Deal social contract was its reliance on the use of mediation to help resolve interest disputes. (The Taft-Hartley Act, for example, established an independent mediation provider, the Federal Mediation and Conciliation Service.) The professional and voluntary nature of the mediation services provided by the federal government (at no cost to the parties) also served to reduce strikes and industrial conflict. In addition, the emergency dispute resolution procedures provided through the Taft-Hartley amendments served to deter or constrain conflict in the few cases where the president exercised his authority under the law to invoke these procedures. In sum, although unions were given the right to strike under the New Deal social contract, the constraints in policy and practice on that right served to reduce the occurrence of strikes in the U.S. system of industrial relations.

The New Deal system of industrial relations also allowed management to exercise an array of management rights and prerogatives. As noted earlier, management could control all strategic decisions on products, prices, investments, and other matters "at the core of entrepreneurial authority."[28]

Management also insisted on its right to manage the workforce. Especially in manufacturing industries, employers negotiated provisions in collective bargaining agreements that reserved for management the right to hire, fire, discipline, and otherwise control decisions affecting their employees, subject to other relevant provisions in their collective bargaining agreement. As the postwar system developed, unions increasingly ceded to management control over the implementation of workplace rules, but insisted that management adhere to certain standards and procedures in making workplace decisions.[29]

Nevertheless, in the three decades that followed World War II, there was an unprecedented level of agreement among management, labor, and public officials on the core characteristics of the U.S. system of employment relations. The first and foremost characteristic was the distinction between unionized and nonunionized employees. In the realm of dispute resolution, unionized employees under nearly all collective bargaining agreements had access to a grievance procedure and, ultimately, to arbitration to resolve disputes arising over the interpretation or application of the agreement. In contrast, nonunionized employees, with very few exceptions, had no means of contesting decisions made by their employers and supervisors. The so-called employment-at-will doctrine meant that these employees could be discharged for any reason at all—for a good reason, a bad reason, or no reason. By applying the concept of just cause to the discipline and discharge of employees, collective bargaining limited the employment-at-will doctrine, although it did not abrogate it.[30]

Dispute Resolution and Labor-Management Relations

In the U.S. system of industrial relations, a sharp distinction is made between disputes over interests and over rights. Negotiations between employers and unions are the principal means of resolving—or avoiding—disputes over interests. If the parties reach an impasse in the negotiation of a new collective bargaining agreement, mediation is typically used to help them resolve their dispute. If the parties are covered by the NLRA, the Federal Mediation and Conciliation Service has jurisdiction over the dispute and provides the parties with a mediator. Arbitration is almost never used in the United States to resolve interest disputes. (In a handful of states, interest arbitration is used to settle police and fire-fighter disputes in the public sector, but it is almost never used in the private sector.)

Almost all collective bargaining agreements in the United States incorporate a grievance procedure for handling disputes over rights. The grievance procedure is negotiated by the parties and almost always provides for the use of arbitration to resolve grievances that have not been settled earlier in the procedure. The arbitrator is an individual, jointly selected and paid by the parties in the dispute. If grievance and arbitration provisions were not included in collective bargaining agreements, unions and employers presumably would need to resolve their rights disputes either by resorting to concerted activity (strikes, lockouts, or other work stoppages) or by suing one another in the courts to enforce their contracts. In large measure, therefore, using grievance procedures and arbitration to resolve disputes over rights is a substitute for using the court system.

Thus, grievance and arbitration procedures in collective bargaining relationships are a form of ADR. Grievance arbitration has been widely considered one of the hallmarks of the collective bargaining system in the United States, and it is reasonable to assume that the successful use of mediation and arbitration in industrial relations in the United States spurred the use of ADR as a means of resolving other types of disputes.

The significance of grievance arbitration was enhanced in a series of landmark decisions by the U.S. Supreme Court. In the so-called Steelworkers Trilogy, three cases decided in 1960 involving the Steelworkers Union, the Court ruled that arbitrator decisions are virtually inviolate and not subject to review in the federal courts except under very special circumstances.[31] If the Court had not severely limited the review of arbitrator decisions, the court system would have been flooded with petitions to review thousands of arbitration awards. This pragmatic consideration was explicitly mentioned as a factor entering into the Court's reasoning. After the Steelworkers Trilogy, grievance arbitration flourished in the United States.

Within a few years, however, President Lyndon Johnson's Great Society triggered a flood of federal legislation matched in volume only by the period of Franklin Roosevelt's New Deal in the 1930s. In the area of employment law alone, between 1960 and 1980 Congress passed at least two dozen major statutes regulating employment conditions. Consequently, arbitrators operating under collective bargaining agreements have increasingly been required not only to interpret those agreements but also to apply the various statutes (in other words, the external law) that may be linked to grievants' complaints. The rise in the prevalence and importance of statutory rights in labor-management arbitration has been a source of considerable concern. The need for arbitrators to apply external law in a growing number of their cases requires that they be expert in the content and application of these statutes. Questions have arisen about the preparation and expertise of arbitrators who are called on to resolve statutory claims. Moreover, the increased arbitration of statutory rights makes considerations of due process more important than in the past. Concerns have been raised, for example, about the adequacy of representation in arbitration cases that involve the application of statutory rights.[32]

FORCES OF CHANGE

The New Deal social contract was a remarkably stable compact for several decades. By the 1990s, however, the glue that had held it together had loosened. The forces bringing about the transformation of the old social contract included the increasing globalization of business, the growth of multinational corporations, and the rapid pace of technological change. These factors required corporations operating in international markets to accelerate the pace of their decision making. No longer did managers have the luxury of tolerating any aspect of their business that dampened their ability to respond to market pressures.

The forces affecting the nature of the social contract included not only globalization and technological change but also the so-called litigation explosion. The number of employment lawsuits grew dramatically following the passage of the many new statutes affecting employment relations in the 1960s. The delays and costs associated with disputes—and particularly with litigation—became a factor that U.S. business needed to manage and control. The decline of unionism also significantly affected the terms of the social contract at the workplace, as did changes in the legal system that served to encourage litigation and brought about a transformation in the corporate legal function.

The Turbulent 1960s and the Strengthening of Individual Rights

The undoing of the New Deal social contract had its roots in the turbulent 1960s. The nation became enmeshed in the quagmire of the Vietnam War. From the 17,000 U.S. military "advisers" in Vietnam at the time of President Kennedy's assassination in November 1963 to the 500,000 military personnel in that country at the time of Richard Nixon's inauguration in January 1969, U.S. involvement in the war had steadily escalated, launching widespread protests and demonstrations by students and their adult allies. At the same time, the civil rights movement, which had steadily gained momentum after the Supreme Court's 1954 decision in *Brown* v. *Board of Education*, reached a new peak of influence after Martin Luther King Jr.'s March on Washington in 1963. Following President Kennedy's assassination, the nation's political climate shifted in a decidedly liberal direction, signified by Lyndon Johnson's landslide victory over Barry Goldwater in the 1964 presidential election. Johnson's Great Society program resulted in a stunning number of new laws being passed in the mid-1960s by an overwhelmingly Democratic Congress.

In the civil rights arena, Congress passed the landmark Civil Rights Act of 1964 and the Voting Rights Act of 1965. These legislative achievements were accompanied by massive nonviolent demonstrations, frequently led by King, and by periodic riots in many urban centers, most notably Los Angeles (Watts), Detroit, and Newark, New Jersey. In the decade's penultimate year, 1968, President Johnson announced in March that he would not be a candidate for reelection, King was assassinated in Memphis in April, Robert Kennedy, in the midst of his bid for the Democratic party's presidential nomination, was assassinated in Los Angeles in June, and at the Democratic party's convention in Chicago that summer, violence erupted in the course of massive demonstrations by civil rights and antiwar activists.

The social movements of the 1960s changed the attitudes of many Americans about the legitimacy of challenging the authority of government and, in fact, all other established institutions. Direct action against lawfully constituted authority became an acceptable means of bringing about social change. Not since the union organizing strikes of the 1930s had the view that mass protest was an appropriate method of affecting change been widely accepted by the U.S. public. The example set by civil rights and antiwar activists inspired the women's movement, which began to take shape after the publication of Betty Friedan's *Feminine Mystique* in 1963.

Insofar as workplace institutions were concerned, the decade of the 1960s, for all its turmoil, affected the fundamental tenets of the

New Deal social contract only marginally. Instead, it tended to strengthen and extend this version of the social contract, at least in the short term. Civil rights legislation, for example, held the promise of covering several groups, especially blacks and women, previously excluded from the social contract. Unionism and collective bargaining expanded into the public sector in the 1960s. Most government employees did not enjoy the right to engage in collective bargaining prior to the 1960s, and the right to strike was uniformly prohibited. Although some groups of public sector employees—school teachers, postal workers, firefighters—had joined unions or employee associations, their organizations were largely confined to lobbying activities. In 1962, President Kennedy fulfilled a campaign pledge by issuing an executive order mandating collective bargaining for federal employees. Kennedy's executive order was a spark that helped ignite the rapid diffusion of unionism and collective bargaining throughout state and local governments. Public sector employees were also clearly inspired by the example set by the antiwar and civil rights movements. By the end of the decade, a majority of public sector employees had gained the right to engage in collective bargaining.[33]

Globalization and the Restructuring of the American Economy

The transformation of the social contract, particularly with regard to workplace institutions, really began in the 1980s. Probably the most important causes of this transformation were the growing globalization and dramatic restructuring of the economy—a restructuring that many consider a second industrial revolution. In the 1960s, U.S. economic strength was still based on its ability to produce and distribute manufactured products, but by the turn of the century, its strength was based on its ability to produce and distribute information. The United States had become a knowledge-based economy, a historic change that necessitated a reworking of the social contract.

By the 1980s, the deindustrialization of the United States was in full swing. In the economic battle against imported products from Germany, Japan, and elsewhere, U.S. manufacturing was in full retreat. In autos, auto parts, steel, aluminum, apparel, and dozens of other industries, plants were closed, jobs were permanently lost, and communities were abandoned. The industrial centers of the Northeast and Midwest were left in shambles.[34] Computing and other high-tech industries were on a growth path, but no one could be certain in the 1980s that these industries would dominate world markets in the future. Indeed, many predicted that the Japanese would ultimately control the microchip and microprocessor markets, gaining success in those sectors as they already had in autos, steel, and electronic products.

A Shift in the Political Climate and the Deregulation of Industry

Ronald Reagan's election to the presidency in 1980 signaled a distinct rightward shift in the nation's political climate. The new conservative political climate of the nation, a reaction in part to the excesses of the 1960s, helped accelerate the move to deregulate U.S. industry. Deregulation had begun in earnest during the Carter presidency, starting with the passage of the Airline Deregulation Act in 1978, which virtually eliminated federal controls of the airline industry.[35] During the Reagan years, it spread rapidly to telephone, telecommunications, trucking, and other heavily regulated industries, supported by Democrats and Republicans alike. In 1983, following federal Judge Harold Green's issuance of a consent decree, AT&T was divested of its operating companies, unleashing serious competition in both local and long-distance service for the first time in history.[36] Perhaps the rapid advance of technological change in telecommunications would inevitably have brought about competitive markets alone, but the court hastened the process. Thus, the combination of globalization, heightened competition, deregulation, and technological change served to undermine the terms and conditions of the New Deal social contract.

THE LITIGATION SOCIETY

A dramatic surge in litigation in the 1970s, particularly in the area of employment relations, is another significant factor that ultimately changed the nature of the social contract. Many observers believe that the perceived litigation explosion that began in the 1960s and, some contend, continues to this day is a principal cause of the rise of alternative methods of dispute resolution in the United States.[37] "Proponents of this view tend to focus primarily on the growth of torts, especially personal injury claims based on product liability theories," according to Dunworth and Rogers.[38] But business litigation has also expanded in other areas, including employment, civil rights, contract, and environmental disputes. Thus, more and more dimensions of the employment relationship were brought under the scrutiny of the court system and a multitude of regulatory agencies.

Documenting the Explosion

Proponents of the view that there has been a litigation explosion cite the fact that since the 1960s, litigation has increased approximately seven times faster than the national population. An estimated 30 million civil cases are now on the dockets of federal, state, and local courts, a number that has grown dramatically in recent years. The United States has about 5 percent of the world's population but 70 percent of the world's lawyers.[39] A 1994 survey by Tillinghast–Towers Perrin estimated that tort liability cost the United States $152 billion a year.[40] Other data show that in the past two decades, the number of suits filed in federal courts concerning employment matters grew by 400 percent.[41] In the 1990s, the number of civil cases in U.S. federal courts involving charges of discrimination alone nearly tripled. Plaintiffs who won their employment discrimination suits received a median award of $200,000 in 1996; one in nine received an award of $1 million or more.[42]

The purported increase in business and employment litigation has been accompanied by delays in the settlement of such cases. According to the Dunlop Commission, "Overburdened federal and state judicial dockets mean that years often pass before an aggrieved employee is able to present his or her claim in court."[43] In 1994, a panel of nine federal judges commissioned by the Judicial Conference of the United States noted that the huge increases in the caseload of the federal courts had further slowed the already languid rate of processing civil cases.[44] In sum, the litigation explosion clogged the dockets of federal and state courts in the United States, leading to longer delays and higher costs in the use of traditional means of dispute resolution.

Some have challenged whether there has been a significant increase in litigation. Dunworth and Rogers, for example, who examined federal litigation involving the two thousand largest U.S. corporations during the period 1971 through 1991, concluded that the litigation explosion is largely a myth: "It may have had some credibility ten years ago, near the peak of the post-1971 rise in litigation levels, but it has much less now. [In] most major categories of litigation, filings have actually declined in recent years. If there ever was a 'litigation explosion' affecting business in the federal courts, it has generally subsided."[45] Although Dunworth and Rogers's research undermines the conventional wisdom to some extent, they do not paint a complete picture. By confining their analysis to the largest business organizations, they leave open the question of litigation trends for smaller businesses. They also omit trends in state courts and in state and federal regulatory agencies.

Whatever the reality, there is a strong perception, confirmed by the interviews we have conducted, that businesses are much more likely to be defendants in civil litigation of all types than they were a generation ago. That perception has translated into action for many businesses as they seek to gain more control over the litigation process and its results.

Legal and Tort Reform

Frustration with the growing burden of litigation led many in the business community to oppose various federal measures to regulate the employment relationship and to lobby for tort (or legal) reforms that would limit the ability of one party to sue another. Proposed measures have included limitations on damages, "loser pays" requirements, caps on contingency fees charged by lawyers, and restrictions on class-action suits. Leading business organizations, including the National Association of Manufacturers and the Chamber of Commerce, became proponents of tort reform. The American Tort Reform Association, also representing business interests, played a major role in the public relations and lobbying efforts to achieve reforms preferred by the business community. Corporations and their allies often join forces with the Republican party to press for tort reform, although the issue was never framed entirely along conventional political lines.

Trial lawyers, civil rights organizations, labor unions, and other liberal groups usually oppose the push for tort reform. In the 1980s and 1990s, most, but certainly not all, Democratic party lawmakers either opposed reform or were selective in their support of reform measures. They argued either that there has not been an authentic litigation explosion or that, if there has been one, it has served a useful social purpose.[46]

The movement for tort reform may have crested with the election of a Republican majority in the 104th Congress. The Republican party's Contract with America contained a provision pledging party support for reform that would curtail the flood of "frivolous lawsuits and outlandish damage rewards [that] make a mockery of our civil justice system."[47] Congressional Republicans failed to achieve comprehensive tort reform, however, although piecemeal measures were passed and signed into law by President Clinton. At the state level, the movement for tort reform has also had mixed and limited success. It is our contention, based on our interviews in the field, that the failure of tort reform in the 1990s is directly linked to the rise of conflict management systems. We elaborate on this contention in Chapter Four. The election of George W. Bush to the presidency in 2000, however, and especially the election of a Republican Congress in 2002 may tip the scales in favor of the proponents of tort reform. Such a shift in the balance of political forces favoring tort reform could have profound implications for the development of conflict management systems.

THE PROFESSIONALIZATION OF HUMAN RESOURCE MANAGEMENT

Another factor that has played a significant role in transforming the social contract has been the professionalization of human resource management. For most of the twentieth century, the responsibility for managing employees in an organization—when it was not in the hands of line managers—resided in the personnel department, often regarded as the backwater of the corporation. It was frequently staffed by managers who were not considered potential candidates for top management positions and had no special training in personnel. The department was usually responsible for only the day-to-day administration of a limited number of functions, such as payroll, hiring, and benefits. In unionized companies, personnel managers often had some responsibility for labor relations, but in many corporations, the departments for personnel and labor relations were separate, with the vice president for labor relations having higher status than the director of personnel. The personnel director, almost never a member of the top management team, played no role in shaping the corporation's business strategy.

As late as the 1960s, the personnel manager was on the bottom of the management totem poll. The status of the personnel function was elevated significantly in the ensuing decades, however, along the way changing its name from "personnel" to "human resource management" as a symbol of its higher status. One leading practitioner, who started his career in the 1950s and rose to become vice president of human resources and a member of the management committee of one of the nation's largest corporations, was fond of saying, "Over the course of my career, personnel moved from the payroll department to the boardroom." Another executive said, "The human resource department is being presented with an opportunity to become a significant player on the management team. This is occurring because the human resource function is being transformed into a significant management function. Environmental changes are confronting organizations with people issues of great importance and uncertainty. People issues are thus becoming formulated as significant business issues."[48]

In the information age, attracting, retaining, and motivating a skilled and diverse workforce has become a strategic issue for the corporation. Employers need employees with the right skills, knowledge, abilities, and attitudes. Employees not only need to have sufficient skills and training; they need to understand the contribution they must make to keep their company competitive. The human resource function has been professionalized because the failure of the organization to attract and retain the types of workers it needs could very well threaten not only its profitability but its survival. As the twentieth century came to an end, the executive in charge of the human resource function in many corporations had become top management's business partner.[49]

Human resource management is one of the fastest-growing occupations in the United States. It is estimated that over a million members of the workforce currently have the term "human resources" in their job title. Most of the organizations that employ human resource managers now require that they have a college degree. The growth of the profession has been accompanied by the growth of professional societies: for example, 28 individuals established the American Society for Personnel Administration in 1948; by 2002, that association, now called the Society for Human Resource Management, had 170,000 members.[50]

The professionalization of human resource management has had significant effects on the social contract governing the workplace. Basically, organizations have become more sophisticated in their handling of people issues.

THE DECLINE OF UNIONISM

Figure 2.1 shows that from its peak of 35 percent of total payroll in 1954, union membership as a proportion of the workforce (often referred to as union density) has steadily declined for nearly fifty years. By 2001, unions represented only 13.6 percent of the U.S. workforce. Although the proportion of unionized employees in the public sector had risen to 37.4 percent, the proportion in the private sector had fallen to only 9 percent.[51]

Management opposition is clearly one important factor explaining this long-term decline, but there are others. Union membership had been concentrated in the smokestack industries, the industries hit hardest by international competition and deindustrialization. In addition, unions, headed mostly by aging white men, found it increasingly difficult to organize the growing number of women, immigrants, and minorities entering the labor force. The shift from a manufacturing to an information economy also brought about an increase in the white-collar, service, and professional segments of the workforce, segments the union movement has had difficulty reaching.

Figure 2.1. Union Membership as a Percentage of Total Payroll, 1930–2001

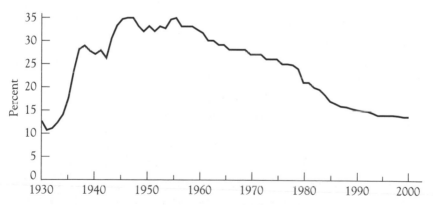

Source: U.S. Bureau of the Census, *Historical Statistics of the United States.* Washington, D.C.: U.S. Government Printing Office, 1970. U.S. Department of Labor, Bureau of Labor Statistics, *Employment and Earnings,* Jan. 2001. Updated data available in the *Statistical Abstract of the United States,* issued annually.

Management Opposition to Unions

Management opposition to unions gained a new legitimacy in the political and economic climate of the 1980s. The key precipitating event for this shift out into the open was President Reagan's firing of twelve thousand air traffic controllers in August 1981. The air traffic controllers were engaged in an illegal strike, and the president acted with the full authority of federal law.[52] Nevertheless, by this action, the president in effect put his stamp of approval on union busting. Many employers needed little coaxing to follow the president's example. As Bluestone and Bluestone note, "They rolled up their sleeves, took a deep breath, and proceeded to imitate a management style pioneered by the Prussian military."[53]

Frank Lorenzo, the CEO of Eastern Airlines, Fred Curry, head of the Greyhound Bus Line, and a handful of other employers hired strikebreakers and used a variety of other tactics designed to break their unions. Ironically, their get-tough tactics often proved ineffective and self-defeating. Eastern and Greyhound were driven into bankruptcy.[54] Lorenzo, Curry, and other union busters may represent the fringe of U.S. management, but many employers in the mainstream embraced union-free and union-avoidance strategies. By the 1980s, one would have to search hard to find a CEO who shared the sentiments expressed by Eric Johnston during President Truman's White House conference. Some scholars maintain that management opposition was the principal cause of the decline of unionism in the United States.[55]

The Weakness of American Labor Law

The transformation of the U.S. economy, the changing composition of the workforce, and management opposition were all critical factors undermining union strength. Still another factor was the weakness of U.S. labor law. The fundamental tenets of the statutory framework had been put in place during the Great Depression, and there was growing recognition by employers and unions alike that the law was steadily losing relevance in an increasingly information-based economy.

Both labor and management became more and more dissatisfied with the law, but the sources of their dissatisfaction differed. Labor complained that the law deterred their efforts to organize the unorganized and lacked adequate sanctions to deal with employer violations. Management asserted that the rights granted to unions interfered with efficient production and feared that the law would obstruct the shift toward team-based work. Although both sides were unhappy with the law, they could not agree on how to change it.

During the Carter presidency, the union movement mounted a major effort to persuade Congress to amend the Taft-Hartley Act. The business community, however, strongly opposed the reforms the unions proposed, and the reforms died in the Senate in 1978.

THE REORGANIZATION OF THE WORKPLACE

All of the forces of change described in this chapter—globalization, rapid technological change, the growing regulation of employment, the decline of unionism—were associated with a significant reorganization of the way work is performed in many U.S. companies. A hallmark of the reorganization of the workplace is the decline in the importance of hierarchy and the rise of team-based work. Many U.S. employers have discovered that employee performance and productivity can be enhanced if employees are empowered to assume more responsibility for the manner in which they perform their work. In many U.S. workplaces, management has removed layers of supervision—often called delayering—and delegated substantial authority to teams of employees to control the direction of their activities. Virtually every corporation we visited in the course of conducting our field research purported to use a team-based system of production.

High-Performance Work Systems

The ultimate form of team-based work is the so-called high-performance work system, which always includes both teams and delayering. In General Motors's Saturn plant in Springhill, Tennessee, for example, management and the union agreed to eliminate all first-line supervisors and instead have teams elect their leaders.[56] Another element of a high-performance work system is the elimination of job classifications. Twenty or more years ago, there might have been as many as three hundred job classifications in many manufacturing plants (such as in the auto industry). That multiple division of the tasks that needed to be performed was an example of Taylorism run rampant. Newer plants opened in the 1980s or later frequently had many fewer job classifications than older plants operating in a more traditional fashion. Verma, for example, did an intensive study of eight plants operated by a manufacturing company. In three aging unionized plants that maintained traditional workplace practices, the average number of job classifications was ninety-six; in three recently opened nonunion plants that had adopted more contemporary forms of work organization, the average number of job classifications was six.[57]

By the 1980s, U.S. companies realized that improved efficiency and performance could be achieved by recombining jobs and eliminating multiple job classifications. The collapse of dozens and dozens of job classifications into a handful is often referred to as broad banding. Instead of having workers perform a fixed set of tasks in a narrowly defined job, employers adopted the practice of having employees rotate across the jobs performed by the members of a team. For members of a team to rotate from job to job, they must have the skills needed to perform the variety of tasks in those jobs. Job rotation, accordingly, gives rise to the concepts of multiskilling and multitasking. To ensure that workers have all of the skills needed for all of the jobs they might perform, employers need to have a commitment to training and retraining of the workforce on an ongoing basis.

Another feature of a high-performance work system is a contingent and flexible compensation scheme. In fact, as the twentieth century came to an end, many employers—even those not relying on team-based production—had abandoned their conventional pay practices and adopted more flexible compensation plans. A growing number of employers no longer increased their employees' base pay annually but instead made improvement in pay contingent on either employee performance and productivity or the profitability of the firm. In many organizations, performance-based pay, profit sharing, lump-sum bonuses, and other contingent pay schemes replaced automatic annual pay adjustments.

Employers, especially after the rapid inflation of the late 1970s, became increasingly reluctant to tie pay to cost-of-living increases. In union-management relations, employers pushed unions to give up cost-of-living adjustment clauses that had been included in many collective bargaining agreements. Thus, the practices that Walter Reuther instituted in the auto industry in the 1950s—an automatic annual pay increase, cost-of-living adjustments, and a three-year contract—that subsequently became the norm for many unionized industries, were undermined by the forces of change affecting the workplace social contract at the end of the century.

Employee Participation

In the last quarter of the twentieth century, many employers came to believe there was a direct link between their employees' participation in workplace decision making and their companies' ability to compete in world markets. Employee participation went hand in hand with team-based production. Companies, often working cooperatively with their unions, experimented with a variety of workplace innovations designed to foster employee involvement in decision making. As Kochan, Katz, and McKersie observed, these innovations had two basic objectives: one was to "increase the participation and involvement of individuals in informal work groups so as to overcome adversarial relations and increase employee motivation, commitment, and problem-solving potential"; a second was to "alter the organization of work so as to simplify work rules, lower costs, and increase flexibility in the management of human resources."[58]

Some of these experiments were based on the apparently successful experience of Japanese manufacturers. For example, in many plants, employers introduced so-called quality circles, an innovation transplanted directly from Japanese firms. Eventually, however, some employers became disenchanted with quality circles and adopted other types of programs to improve the quality of working life. Over time, U.S. companies relied less on Japanese approaches and more on participation programs tailored to the culture and norms of the American workplace.

Teams, delayering, multiskilling, multitasking, contingent pay, empowerment, and participation are all elements of a full-fledged high-performance work system. Not all U.S. employers embraced all of these elements, but a majority adopted one or more of them.[59] The reorganization of the workplace was a consequence of management's drive for increased flexibility in employment relations. To become and remain competitive, U.S. employers realized they needed greater flexibility in the workplace. Flexibility would allow them to shed outdated work rules and practices, motivate employees, and boost employee productivity.

The reorganization of the workplace has also had pronounced implications for conflict management in that a workplace conflict management system is the logical handmaiden of a high-performance work system. In our survey of the Fortune 1000 and our fieldwork, we discovered that a company that had adopted advanced workplace practices, such as team-based production, was more likely to have a conflict management system. The correlation between the use of a conflict management system and the use of advanced human resource practices is not a perfect one. Nevertheless, a growing number of managers have come to realize that delegating responsibility for controlling work to teams is consistent with delegating authority for preventing or resolving conflict to the members of those teams. Through most of the twentieth century, management had the authority to direct employees in all aspects of their working life and to resolve conflicts arising in the workplace. Even the rise of unionism did not fundamentally alter management's decision-making authority. But the ineluctable forces that have transformed U.S. society are producing a new social contract at the workplace that requires new strategies of managing workplace conflict.

CONCLUSION

Table 2.1 provides a summary of the various conceptions of the social contract discussed in this chapter and the implications of these conceptions for workplace dispute resolution.

The classical conception of the social contract served to justify the authority of the sovereign, or more generally government, to control and resolve conflict. In classical theory, the use of private forums to resolve public claims was scarcely imagined. It was the rise of capitalism and democracy that eventually gave new meaning to the concept of a social contract. First in Europe and later in the newly formed United States, the growth of private enterprise and reliance on free markets resulted in private parties' assuming more responsibility for the resolution of conflict. Governments recognized the sanctity of private contracts, and private parties could negotiate those contracts with little interference from the state. Disputes arising under such contracts could be resolved in the courts, but in the United States and most other Western countries, the use of private means—negotiation, mediation, and commercial arbitration—to resolve such disputes came to be recognized as legitimate forms of conflict resolution.

In U.S. employment relations, the integrity of private employment contracts was highly respected under the traditional social contract. The imbalance of power between employers and employees, however, meant that in most instances, employers could effectively dictate the terms and conditions under which employees

Table 2.1. Conceptions of the Social Contract and Their Implications for Workplace Dispute Resolution

Social Contract	Era	Forces of Change	Breadth of Coverage	Purposes and Objectives	Effect on the Workplace	Disposition Toward Conflict and Dissent	Effect on Workplace Dispute Resolution
Classical	Seventeenth and eighteenth centuries	Decline of authority of the church and monarch	Very narrow: rulers and property-holding subjects	Justify authority of the sovereign and civil government	Supports authority of employer and master-servant doctrine	Conflict prevented or stringently controlled; dissent limited or suppressed	Reinforces authority of the sovereign, courts, and employers over workplace disputes
Traditional	Nineteenth and early twentieth centuries	Industrialization and the rise of the market economy	Narrow: Owners of capital, managers, and the state	Justify capitalism, free markets, and authority of owners and managers	Supports hierarchical structure of workplace and management's authority and prerogatives	Conflict considered dysfunctional; some tolerance of dissent; strikes generally unlawful	Heavy reliance on authority of employers and courts to control and resolve workplace disputes

New Deal	1930s to 1980s	Great Depression, challenge of communism, strikes and violence in labor disputes	Broad: Owners, managers, many workers (but not all), and the state	Justify capitalism and continuing authority of owners and managers but recognize legitimacy of unions	Supports management's authority and prerogatives except where modified by collective bargaining contracts	Recognition of some positive aspects of conflict; strikes lawful but regulated	Recognition of union and employee role in workplace dispute resolution; fosters use of mediation and arbitration, especially in union-management disputes
Emerging	1990s and beyond	Globalization, technological change, decline of unionism, and rise of information economy	Very broad: All stakeholders and most segments of society	Justify global capitalism, free markets, and competition; achieve balance between management authority and stakeholder rights	Hierarchy replaced by team-based work; professionalization of human resource function; growing use of high-performance work systems; employee participation in decision making	Conflict legitimate but needs to be managed; dissent tolerated and even encouraged; strikes lawful but less effective	Institutionalization of ADR and emergence of workplace conflict management systems

worked. Moreover, employers had the authority unilaterally to change the terms and conditions of employment. They could, for example, terminate employees at will. The employment-at-will doctrine, borrowed from British common law, allowed U.S. employers to discharge employees for virtually any reason whatsoever. The implicit social contract governing the workplace did not recognize the legitimacy of worker participation in any aspect of decision making at the workplace, unless employers on their own volition invited employees to play such a role. Throughout the nineteenth and early twentieth centuries, neither federal nor state courts in the United States were inclined to side with employees in disputes they might have with their employers. The courts enforced the employment-at-will doctrine and respected management's authority in the workplace.

The rise of unionism modified the traditional social contract, at least for employees who successfully formed unions. The New Deal social contract, the consequence of both the rise of unionism and the passage of legislation during the Roosevelt era, provided employees with protections and privileges they had never before enjoyed. The growth of collective bargaining changed the handling of workplace disputes. It made the use of mediation in new contract disputes and arbitration in grievance disputes the standard practice in many industries. The use of these dispute resolution techniques fostered the development of a skilled cadre of professional arbitrators and mediators. The successful use of arbitration and mediation to resolve labor disputes proved to be a benchmark for those who later championed the use of alternative dispute resolution. Although collective bargaining amended the traditional social contract and led to the introduction of new methods of dispute resolution, the New Deal social contract did not diminish management's ultimate authority in the workplace.

In this chapter we have described the forces of change that have brought about the transformation of the workplace social contract. Globalization, competition, technological change, the growing regulation of employment, and the litigation explosion are some of the critical environmental factors that have brought about a new social contract at the workplace. The rise of human resource management, the decline of unionism, and the reorganization of the workplace are some of the critical organizational factors associated with the new social contract. All of these forces, we maintain, have caused a transformation in conflict management in the United States. Under the traditional social contract, management's authority to manage and control conflict was largely unquestioned. Under the New Deal social contract, unions were given the right, under certain conditions, to challenge management's authority. Under the still-emerging new social contract, entirely new strategies and techniques are being used to manage and resolve conflict. We now turn to those new strategies and techniques.

Chapter Three

The Rise of Alternative
Dispute Resolution

For nearly three decades, a quiet revolution has been occurring in the U.S. system of justice: a dramatic growth in the use of alternative dispute resolution (ADR) to resolve disputes that might otherwise have to be handled through litigation. ADR techniques (arbitration, mediation, and so forth) probably have their roots in antiquity. According to Riskin and Westbrook, "Arbitration has an ancient lineage and an active present. King Solomon, Phillip II of Macedon and George Washington employed arbitration. Commercial arbitration has been used in England and the United States for hundreds of years."[1] By the nineteenth century, commercial arbitration had proved to be especially effective in resolving breach-of-contract claims between corporations. International arbitration has also long been used not only in commercial disputes but as a means of settling differences between nations.

Although ADR has had a long history, the contemporary growth in its use developed as a consequence of increasing dissatisfaction with the U.S. judicial system in the 1960s and 1970s. Complaints about the excessive costs and delays associated with litigation are not new, of course. Charles Dickens included a vivid depiction of the never-ending civil suit *Jarndyce* v. *Jarndyce* in *Bleak House*. A seminal event in the more recent development of ADR was the Pound Conference, "The Causes of Popular Dissatisfaction with the Administration of Justice," held in April 1976. At that conference, attended by more than two hundred judges, scholars, and leaders of the bar, Chief Justice Warren Burger called for the development of informal dispute resolution processes.[2]

Observers believe that the litigation explosion we described in Chapter Two is a principal cause of the rise of ADR. Over a thirty-year period, from 1963 to 1993, Congress passed at least two dozen major statutes regulating employment conditions, including the Civil Rights Act of 1964, the Occupational Safety and Health Act in 1970, the Employee Retirement Income Security Act in 1974, the Americans with Disabilities Act in 1990, the Civil Rights Act of 1991, and the Family and Medical Leave Act of 1993. These statutes gave rise to new areas of litigation, ranging from sexual harassment and accommodation of the disabled to age discrimination and wrongful termination. More and more dimensions of the employment relationship were brought under the scrutiny of the court system and a multitude of regulatory agencies.

Over time, litigants (especially employers) expressed increasing frustration with the legal system because of the long delays in resolving disputes, the expenses associated with the delays, and the often unsatisfactory outcomes. Increasingly, they turned to ADR as a means of avoiding these costs and delays. As critical actors in this changing milieu, corporations have recently been promoting the use of ADR in a wide range of conflicts with businesses, clients, customers, and their own employees. The time and cost associated with traditional litigation in each of these areas have been important factors pushing corporations toward the growing use of ADR processes.

THE PROS AND CONS OF ADR

From its inception, ADR has been controversial. On the one hand, it has been embraced by a coterie of champions who have always believed that its advantages over litigation were so obvious and compelling it would be only a matter of time before it was adopted universally. These champions have also been missionaries, proselytizing their faith in all quarters and making numerous converts. Like all true believers, ADR champions cannot understand why others have not yet "got the faith." Nevertheless, there has always been a group of ADR opponents who believe ADR undercuts our system of justice and must be resisted. ADR champions believe in the inevitability of ADR, while ADR opponents believe the move-ment to ADR can be stopped and even reversed.

The Advantages of ADR

Compared to litigation, the use of ADR has the great advantage of providing a faster, cheaper, and more efficient means of resolving disputes. The parties in a conventional court proceeding often invest considerable funds and energy from the time of the initial fil-ings in court, through interrogatories, depositions, and preparation for the trial itself, and then, 90 percent of the time, they negotiate a settlement on the courthouse steps or in the judge's chambers. The costs of litigation therefore include not only the awards or set-tlements themselves but also the so-called transaction costs of inside and outside legal counsel, expert witnesses, gathering docu-ments and engaging in discovery, and so forth. In the United States, the transaction costs of litigation are often two or three times greater than the settlements themselves.[3] Moreover, this cal-culation does not include the value of the time saved as a conse-quence of resolving disputes quickly. Reducing these opportunity costs may be the largest benefit of using ADR.

In theory, ADR is a means of circumventing the expensive, time-consuming features of conventional litigation. ADR processes are not usually confined by the legal rules that govern court pro-ceedings, such as those regarding the admissibility of evidence and the examination of witnesses. Arbitrators, for example, may con-duct expedited hearings, dispense with pre- or posthearing briefs, consider hearsay evidence, and allow advocates to lead their wit-nesses. Discovery is almost never a part of the mediation process and is used only slightly more often in arbitration, usually when the parties request it. (For a definition of *discovery*, see the glossary in Appendix B.) The parties have significantly more control over the ADR process than they would over a court proceeding. Within broad limits, they can design the ADR procedure themselves.

Because the disputants often jointly select the neutral (such as an impartial mediator or arbitrator), they are likely to have more trust and confidence in that person's ability than they would in a judge assigned to hear the case. Moreover, compliance with the eventual settlement is less likely to be a problem when the disputants have controlled the process that produced that outcome.

The Disadvantages of ADR

Although there are many advantages in using ADR, some observers contend that it poses a substantial threat to the system of justice in the United States. In effect, ADR transfers the dispute resolution function from public forums (the courts or regulatory agencies, for example) to private ones. Typically, ADR proceedings are private and confidential. In contrast to court decisions, arbitration decisions are seldom published because they are considered the property of the disputants. Proponents of ADR view the private and confidential nature of various ADR procedures as advantageous, but opponents worry that critical employment matters, often involving statutory claims and matters of public rights, are being resolved behind closed doors, beyond the scrutiny of public authority.

Critics also dislike arbitration because arbitrators' decisions are difficult to appeal. As we note later, there are only four grounds to vacate an award under the Federal Arbitration Act of 1925: (1) corruption, fraud, or undue means; (b) evident partiality; (3) arbitrator misconduct; or (4) excess or imperfect execution of arbitrator powers. As long as the arbitrator conducts a full and fair hearing (absent the four conditions), his or her decision will be truly final and binding. Although many employers believe the finality of arbitration is one of its advantages, later in this chapter we present results showing that over half of the respondents in our Fortune 1000 survey criticized arbitration because of the difficulty of appealing arbitrators' decisions.

Critics are also concerned about the difficulty of achieving a level playing field when ADR techniques are used. In fact, an increasing number of employers are requiring their employees, *as a condition of continued employment,* to waive their right to sue and to accept arbitration as a substitute means of resolving future disputes. We discuss this use of mandatory arbitration in employment relations elsewhere in this book. In a nutshell, ADR opponents maintain that there is an imbalance of power between employers and most employees, so employees have little choice but to accept a mandatory arbitration provision even if they would prefer not to. One critic has called mandatory predispute arbitration the "yellow dog contract" of contemporary employment relations.[4]

Another concern revolves around the question of representation in ADR proceedings. In arbitration and mediation cases, employees are not necessarily represented by attorneys or advocates of their own choosing, whereas employers are almost always represented by experienced attorneys and skilled professionals. Many employees cannot afford to hire attorneys; most employers can. Furthermore, critics say, employers have more experience and skill in selecting their legal counsel than do employees. Thus, even if an employee can retain an attorney, critics purport, the quality of his or her representation is likely to be inferior to the quality of representation on the employer's side of the table.

One line of research on employment arbitration has focused on the so-called repeat player effect. Bingham analyzed a large sample of employment arbitration awards and discovered that employers who made repeated use of arbitration won the great majority of their cases, while employers who used arbitration only once lost most of their cases.[5] Her research raises the possibility that repeat players, normally employers, have advantages in ADR because of their experience and expertise that one-shot players, normally employees, lack. Bingham's research has been highly controversial, but if she is right, the repeat-player phenomenon makes it all the more difficult to achieve a level playing field in employment ADR. In Chapter Five, we discuss safeguards that can be built into the design of conflict management systems that help ensure the existence of a level playing field. According to ADR critics, however,

the increasing privatization of the U.S. system of justice poses serious challenges for the guarantees of due process and equality under
the law.[6]

PATTERNS OF ADR USE

The apparent trend of corporations to rely more and more on the
use of ADR motivated us to conduct a survey in 1997 of the general counsel of the Fortune 1000 corporations.

A Survey of the Fortune 1000

During the first four months of 1997, the Institute on Conflict Resolution at Cornell University ran a mail and telephone survey of
the corporate counsel of the one thousand largest U.S.-based corporations. The objective of the survey was to obtain comprehensive information about each corporation's use of ADR from the
person in the organization responsible for, or most knowledgeable
about, the processes. Interviews were completed with 606 respondents. Given that surveys of high-level corporate populations usually generate response rates of less than 20 percent, this is a very
high rate.[7]

Although several years have passed since we conducted that
survey, it remains the only comprehensive survey of the use of
ADR in the U.S. corporate world. We are quite confident that the
evidence revealed in our data on the patterns of ADR usage, levels
of satisfaction, and emerging trends continues to have validity. Our
faith in the validity of our survey results is buttressed by several
years of conducting field studies in some of the corporations we surveyed. In fact, based on subsequent research and evidence, we
believe that corporate use of ADR has increased since we conducted the 1997 survey.

In roughly half the cases, the respondent in our survey was the
general counsel and in the other half, a deputy counsel or chief litigator. The survey instrument contained fixed-choice questions,

but the interviewers asked open-ended questions as well, which yielded valuable anecdotal material. The result was a rich harvest of information about the use of ADR by major U.S. corporations.

Prior to our research, only a handful of limited surveys sought data on how many corporations used ADR, what forms they used, what kinds of disputes they used ADR to resolve, and, perhaps most important for the purposes of this book, what they believed about the future of ADR in business in the United States.[8] In their 1999 review of research on ADR, Bingham and Chachere concluded that "about half of 'large' private employers ha[d] established some sort of formal dispute resolution procedure for their nonunion employees."[9] By the time of our survey, ADR had been in place long enough to permit corporate respondents to make judgments about some of the critical issues surrounding its use, including whether ADR had resulted in significant changes in the way disputes were resolved by U.S. corporations.

Experience with Forms of ADR

We asked respondents about eight forms of ADR we suspected were in wide use. Five of the forms involved the use of a process or procedure external to the organization: mediation, arbitration, mediation-arbitration, minitrials, and fact finding. Three of the forms involved the use of an in-house (or internal) process (in-house nonunion grievance procedure, peer review, and ombudsperson). It might be noted that in contrast to grievance procedures in collective bargaining relationships, the majority of the nonunion grievance procedures in these corporations did not culminate in arbitration. Rather, management reserved the right to make the final decision.

Figure 3.1 reports respondents' experiences with the eight forms of ADR we asked about. Nearly all reported some experience with ADR, with an overwhelming 87 percent having used mediation and 80 percent having used arbitration at least once in the three years prior to the survey. More than 20 percent said they had

**Figure 3.1. Experience with Forms of ADR
Among Fortune 1000 Companies**

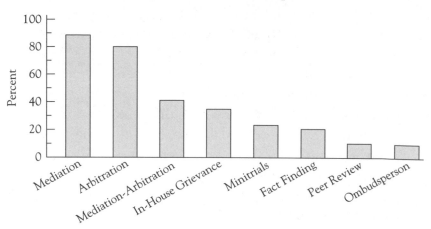

used mediation-arbitration, minitrials, fact finding, or employee in-house grievance procedures in the three prior years. Finally, respondents from about sixty corporations (10 percent) had had experience with ombudspersons and peer reviews.

Thus, the breadth of penetration of ADR into U.S. business was substantial, even surprisingly so. When asked their favorite form of ADR process, respondents overwhelmingly reported mediation (63 percent), with arbitration a distant second at 18 percent. Other forms of ADR appeared to remain significant choices in the corporation's tool kit, although they had clearly not replaced tried-and-true tactics. Because arbitration and mediation seem to dominate the use of ADR by the U.S. corporate world, we will focus on those two techniques.

Frequency of ADR Use

We also sought to learn about the depth of the penetration of ADR into the dispute resolution procedures of individual firms. In other words, having tried a process, does a firm resort to it again? Our survey asked respondents about the frequency of their use of media-

tion and arbitration in the prior three years (see Table 3.1).[10] Only
19 percent of those who had used mediation reported using it frequently or very frequently, almost 30 percent said they used it
rarely, and the largest group (43 percent) reported that they used it
occasionally. The pattern is similar for arbitration: 21 percent
reported frequent or very frequent use, 33 percent rare use, and 42
percent occasional use. These numbers are significantly smaller
than the responses to the question simply about use, indicating that
a much smaller group of firms had what could be called extensive
ADR experience. Thus, the reality of corporate ADR experience
was one of significant breadth but little depth.

Table 3.1 shows the frequency of ADR use in so-called rights
disputes. We were also interested in the frequency of ADR use in
so-called interest disputes. These two terms, which are commonly
applied in such fields as employment, have different meanings in
different arenas. We define a *rights dispute* as a conflict that arises
out of the administration of an already existing agreement and an
interest dispute as a conflict that arises during the negotiation of a
new agreement. In practical terms, interest disputes arise between
parties trying to forge a relationship, whereas rights disputes arise
between parties already in a relationship.

Table 3.1. Frequency of ADR Use in Rights Disputes

Frequency	Mediation	Arbitration
Company uses	87.0%	78.0%
Very frequently	5.6	7.5
Frequently	13.1	13.1
Occasionally	43.2	41.6
Rarely	29.9	33.2
Not at all	8.1	4.5
Company does not use	13.0	22.0

Note: In this table and Tables 3.2 and 3.3, the percentages on frequency of ADR
use apply only to the companies that reported that they had used mediation or
arbitration at least once in the preceding three years.

We found significantly different patterns in the forms of ADR used for rights disputes and interest disputes. To make it easy to compare results, Table 3.2 compares the use of mediation and arbitration in rights disputes (repeating data in Table 3.1) with the use of these techniques in interest disputes. Table 3.2 shows that almost 92 percent of the respondents had used mediation in rights disputes, but more than 60 percent had never used it for interest disputes. The table indicates a similar pattern for arbitration, with over 95 percent of the respondents reporting some use of arbitration in rights disputes, but nearly 64 percent having never used it in interest disputes. Therefore, wherever we examine frequency data in this book, we use only the findings concerning rights disputes.

In sum, according to the data from our survey, nearly all corporations have experience with ADR, primarily mediation and arbitration. A much smaller number use ADR frequently, even in rights disputes, and an even smaller number in interest disputes.

Table 3.2. Use of Mediation and Arbitration in Rights and Interest Disputes

Frequency	Rights Disputes (Administration of Contracts)	Interest Disputes (Negotiation of Contracts)
Mediation		
Very frequently	5.6%	1.7%
Frequently	13.1	2.1
Occasionally	43.2	7.6
Rarely	29.9	28.2
Not at all	8.1	60.4
Arbitration		
Very frequently	7.5	3.0
Frequently	13.1	2.1
Occasionally	41.6	10.7
Rarely	33.2	20.5
Not at all	4.5	63.7

We expected that corporations that had tried mediation or arbitration would be more likely to have also tried the other six ADR processes included in our survey, and the survey responses confirmed this. Companies that used mediation or arbitration frequently were much more likely to have experimented with less commonly used methods, such as ombudspersons or peer-based processes. Table 3.3 reports the data for this analysis. The mediation column shows that companies that used mediation very frequently had, on average, used four of the eight processes. Going down the column from "very frequent" to "not at all," there is a consistent decline in the average number of other processes used.

The arbitration column reveals a similar tendency among companies that frequently used arbitration. They were also more likely to have experimented with other ADR processes. In sum, the average Fortune 1000 company in 1997 used four of the eight processes included in our survey.

Contingent Use of ADR

Our survey also asked about the circumstances in which ADR was appropriate, including each corporation's general strategies when it was the initiating party and when it was the defending party. We thought that a company might prefer to litigate when initiating and negotiate when defending and that corporations could vary their strategy depending on the situation. Company A may sue

Table 3.3. Mean Number of ADR Processes Used by Fortune 1000 Companies in Mediation and Arbitration

Frequency of Use	Mediation	Arbitration
Very frequently	4.2	3.9
Frequently	3.7	3.9
Occasionally	3.4	3.3
Rarely	2.9	3.0
Not at all	2.7	2.5

Company B, and although B may want to negotiate a resolution, it may be obligated to defend itself in court. With those notions in mind, we asked questions relating to companies' overall strategy toward conflict resolution (see Table 3.4).

We found that most U.S. corporations used ADR on a contingency basis rather than as a matter of policy. Although most firms adopted a conditional posture, in general they were nevertheless open to the use of ADR. Combining the second and third categories in Table 3.4 shows that nearly half the major corporations in the United States had a contingent approach to ADR. A reasonably large proportion of the corporations (about one-fifth) had no policy on this matter, and their comments indicated that they set strategy on a dispute-by-dispute basis.

Only 5 percent and 6 percent of the corporations responded that they "always choose to litigate" when they are the defending and initiating parties, respectively. A larger group of the Fortune 1000 (approximately 11 percent) told us they "always choose ADR," whether defending or initiating. Our subsequent research reveals that a substantial number of these major U.S. corporations have developed conflict management systems for workplace disputes.

Table 3.4. Conflict Resolution Policies of Corporations

Strategy	Defending Party	Initiating Party
Always litigate	5.0%	6.1%
Litigate first; move to ADR when appropriate	24.7	21.4
Litigate only when appropriate; use ADR for all other disputes	25.2	27.0
Always try to use ADR	11.7	11.3
No company policy	20.8	22.1
Other	12.6	12.1

Before analyzing the 1997 data, we believed that if a corporation was the initiating party and at least was initially in control, its decision to use or not use ADR might better reflect corporate policy. Based on our data, it appears to make no difference. Corporate policy seems to be largely independent of a company's status as the defending or initiating party.

ADR Use by Type of Dispute

Although we focus on employment relations in this book, it is of interest to know to what extent corporations use ADR in other types of disputes as well. Initially, we suspected that the subject matter of a dispute might affect a corporation's preference for ADR rather than conventional litigation. We speculated that corporations might see it as advantageous to litigate certain types of disputes that the courts or administrative agencies were particularly well positioned to resolve or were more likely to produce a favorable outcome for the corporations. And we thought that corporations might see the conditions surrounding some areas of conflict as more favorable to negotiation. To ascertain whether these differences affected a corporation's preference for ADR, we asked the respondents whether they had used mediation or arbitration in eleven specific dispute situations (Table 3.5).

As the data indicate, the proportion of firms that had used mediation or arbitration to resolve different types of disputes varied widely. The raw rankings from high to low were similar for mediation and arbitration, with commercial and contract disputes and employment disputes leading both lists. Financial disputes of all types, including corporate finance, were rarely submitted to either form of ADR. The other types of disputes fell into a middle range. Mediation was used more extensively than arbitration in employment disputes, but the reverse was true of commercial disputes. Apparently, U.S. corporations use ADR selectively, the workplace being one arena in which it has found widespread acceptance.

Table 3.5. ADR Use by Type of Dispute

Type of Dispute	Mediation	Arbitration
Commercial, contract	77.7%	85.0%
Financial reorganization, workout	10.3	8.1
Consumer rights	24.1	17.4
Corporate finance	13.3	12.3
Employment	78.6	62.2
Environmental	30.8	20.3
Intellectual property	28.6	21.0
Personal injury	56.5	31.8
Product liability	39.3	23.3
Real estate	31.9	25.5
Construction	39.3	40.1

ADR Use by Industry

ADR use is not uniform. There are important variations among corporations in their preferences for one dispute process over another and in the kinds of cases for which they use ADR. Its use also varies significantly by industry, and we see at least two plausible reasons for this. First, within a particular industry, behavior patterns or norms tend to be uniform, and the use of ADR may be one such norm. Negotiation may be the preferred method of dispute resolution in one industry, for example, simply because it has always been used. Second, industry variation in ADR use may be attributable to the fact that conflicts in certain industries, such as construction, are more amenable to resolution with ADR techniques than conflicts in other industries.

Table 3.6 shows the proportion of corporations in each of the major industrial groups that have had some experience with each of the eight ADR procedures. These findings indicate that nearly all corporations have had some experience with mediation and with arbitration. All the firms in mining and construction reported having used both, and even in the service sector, where the levels

Table 3.6. Use of ADR Procedures by Industry

Procedure	Mining, Construction	Durable Manufacturing	Nondurable Manufacturing	Transportation, Communications, Utilities	Trade	Finance	Insurance	Service
Mediation	100%	87%	88%	90%	89%	90%	87%	84%
Ombudsperson	27	11	6	8	13	15	12	5
Fact-finding	9	20	15	21	30	22	20	23
Peer review	9	9	10	9	14	8	8	14
Arbitration	100	74	84	86	73	80	79	75
Minitrials	36	29	25	23	18	22	16	11
Mediation/ arbitration	45	41	37	42	40	41	49	46
In-house grievance procedure	27	28	24	41	34	49	39	35

of experience were the lowest overall, well over four-fifths of the firms had used mediation in the previous three years.

An examination of the less commonly used ADR techniques reveals more significant variation by industry. For example, nearly half the financial firms had an in-house grievance procedure, whereas only 24 percent of the nondurable manufacturing firms did. For ombudspersons and minitrials, firms in the mining and construction sector had significantly more experience than did firms in other industries. Thirty-six percent of mining and construction firms had used minitrials, as compared with only 11 percent of service firms. More than 27 percent of the mining and construction firms reported having an ombudsperson, whereas only 5 percent of the service firms did. Mining and construction firms were less likely than other firms to use fact finding. Finally, the use of peer review and mediation-arbitration did not seem to vary much across industries.

Most firms across all industries listed mediation as their preferred ADR technique, although the mining and construction sector had a substantial proportion (30 percent) preferring arbitration (see Table 3.7).

Corporate Conflict Resolution Policy by Industry

Industry differences may also account for differences in corporate policy. We classified all respondents into two policy groups: companies that tended always to litigate or to litigate first when they were the initiating party and companies that always used ADR, or sought to, and litigated only as a last resort. For this analysis, we eliminated companies with no stated ADR policy. As previously noted, many of the companies that always used ADR in fact had developed a conflict management system. In the next chapter, we discuss an analytical model that we believe explains a corporation's choice of conflict management strategy. Here we describe how corporate conflict resolution policies vary across industries.

As Figure 3.2 indicates, some industry differences are apparent. A raw ranking reveals that the mining and construction sector

Table 3.7. Preferred ADR Procedure by Industry

Procedure	Mining, Construction	Durable Manufacturing	Nondurable Manufacturing	Transportation, Communications, Utilities	Trade	Finance	Insurance	Service
Mediation	60%	70%	65%	63%	56%	68%	59%	50%
Ombudsperson	10	1	0	4	2	4	3	0
Fact-finding	0	1	3	0	3	6	0	0
Peer review	0	0	1	0	0	0	3	0
Arbitration	30	16	23	18	18	17	19	17
Minitrials	0	1	0	0	0	0	0	0
Mediation/arbitration	0	6	3	13	8	2	5	23
In-house grievance procedure	0	5	4	4	13	2	11	10

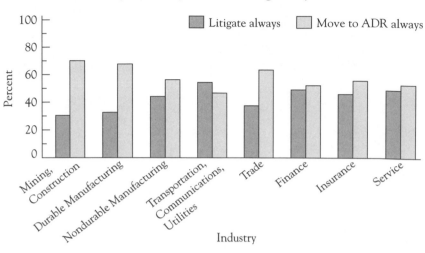

Figure 3.2. Corporate Conflict Resolution Policy
by Industry, for Initiating Party

tends to use ADR; in this group, 70 percent of the respondents reported that their firms used ADR most or all of the time to resolve disputes. By stark contrast, 54 percent of the firms in the transportation, communications, and utilities sector reported that they preferred to litigate, making this the industry group most likely to do so.

Up to this point, we have examined industry differences in the use of ADR, but not how often firms in these industries use the various processes. Table 3.8 shows how frequently firms in eight industries used mediation and arbitration. In the upper half of the table, the figure for the mining and construction sector stands out: 54 percent of the firms in this sector reported using mediation frequently or very frequently—more than twice the next-highest percentage, for the service sector.

The results are similar on the use of arbitration, with the percentage for firms in mining and construction higher than that in other industries: 60 percent of the firms in this sector reported that they use arbitration frequently or very frequently. Companies in all the other industries reported using arbitration much less frequently:

Table 3.8. Frequency in Use of Mediation and Arbitration by Industry

Frequency	Mining, Construction	Durable Manufacturing	Nondurable Manufacturing	Transportation, Communications, Utilities	Trade	Finance	Insurance	Service
Mediation								
Very frequently	9%	6%	1%	5%	1%	10%	14%	6%
Frequently	45	14	18	9	15	6	7	17
Occasionally	36	42	43	55	41	35	50	43
Rarely	0	31	32	26	35	31	20	29
Not at all	9	6	6	6	8	19	9	6
Arbitration								
Very frequently	10	4	5	8	9	8	10	6
Frequently	50	9	18	19	9	6	13	12
Occasionally	30	49	45	42	26	38	41	41
Rarely	10	34	28	28	49	34	31	41
Not at all	0	3	3	3	7	14	5	0

only 14 percent of the respondents in finance reported using arbitration very frequently or frequently; in durable manufacturing, the figure was 13 percent.

Why are the mining and construction industries so different from the other industries? In our fieldwork, we interviewed respondents at two major construction companies, Bechtel and Halliburton. They told us that construction may be the industry most in need of ADR because delay caused by a dispute can destroy a project or even a business. A construction project cannot be held up while a dispute with a supplier is being resolved in the courts. This industry has had to develop and nurture ADR procedures that allow work to continue while a dispute is being resolved.

Finally, we examined the use of mediation and arbitration by industry for different types of disputes (see Table 3.9). As we observed earlier, nearly all the industries reported heavy use of ADR for employment disputes: from a low of 64 percent in mining and construction to a high of 91 percent in service, most firms have used mediation. Nearly all the firms also reported using mediation in commercial and contract disputes. In disputes for which ADR use is less universal, however, there is significant variation by industry. Manufacturing firms used ADR to resolve environmental and intellectual property disputes more than firms in any of the other industries. Furthermore, finance firms showed substantially higher-than-average use of mediation for disputes about financial reorganization, consumer rights, and corporate finance. The result for consumer rights in the finance industry (57 percent) is easily explainable because ADR has long been established as the appropriate means for handling disputes between brokers and customers. The explanation for the higher use of mediation in financial reorganization or corporate finance disputes is not so straightforward. In some industries, below-average use clearly occurs because the concept of a dispute is irrelevant. A very small number of firms in finance report using mediation to resolve product liability cases, for example (they have no products in a conventional sense), and no mining or construction firms had used mediation to resolve disputes involving corporate finance.

Table 3.9. Firms Using Mediation and Arbitration by Type of Dispute and Industry

Type of Dispute	Mining, Construction	Durable Manufacturing	Nondurable Manufacturing	Transportation, Communications, Utilities	Trade	Finance	Insurance	Service
Mediation								
Commercial, contract	100%	90%	84%	83%	77%	91%	89%	79%
Financial reorganization	13	15	12	14	15	38	30	5
Consumer rights	29	33	25	43	27	57	52	45
Corporate finance	0	19	22	12	20	46	13	19
Employment	64	85	84	84	88	75	81	91
Environment	43	54	56	51	27	21	29	42
Intellectual property	17	64	55	23	31	18	15	44
Personal injury	67	72	74	70	69	45	71	60
Product liability	50	76	71	26	55	10	55	53
Real estate	50	33	36	54	51	59	50	47
Construction	100	48	60	65	55	47	50	42

(Continued)

Table 3.9. Continued

Type of Dispute	Mining, Construction	Durable Manufacturing	Nondurable Manufacturing	Transportation, Communications, Utilities	Trade	Finance	Insurance	Service
Arbitration								
Commercial, contract	100	88	91	92	85	87	81	94
Financial reorganization	0	12	20	15	13	15	18	7
Consumer rights	50	22	25	15	19	50	43	28
Corporate finance	0	20	21	6	17	40	24	18
Employment	71	69	71	73	76	58	58	71
Environment	40	45	35	33	31	9	5	12
Intellectual property	0	39	49	13	22	22	4	38
Personal injury	67	31	45	43	59	26	48	48
Product liability	60	38	48	14	46	7	33	26
Real estate	67	28	38	30	49	37	21	53
Construction	100	50	59	58	54	49	33	55

Clearly, the data show that significant differences exist in both practice and policy across industries and different patterns of use are developing, although nearly all U.S. corporations have had some experience with the basic ADR processes of arbitration and mediation. As we inspect the data more carefully, however, we see that ADR is used primarily to resolve specific types of disputes under specific circumstances. A much smaller number of companies have had extensive experience with ADR or have tried to use it as a general mechanism for dispute resolution.

WHY DO CORPORATIONS USE ADR?

Although there clearly is widespread experience with ADR in major U.S. companies, the reasons for its popularity need further explication. Fundamentally, three situations lead corporations to the use of ADR. First, in the course of doing business, a particular dispute may arise for which opting for an alternative to litigation may be desirable. Such ad hoc, case-by-case decision making may characterize much of corporate use of ADR. Second, corporations may agree in advance to use mediation or arbitration to resolve disputes that arise in the future. Our survey results suggest that a growing number of corporations are, in fact, incorporating ADR provisions in their contracts, warranties, and other agreements. Third, corporations may be ordered by a court or an administrative agency to attempt to resolve a dispute through mediation or arbitration. Such court-ordered ADR, which has become prevalent in some jurisdictions in recent years, plays a significant role in encouraging corporations to negotiate when they might not otherwise do so.[11]

In our 1997 survey, we discovered that the companies with the strongest pro-ADR policies tended to be the very largest companies in the Fortune 1000 and to be known for adopting so-called progressive policies in other areas. Many pro-ADR companies, for example, were among the first to embrace Total Quality Management and team-based production systems. Several were leaders in introducing high-performance work systems. Most faced significant global competitive pressures and had engaged in downsizing in the 1980s. A pro-ADR policy seems closely linked to this array of corporate policies.

Triggers for ADR

Our survey asked about the specific triggers for the use of mediation or arbitration. As Figure 3.3 shows, two primary mechanisms triggered the use of mediation: either circumstance led to an ad hoc, voluntary decision to mediate or a court ordered it. The decision to mediate in advance as part of a contract or as company policy was much less common. Few corporations mediated as a matter of company policy, although many had signed the CPR Institute for Dispute Resolution pledge to try ADR before litigation.[12]

In stark contrast to the triggers initiating mediation, corporations overwhelmingly pursued a process of arbitration because the parties had agreed to it in advance and had included it as a provision in a contract. The counsel for a mutual life insurance company, for example, told us, "My company generally does not volunteer to use arbitration. We only use it when we are required to do so contractually. We operate a registered brokerage, which is

Figure 3.3. ADR Triggers for Mediation and Arbitration in U.S. Corporations

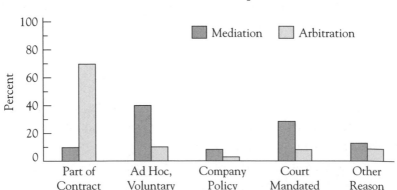

a member of the National Association of Securities Dealers [NASD]. NASD requires arbitration, and so we use it under that agreement." This typifies corporations' experience overall. Only rarely (in 8 percent of the cases) did corporations report using arbitration because courts ordered them to do so, and parties chose to arbitrate only 10 percent of the time.

We surmise that mediation is tried more experimentally and more readily, compared with arbitration, because the stakes are lower. If mediation does not work out, the parties can always revert to litigation. The courts seem to be in concert with that view in that they are ordering mediation much more frequently than they are advisory arbitration. Even when the courts urge the parties to mediate, however, there is no assurance that the parties will make serious efforts to reach agreement. The decision to arbitrate, on the other hand, except in rare cases means the parties must accept the outcome of the process. Consequently, their decisions to enter into this form of ADR are much more deliberate.

We have observed in our research that the corporations most likely to agree in advance to use mediation or arbitration are those most experienced in using ADR.[13] This observation leads us to speculate that employers' growing experience with ADR will lead to their greater reliance in the future on incorporating mediation and arbitration provisions in agreements signed in advance of the actual occurrence of disputes—that is, to mandatory predispute arbitration or mediation. This trend has been fostered by a series of Supreme Court decisions favoring mandatory arbitration. Indeed, if key players in a growing number of companies are comfortable with arbitration or mediation, knowledgeable about its workings, and satisfied with the outcomes produced, we would expect in the future to see more companies signing agreements in advance and moving toward the use of conflict management systems and fewer companies subject to court-ordered arbitration or mediation, or using ADR on an ad hoc, case-by-case basis.

These observations are supported by the data in Table 3.10. We compared the triggers for mediation with the frequency of its use

Table 3.10. Triggers for Use of Mediation and
Arbitration by Frequency of Use

Frequency	Required by Contract	Ad Hoc	Company Policy	Court Ordered	Other
Mediation					
Very frequently	14%	17%	34%	21%	14%
Frequently	13	35	25	16	10
Occasionally	11	47	5	25	13
Rarely	7	38	2	39	14
Not at all	7	36	2	38	17
Arbitration					
Very frequently	82	6	9	0	3
Frequently	82	2	3	3	10
Occasionally	73	9	2	8	7
Rarely	63	14	2	11	10
Not at all	43	14	5	14	24

and found that the more frequently a company mediated, the more likely it was to agree in advance (by contractual clause or company policy) to use mediation. Among companies that used mediation very frequently, 14 percent reported they used it because it was contractually required, compared with only 7 percent for companies that rarely used the process. Companies that used mediation very frequently were the least likely to use it on a case-by-case basis. Only 17 percent of companies that mediated very frequently decide to do so on a case-by-case basis; for companies that went to mediation frequently, the figure was 35 percent, and it was even higher for companies that used mediation less frequently.

Company policy drove the decision to mediate only among companies that used mediation frequently or very frequently and almost never among those that used the process less often. The frequency of court-ordered mediation, with the decision to do so outside the control of the parties, does not seem to have varied as significantly, although it was ordered somewhat less frequently if the companies involved in the dispute generally used mediation a great deal. This may very well indicate that parties predisposed to mediate disputes were rarely ordered to do so by the courts, in all likelihood because they had already exhausted mediation as a means of dispute resolution.

Table 3.10 shows that we also examined triggers for the use of arbitration by the frequency of its use. As might be expected, the more frequently a company had previously used arbitration, the more a contract or company policy triggered its use. The vast majority of companies that used arbitration frequently or very frequently did so because of contractual arrangements. As already noted, court-ordered arbitration was relatively rare. When it did occur, it was almost always imposed on parties that rarely used arbitration, and in our sample, it was never ordered for companies that used arbitration very frequently. Companies that used arbitration frequently also rarely chose to use it on a case-by-case basis, whereas companies that used the process less frequently were more likely to choose it under ad hoc circumstances.

Overall, these data indicate that arbitration is a relatively fixed process, favored by those who have more experience with it and agree in advance that it will be the means of resolving disputes. By contrast, mediation is triggered in many different ways. In addition, the survey data suggest that those who have used mediation relatively frequently exhibit an increased preference for using it again.

Economic Reasons for Using ADR

Our survey asked respondents why their corporations used mediation and arbitration and allowed them to choose any of fourteen possible reasons for doing so. These responses provide us with a reasonably complete understanding of the forces that cause a company to decide to mediate or arbitrate a particular dispute.

One of the more significant forces that appears to have been driving corporations toward the use of ADR was the cost of litigation and the length of time needed to reach a settlement. In many cases, ADR offered a significant financial carrot for corporations. All else being equal, it is widely believed that it is cheaper and more time efficient to use ADR. According to our respondents, this is the case. In Figure 3.4, we present the responses to two questions: Does the use of mediation (arbitration) save time, and Does the use of mediation (arbitration) save money? Overwhelmingly, respondents answered yes, although the percentage answering yes for arbitration was slightly lower. More than 80 percent of the respondents believed that mediation saves time and money, while slightly less than 70 percent believed that arbitration saves time and money.

Saving time and money may be the reasons most widely cited for using ADR, but corporations cite many other reasons as well. Our survey results suggest that some corporations use ADR without obtaining adequate evidence that it will actually save their organization money. Indeed, a few corporations choose to use ADR even if doing so might cost more money than litigation. In most cases, corporations use ADR for a combination of reasons: to save time and money and to achieve other objectives as well. Table 3.11 shows the percentage of respondents who told us that the factor listed in the table was a reason their corporation used either mediation or arbitration.

**Figure 3.4. Instrumental Value of ADR
to Companies That Use It**

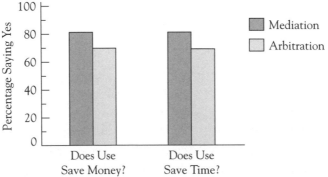

Table 3.11. Reasons Companies Use Mediation and Arbitration

Reasons	Mediation	Arbitration
Uses expertise of neutral	53.2%	49.9%
Preserves good relationships	58.7	41.3
Required by contract	43.4	91.6
Provides more durable resolution	31.7	28.3
Preserves confidentiality	44.9	43.2
Avoids legal precedents	44.4	36.9
More satisfactory settlements	67.1	34.8
More satisfactory process	81.1	60.5
Court mandated	63.1	41.9
Dispute involves international parties	15.3	31.9
Allows parties to resolve disputes themselves	82.9	—
Has limited discovery	—	59.3
Standard industry practice	—	33.7

The most often cited reason for using mediation was that the process allows the parties to resolve the dispute themselves; no settlement can be reached unless both sides agree to it. About 83 percent of the respondents said that this was one of the reasons they used mediation. In contrast to mediation, of course, the use of arbitration or the court system will lead to decisions being imposed on the parties.

Three of the next four reasons for using mediation are also linked to the same theme: that it offers the corporation greater control over the dispute resolution process and its outcome. Eighty-one percent of those surveyed said that mediation provided a more satisfactory process than litigation, 67 percent said it provided more satisfactory settlements, and 59 percent reported that it preserved good relationships. These responses indicate that mediation provides not just an alternative but a superior process for reaching a resolution.

The remaining reasons for using mediation were not as widely supported by our respondents. Just over half the respondents saw the mediator's expertise as an advantage of the process. Many of the respondents appear, however, to have some ambivalence about the qualifications of mediators and arbitrators, a finding we discuss later in this chapter. Finally, some parties engaged in mediation because it was required by contract (43 percent) or was court mandated (63 percent).

In the open-ended portion of our interviews, our respondents elaborated on their reasons for choosing to mediate, as the following comments illustrate:

> One reason we use mediation is because we have a lot of environmental disputes involving complicated scientific issues, and we can select a mediator who knows more about such issues than a judge would.

> Mediation creates an environment in which the parties can speak freely about their perspective on the merits of the claim. There doesn't seem to be the filtering that occurs in the courtroom.

> Mediation allows each side to understand what's really important to the other side. It's not always simply a matter of money. Sometimes a simple apology can go a long way to resolving a dispute.

> In employment law disputes, mediation provides a catharsis for people who think they've been wrongly injured. It helps them get over their problem.

Now let us turn to the results presented in Table 3.11 regarding the respondents' reasons for using arbitration. The overwhelming reason respondents gave was that arbitration was required by contract: the corporation had agreed to pursue this route before the dispute arose.

In general, the support for arbitration among corporations was not as strong as it was for mediation.[14] Just over 60 percent of respondents, for example, said they believed arbitration provides a more satisfactory process than litigation. Although this suggests that "more satisfactory process" is a strong motive for using arbitration, it is clearly a much stronger motive for using mediation. Respondents also supported the other process-control reasons for using arbitration in smaller, albeit significant, numbers. As one respondent representing the view of a large insurance company said, "Arbitration is cheaper [than litigation], faster, confidential, final, and binding. What more can I say?" Some other differences also emerged in respondents' views of mediation and arbitration. Although two-thirds thought that mediation produced more satisfactory settlements than litigation, only about one-third had that view of arbitration. Nearly 60 percent believed that mediation preserves good relationships, while 41 percent believed arbitration did. Thus, although there is strong support for the belief that arbitration saves time and money, there is much less for the notion that arbitration has value as a means of controlling the process of dispute resolution.

WHY SOME CORPORATIONS DO NOT USE ADR

Of the more than six hundred corporations in our sample, respondents from only thirty-five told us their corporations never used ADR. Some were adamantly opposed to its use. One told us, "ADR is a response to perceived problems in a system that's worked for two hundred years. Let's fix the problems rather than develop new ones." The corporations in this group tended to be smaller than average (although all corporations listed in the Fortune 1000 are very large indeed). They also tended to be very profitable corporations under much less cost pressure than the pro-ADR group. Several have had reputations for dealing with unions in a militant fashion.

In our interviews with corporate counsel, we discovered several key reasons that some corporations chose not to use ADR. Some of the lawyers told us that they would use ADR only if and when senior management supported it. Although many senior managers approved of ADR and supported its use and the counsel's office could exercise broad discretion in its choice to use ADR in routine disputes, the use of ADR ordinarily requires the support of top managers in disputes involving important legal principles or potentially large settlements. The bigger the case and the higher the stakes, the more likely it is that the CEO or the chairman of the board will participate in the decision to use ADR. Also, adopting a set of strong ADR policies usually requires the participation of both the counsel's office and other top managers. The corporate decision to use a conflict management system, which we discuss in Chapter Four, is often a strategic decision and is likely to involve the CEO and other top managers in addition to the general counsel.

Our interviews also suggested that the use of ADR was sometimes viewed as threatening by middle managers who make many decisions that are the source of corporate disputes yet want their decisions to be supported by the corporation. If top management uses ADR to arrive at negotiated agreements that compromise those decisions, middle managers may feel that their authority is undermined.

Some of our respondents told us that they did not use ADR because it was too difficult to initiate. That is, in some respects, it was easier to initiate a court suit than to pursue mediation or arbitration. Why is this? Quite simply because using ADR usually requires the agreement of the opposing party in a dispute and reaching such an agreement through negotiations with an adversary can be difficult. Even initiating a discussion of the possibility of a negotiated settlement can be seen as a sign of weakness. Thus, in some disputes, both parties may even prefer to settle but be unable to initiate a negotiation process because they do not want to signal anything but a determination to litigate to the end.

Even if one party sees potential gains to both disputants from opting for ADR, there is no guarantee that its adversary will have the same assessment. The use of ADR requires a level of sophistication that both parties may not have. The opposing party in a lawsuit brought against a corporation may have an emotional investment in the dispute that prevents it from understanding the potential benefits of ADR. Moreover, the use of ADR to resolve disputes tends to blur, if not eliminate, the distinction between winners and losers. This is particularly true for negotiated settlements, and sometimes for arbitrated settlements in which the arbitrator has split the difference. Corporate counsel may not care, but this distinction may be important to an opposing lawyer. If both the opposing counsel and client believe there is a chance for a big victory in a suit against a major corporation, their inclination to agree to use ADR may be seriously limited.

Therefore, because the use of ADR generally requires a negotiated agreement between the complaining and responding disputants and because there are numerous impediments to achieving such agreements, there may be a tendency to resort to litigation even when the benefits of using ADR are apparent. Several of our respondents in fact emphasized that using ADR requires a change in the disputants' mind-sets—that is, in the culture of handling disputes—and not merely the ad hoc consideration of alternative methods for resolving them.

Aspects of ADR Processes Companies Find Disadvantageous

Some companies do not use ADR because they find aspects of the mediation or arbitration process undesirable, some of them the very same characteristics that other companies find advantageous. A general counsel from a public utility told us, for example, "Cost isn't the issue—it's the lack of rules. Litigation may be expensive, but it does have rules. Unless we see a fair and quick resolution, we don't use mediation." In some disputes, the lack of legal rules and constraints helps expedite settlement, but in others, corporate lawyers prefer the procedural safeguards provided by conventional litigation. This especially appears to be the case in disputes that involve important legal principles.

For decades, federal courts have been inclined to defer to decisions made by arbitrators. Most state courts have developed comparable policies. The courts have consistently supported the

enforceability of agreements to arbitrate entered into by the disputants. At the same time, they have granted arbitrators broad discretion to decide issues of arbitrability—that is, what matters are or
are not arbitrable under arbitration agreements. The courts have
also allowed arbitrators considerable latitude in fashioning appropriate remedies. As long as an arbitrator holds a full and fair hearing, allows each party to make a full and complete presentation of
its case, and arrives at a decision that is not arbitrary, or capricious,
or "repugnant" to public policy, the courts will normally refuse to
consider an appeal.[15] The broad discretion the courts have granted
arbitrators and the virtual finality of arbitrators' decisions have
made arbitration a desirable alternative to litigation in many cases.
In other cases, however, as our respondents noted, these characteristics are the reasons corporations may choose not to use it.

Several respondents noted that the arbitration process is beginning to match litigation in costliness and complexity. The counsel
from a large energy company said, "Arbitration is proving to be just
as burdensome as litigation. The opposition can use arbitration to
elongate the process. It can take over six months simply to agree on
an arbitration panel. You can be constantly running back to arbitrators for decisions on discovery. It is a process fraught with potential
abuse." This view was echoed in the comments of a respondent from
a major paper products corporation: "Arbitration oftentimes includes
the worst characteristics of litigation without any of the benefits. The
arbitrator can let anything into the record, and the process can be
every bit as expensive and burdensome as civil litigation."

For many corporations, the decision to use ADR (or to adopt
pro-ADR policies) is apparently a pragmatic one, based largely on
an analysis of the costs and benefits of using ADR compared with
the costs and benefits of resorting to litigation. One respondent
told us, "In some cases, it's simply not appropriate to use mediation,
and in other cases it is. In some cases, the dollar amount of the
claim isn't high enough to waste our time on mediation. We
believe the benefit from mediation comes in cases involving multiple claimants and more than $1 million in claims."

It is widely recognized that the use of either mediation or arbitration tends to result in compromise settlements. Mediators attempt to persuade negotiators to make offers and counteroffers until a compromise agreement is reached. Arbitrators, in the minds of some, consider the positions the parties have presented at the hearing and then make an award that splits the difference between the parties' positions. The perceived tendency of ADR to produce compromise settlements can serve as a barrier to the use of mediation and arbitration, according to a significant number of our respondents. The counsel for a food products corporation told us, "We're reluctant to use binding arbitration. If the matter in dispute is very serious or involves great amounts of money, then we don't use arbitration because arbitrators have a strong tendency to compromise rather than do what may be right. Minor matters may be arbitrated but not major ones. We may be more likely to use mediation in both major and minor cases, but we don't have a set policy."

Again, when a corporation believes that a dispute involves an important matter of principle, it is less willing to consider a process in which concession and compromise are inherent characteristics. A lawyer from a prominent midwestern manufacturing company told us that the organization avoided the use of ADR because it wanted to establish a reputation as a company that would never compromise in critical disputes. In the long run, this company maintained, a reputation for fighting in every major dispute would serve as a deterrent to lawsuits and save it money. Another respondent, from a corporation based in California, said, "Sometimes we want a total victory in a lawsuit. We want to inflict some pain and suffering on our adversary. In those cases, we're not likely to use mediation."

Finally, a surprising number of respondents told us they did not use ADR because they lacked trust and confidence in ADR neutrals, especially arbitrators. Although there is no shortage of individuals available to serve as mediators and arbitrators, many of our respondents believed there is a shortage of truly qualified neutrals. For example, a company in the maritime business had trouble finding an arbitrator with special knowledge of both maritime law and the international law of the sea. Under the circumstances, it preferred to litigate the dispute rather than take a chance on an arbitrator's lacking the expertise the corporation thought was necessary.

The various influences impeding the use of ADR can be summarized as follows:

- Senior managers are opposed.
- Middle managers fear loss of control.
- ADR is too difficult or too complicated to initiate.
- Arbitration and mediation are not confined to legal rules.
- Opposing parties are unwilling to consider using ADR.
- ADR results in too many compromise settlements.
- Managers lack confidence in neutrals.

In our survey, we asked the respondents to tell us whether these factors were important in their companies' decision not to use ADR. Table 3.12 summarizes these results. Overwhelmingly, our respondents indicated that the principal reason they did not use either mediation or arbitration was that the opposing party in the dispute was unwilling to agree to it. In the case of mediation, three-quarters of the respondents said they did not use it because the opposing party was unwilling; the figure for arbitration was 63 percent. About 40 percent of respondents said they did not use mediation because it was a nonbinding procedure and resulted in compromise outcomes. In the case of arbitration, 54 percent said they did not use it because arbitrators' decisions were difficult to appeal. About 49 percent did not like the fact that arbitration hearings are not confined to legal rules, and about half indicated that they sometimes did not use arbitration because it resulted in compromise outcomes. Thus, many of our respondents viewed these features, often seen as advantages of the arbitration process, as barriers to its use.

A significant proportion of our respondents (29 percent in the case of mediation and 35 percent in the case of arbitration) said

Table 3.12. Reasons Corporations Do Not Use ADR

Reason	Mediation	Arbitration
No desire from senior management	28.6%	35.0%
Too costly	3.9	14.8
Too complicated	4.6	9.9
Nonbinding	40.9	—
Difficult to appeal	—	54.3
Not confined to legal rules	28.1	48.6
Lack of corporate experience	24.7	25.9
Unwillingness of opposing party	75.7	62.8
Results in compromise outcomes	39.8	49.7
Lack of confidence in neutrals	29.0	48.3
Lack of qualified neutrals	20.2	28.4
Risk of exposing strategy	28.6	—

they did not use ADR techniques because senior management had no desire to use them. As we have noted, the active involvement and support of senior management is especially necessary when important matters of strategy, policy, or principle are involved.

Very few respondents indicated that they did not use mediation because it was "too costly" or "too complicated." As Table 3.12 shows, these considerations were somewhat more important in the decision not to use arbitration but much less important than the other barriers listed. A respondent who had a negative view of mediation represented a corporation headquartered in Indiana. She told us, "We've decided as a company we don't want to use mediation. We feel in nonbinding situations it's just an added step. It costs us time and money, and it just leads into other steps in the litigation process. We don't think we're achieving anything when we use mediation."

The following negative views reflect the opinions of a small minority of the respondents in our study. Nonetheless, they provide some understanding of why other companies do not use mediation:

Generally mediation is used only at the end of the long drawn-out part of the discovery process, and you're pretty much into trial by then. It really doesn't save time.

Using mediation can be more complicated than litigation. When it works, it avoids costs, but when it doesn't work, it is basically going to trial twice.

We don't use mediation anymore. I can't think of any circumstance where we found mediation to be productive.

Not a lot of people are familiar with mediation, and it's always a battle to get people to agree to it unless they've been through it before. And lawyers are more afraid of it than the parties.

Concerns About Neutrals' Qualifications

The respondents' concern about the qualifications of neutrals requires elaboration. Our respondents told us they chose their neutrals primarily from private ADR providers—like the American Arbitration Association (AAA) or JAMS—or from their own previous experience or recommendations from colleagues by word of mouth. Their views of the qualifications of the neutrals they used are summarized in Table 3.13. The level of satisfaction is generally high: more than 94 percent of the mediators they had used (and 93 percent of the arbitrators) were seen as somewhat qualified or very qualified. These results need to be interpreted carefully, however. As Table 3.13 shows, only 27 percent of the respondents thought the arbitrators they had used were *very* qualified, whereas two-thirds thought they were only *somewhat* qualified. We cannot say with certainty what each respondent actually meant by "somewhat qualified," although a comment made by one respondent may provide a clue. He told us that his corporation had been involved in quite a few arbitration cases and that the qualifications of the arbitrators in these cases varied significantly. Some were very qualified,

Table 3.13. Satisfaction with Qualifications of ADR Neutrals

Opinion	Mediators	Arbitrators
Very qualified	41.2%	26.8%
Somewhat qualified	53.3	66.1
Not qualified	1.0	1.7
Don't know	4.6	5.4
Percentage who have a lack of confidence in mediators or arbitrators	29.0	48.3
Percentage who say there is a lack of qualified mediators or arbitrators	20.2	28.4

and others were not. In our survey, he answered "somewhat qualified" as a way of suggesting the average quality of the arbitrators his company had used. The fact that so many respondents thought their arbitrators were only somewhat qualified is disturbing, especially because nearly half of our respondents reported that they lacked confidence in arbitrators.

Overall, it appears that our respondents' evaluations of mediators and arbitrators are mixed. They are generally satisfied with the qualifications of the neutrals they have used, but have reservations about some of them, especially when specialized expertise is required. As one respondent said, "We have a lot of intellectual property disputes, but we don't think arbitrators do a good job with them. There simply aren't any qualified arbitrators in this area." Several respondents thought that better training programs for neutrals were needed, and others recommended improving the means of certifying neutrals' expertise.

CONCLUSION

Nearly all U.S. corporations have some experience with the basic ADR processes of arbitration and mediation. A much smaller number of companies have extensive experience with ADR or have tried to use it as a general mechanism for dispute resolution.

Our findings show that in most U.S. corporations, mediation, arbitration, and other ADR processes are not yet institutionalized. In general, parties are reluctant to agree in advance to mediate and make that decision on a case-by-case basis. Arbitration, although less widely used, is almost always agreed to in advance. The companies that use both mediation and arbitration more frequently seem much more willing to incorporate these processes into contracts and to try ADR processes as a matter of company policy.

The reasons corporations have moved toward using ADR can be divided broadly into cost and process-control categories. Most of the participants in our study believed that there were instrumental reasons to use ADR processes; compared with conventional dispute resolution processes, they saved their companies time and money. But there was strong support for the notion that regaining control of the dispute resolution process was an important motivation as well. For some corporations, in fact, particularly those that were not under significant cost pressures, the opportunity to regain control may have been their most important motivation.

There were several important reasons major U.S. corporations did not use ADR. The difficulty of negotiating ADR agreements with reluctant adversaries appears to have been the principal impediment. This barrier may become less important in the future as the parties in disputes learn more about the benefits of ADR. But the use of ADR was also impeded in part by certain intrinsic characteristics of mediation and arbitration, for example, the tendency of these processes to result in compromise settlements. As parties in disputes acquire more sophisticated knowledge about the nature of ADR, they will learn more about the nature of mediation and arbitration. Their use of ADR in the future will depend on whether the potential benefits of ADR are greater than the impediments.

The ADR policy that a corporation adopts appears to be systematically related to a set of economic and market factors, as well as the corporation's conscious strategies. Large corporations that have faced intense competitive pressures and have engaged in downsizing and reengineering appeared more likely to have had strong pro-ADR policies. Corporations that have adopted cutting-edge management strategies also seem likelier to be pro ADR. Smaller, more profitable corporations, sometimes controlled by one or two families, were more likely to favor litigation. When it comes to choosing between litigation and ADR, these companies would rather fight than switch. In the next chapter, we present an analytical model of the corporation's choice of a conflict management strategy that incorporates these findings.

A logical question that follows is whether corporate policies have an effect on the actual disposition and real cost of disputes. Our 1997 survey did not provide a clear answer to this question, and there has not been very much systematic research on these critical questions conducted by other researchers. We do know, however, that our survey respondents believed overwhelmingly that the use of ADR had saved them time and money.

Chapter Four

New Strategies of Conflict Management

The Emergence of a New Paradigm

We have concluded, based on our research, that there is a great deal of variance in the choice of conflict management strategy by U.S. corporations, ranging from traditional reliance on litigation to experimentation with various ADR techniques to the adoption of a conflict management system.[1]

In this chapter we discuss the emergence of workplace conflict management systems and analyze the environmental and organizational factors that seem to explain the variance concerning the choice of a conflict management strategy by an organization. Drawing on our field research, we then describe three conflict management strategies that U.S. corporations and other organizations use, illustrating the discussion with examples based on our fieldwork.

AN ANALYTICAL MODEL OF THE CHOICE OF CONFLICT MANAGEMENT STRATEGY

ADR and conflict management systems seem to have arisen largely as a response to changes—some long term and some short term—in the organizational environment that made their use an effective alternative to conventional litigation. These environmental changes were filtered through a set of the organizations' motivations, resulting in some organizations' choice of a conflict management strategy.

Three Strategies of Conflict Management

As the model depicted in Figure 4.1 shows, we divide the dependent variable in our model, the organization's choice of conflict
management strategy, into three categories: contend, settle, and
prevent. These categories are obviously somewhat arbitrary. In
truth, organizational strategy ranges across a spectrum, and group-
ing large numbers of organizations in a particular category may blur
important differences across organizations within that category. To
some degree, each organization we studied had its own unique conflict management strategy, tailored to fit its own objectives and circumstances. Nevertheless, we believe that our three-part
categorization captures the most fundamental differences in organizational strategy that we observed in our research.

In the *contend* category are organizations that clearly prefer litigation to ADR; they never or rarely use any ADR technique to
resolve a dispute. They reject the use of ADR as a matter of organizational policy, although occasionally some of them accept the
use of mediation or arbitration in a particular dispute.

In the *settle* category are a majority of the major corporations in
the United States. Again, we recognize that there are critical differences in organizational strategy across this large group of companies, but in general these corporations, and most other large

Figure 4.1. Organizational Strategic Approaches
to Conflict Management

organizations, use ADR either as a matter of policy or on an ad hoc basis in a variety of different types of disputes.

In the *prevent* category are organizations that apparently use ADR in all types of disputes as a matter of policy. Many of these organizations have developed conflict management systems; rather than merely use a particular dispute resolution technique as a matter of practice or even policy, they have developed a comprehensive set of policies designed to prevent (if possible) or to manage conflict.

The Disposition of Decision Makers

The choice of an organization's conflict management strategy, we discovered, often reflects the decision makers' dominant disposition regarding the nature of conflict. Many decision makers view conflict as being either *zero sum* or *variable sum*, terms we borrow from game theory. Others have frequently applied these terms to the choice of a negotiating strategy and we apply them here in the context of conflict management.[2]

Zero-Sum Strategies. Decision makers who view conflict as primarily a zero-sum game believe that the resolution of conflict always (or at least usually) results in there being a winner and a loser. They view every conflict as a contest over the allocation of a fixed sum of benefits or rewards. At the start of a "game," each party has a proportion of the available rewards. Each side would like to increase its share of the rewards—in the extreme, to capture all of the available rewards. Under those circumstances, one party's gain necessarily comes at the expense of the other. The more one party is able to increase its share of the rewards, the smaller the share received by the other party (or parties) in the contest. The proverbial pie is fixed in size and divided between the parties. Each party would like to have the entire pie, but failing to obtain all of it, a "winner" in the conflict at least manages to obtain most of it. Because one party's gain can come only at the other party's expense, zero-sum games result in win-lose outcomes.

Some of the managers and lawyers we interviewed in our study seemed to view conflict through a zero-sum prism. For these decision makers, victory was essential in every contest they entered. Very often victory was not defined in terms of actual benefits and costs but rather in terms of perceived benefits and costs. It was important to these managers to appear to have won disputes that arose with employees and others. Often a contestant in a zero-sum game attaches value not only to how much he or she receives but also to how much his or her opponent loses. Even if winning on the corporation's terms were not possible, these managers attached great value to "fighting the good fight." They believed that contesting every claim made by an employee served to build the employer's reputation for toughness and to deter other employees from making claims in the future. Like the philosopher Thomas Hobbes, some of them believe "nature is red in tooth and claw" and organizational survival is a Darwinian struggle in which only the fittest survive. Decision makers who view conflict as a zero-sum game naturally tend to choose the contend approach to conflict management.

Not all of the decision makers in the contend category in our research had a zero-sum view of conflict, but many did. Among managers of companies in this category, even those who had a less drastic view of the nature of conflict thought it was important to protect the corporation's reputation by using litigation to deter future claims. They may have had a more pragmatic—and less dogmatic—view of the nature of conflict, but they thought the use of negotiation, mediation, and other ADR techniques invariably resulted in compromises and concessions that did not serve the interests of their organizations. Compromise and concession, in their view, were signs of weakness and served only to encourage adversaries to bring claims against the corporation.

Decision makers with a zero-sum disposition toward conflict do not believe that the benefits of using any form of ADR outweigh the costs. They believe that in the longer term, their interests are best served by using a strategy of litigating virtually every claim brought against them. We do not share this point of view. We do believe, however, that an organization's choice of conflict management strategy needs to be tailored to its philosophy, values, and objectives. Insofar as an organization's choice of a conflict management strategy is concerned, we do not want to be presumptuous and claim that one size fits all. Clearly, many of the companies that have chosen the contend strategy are satisfied with this approach and have no intention of changing in the near future.

Variable-Sum Strategies. Many decision makers who strongly favor ADR and the prevent strategy of conflict management consciously or implicitly view conflict as primarily a variable-sum game. That is, they do not necessarily believe that one side's gain in the resolution of a conflict is the other side's loss. They do not view every conflict as a contest over the allocation of a fixed sum of rewards. Rather, they believe that in most conflicts, there is a possibility of both parties' winning. The sum of the rewards—the size of the pie—available to the parties is not fixed but can be expanded, and both (or all) parties can end up in a more advantageous position than they were before the conflict arose. For a party in a variable-sum contest, winning the contest does not mean that the other side loses. Variable-sum games, if played correctly, can result in win-win outcomes.

There were clearly decision makers in our study who viewed conflict through a variable-sum prism. For them, being the victor was not an important objective; rather, doing their utmost to achieve outcomes that served the organization's best interests was the target. Managers who pursue variable-sum conflict management strategies do not attach great value to winning and losing, nor are they concerned about maintaining their reputations for toughness. They do not believe that fighting the good fight is ordinarily an efficient means of achieving an organization's objectives because contending every claim may consume the organization's time and money, with little discernible effect on the achievement of desirable outcomes. They believe that most, if not all, situations that initially appear to be zero sum in nature can be converted into variable-sum opportunities if only the participants are wise enough to see the potential for joint gains. Although these decision makers can be vigorous defenders of their vital interests, they do not believe that compromise and concession are necessarily signs of weakness. Rather, they believe that a principled but flexible approach to conflict resolution is the best strategy. In sum, decision makers with a variable-sum view of conflict tended to adopt pro-ADR policies and prevent strategies of conflict management.

Mixed-Motive Decision Making.   Many of the managers we interviewed did not view conflict as always being either a zero-sum game or a variable-sum game. We often talked to managers who seemed to have an instrumental view of conflict management: they adopted one strategy or another (or none at all) depending on the circumstances of their organization and the nature of the conflicts they faced. They were neither dogmatic nor ideological about the strategy they pursued. Rather, they were flexible and pragmatic, choosing policies, procedures, and strategies that they thought best suited the values and objectives of their organizations. The vast majority of these decision makers, in our view, used a settle strategy of conflict management, although some of the pragmatists had moved into the prevent category.

In real life, conflicts are seldom purely zero-sum games. Rather, they usually combine elements of both zero-sum and variable-sum games. That is, conflicts typically have both competitive and cooperative elements. Opposing parties in a conflict may find they have opportunities to expand the proverbial pie (the cooperative element), but ultimately resolving the conflict requires them to divide the pie (the competitive element). Thus, many scholars maintain that resolving conflict is typically an exercise in mixed-motive decision making. The successful resolution of conflict requires an understanding of how to mix competitive (zero-sum) and cooperative (variable-sum) strategies. Successful conflict management strategies, we maintain, recognize the mixed-motive nature of conflict. Like Goldilocks, conflict managers often adopt strategies that are neither too hot nor too cold, neither too hard nor too soft.

Some of the companies we examined, recognizing the mixed-motive nature of conflict, were experimenting with conflict management strategies, testing the effectiveness of harder strategies in some cases and softer strategies in others. They had not yet adopted full-fledged systems and their companies could not yet be classified in the prevent category. They were, however, testing the waters, benchmarking the experience other companies were having with prevent strategies, and using pilot programs to evaluate the effectiveness of the systems approach. We placed companies using this approach to conflict management in the settle category.

Alignment Between Conviction and Strategy. In sum, we talked with managers who seemed temperamentally disposed to view all conflict as either zero sum or variable sum in nature. These managers, we believe, tend to choose conflict management strategies that fit their worldview. It is very difficult, if not impossible, for a manager with a zero-sum view of the world to adopt a prevent strategy of conflict management. Similarly, it is equally difficult for a manager with a variable-sum view of the world to adopt a contend strategy. Most managers do not view the world through either prism but recognize the mixed-motive nature of conflict. These managers tend to adopt a pragmatic approach to conflict management. In most companies we studied, we found a close alignment between the decision makers' convictions and the strategy adopted by their organizations.

The Operation of the Model

We believe that an organization's choice of conflict management strategy is a function of two types of factors, environmental and organizational, as we show in Figure 4.1. In the environmental category, we hypothesize that several exogenous variables influence the organization's choice of strategy. For example, we suspect that market factors influence the organization's choice: corporations operating in more competitive, global markets tend to rely on ADR more heavily than do organizations in less competitive markets. The underlying logic supporting this proposition is straightforward: corporations in competitive markets need to be more diligent about controlling and reducing their costs, and ADR is a means of controlling and reducing the costs of dispute resolution. Corporations in less competitive markets have less need to be concerned with the costs of litigation.[3]

Our model postulates that these environmental variables operate through a set of organizational motivations. We hypothesize, for example, that an organization that has experienced a precipitating event, such as a major multimillion dollar lawsuit, is more likely to rely on ADR than one that has not. Exogenous environmental factors may be necessary conditions for an organization to adopt a pro-ADR policy, but they are not sufficient conditions. The growth of government regulation, for example, might cause a company to adopt pro-ADR policies, but the influence of this environmental factor is filtered through organizational factors such as culture and management commitment. As another example of how our model operates, we hypothesize that an organization that both operates in a competitive market and has been a defendant in a major lawsuit is much more likely to have a pro-ADR policy than an organization that operates in a competitive market but has not experienced that type of precipitating event. Thus, it is the interaction of environmental and organizational (or exogenous and endogenous) variables that in our model influences an organization's choice of strategy.

Our model does not suggest that environmental factors invariably lead to a particular conflict management strategy. Many organizations experienced rising litigation costs in the 1970s and 1980s, but not all responded by adopting pro-ADR policies. An organization that faces an escalation in litigation costs presumably considers how it might reduce or minimize those costs. It might choose ADR as a cost-saving measure, or it might respond in a different fashion, such as by seeking other means of more efficiently managing litigation. Indeed, if the organization has reason to believe the rise of litigation costs is a transient phenomenon, it may decide to do nothing in response. How an organization makes decisions in the face of changing environmental conditions is a complex matter. Clearly, organizational culture, which reflects the values, experiences, and belief structures of the organization's decision makers, plays a critical role.

Similar organizations faced with a common set of environmental challenges might choose very different conflict management strategies, and, in fact, this is the situation we observed in our research. One of the companies in our study, PECO Energy, adopted a sophisticated conflict management system, whereas most other utility companies had not. After PECO merged with the Unicom Corporation, headquartered in Illinois, to form the Exelon Corporation, it discovered that managers at Unicom resisted the adoption of the conflict management system favored by PECO managers. The two utilities were similar, if not identical, in most characteristics, but one strongly favored a prevent strategy and the other did not.

Another company in our study, Halliburton (and its construction subsidiary, Brown and Root), pioneered the use of mandatory predispute arbitration agreements in employment, but most other companies in the construction business have not. The Zachry Construction Company, a large contractor also headquartered in Texas, has consciously considered Brown and Root's approach and decided not to adopt it. Conversations with the senior author showed that Zachry managers were not only aware of Halliburton's approach but had tracked Halliburton's experience with it carefully. Zachry had consciously chosen the contend strategy but was benchmarking its key competitors, including Halliburton, and was prepared to consider an alternative conflict management strategy under the right circumstances. In sum, the decision to adopt a particular conflict management strategy is strongly influenced by the environmental factors listed in Figure 4.1, but the organization's actual choice of strategy is ultimately determined by organizational motivations.

Some Correlates of the Choice of Strategy

In our 1997 survey of corporate counsels, we asked a series of questions regarding how the respondents would characterize their organizations' conflict management strategies. On the basis of their responses, we were able to group the corporations into the contend, settle, and prevent categories (see Table 4.1). The proportions listed, which must be considered rough estimates subject to the caveats previously discussed, are constantly shifting. Presumably, though, the number of corporations in the contend category is shrinking and the number in the prevent category is growing, but this is by no means certain. We estimate, nevertheless, that in 1997, about 9 percent of the major U.S. corporations studied rejected ADR and elected to be in the contend category, 74 percent fit in the broad settle category, and 17 percent strongly favored ADR, had some form of a system, and accordingly belonged in the prevent category.

Table 4.1. Corporate Conflict Management Strategies
of the Fortune 1000 Companies, 1997

Strategy	Percentage	Size	Market Pressure	Industries
Contend	9	Smaller	Less pressure	Service, durable manufacturing, construction
Settle	74	Medium	Some pressure	Transportation, communications, utilities, trade, finance
Prevent	17	Larger	More pressure	Financial services, insurance, construction, nondurable manufacturing

After we grouped the corporations in our sample into the three conflict management strategies, we were able to perform some simple analyses to determine the correlates of the organization's choice of strategy. Although we had not collected sufficient data in our survey to be able to do a test of the model depicted in Figure 4.1, we had collected enough on the basic characteristics of the corporations in our sample to perform a few elementary tests.

Size. We found that the corporation's choice of conflict management strategy was highly correlated with size, as measured by either revenue or number of employees. Corporations in the prevent category tended to be significantly larger than corporations in the contend category (albeit all corporations in the Fortune 1000 have revenues greater than $1 billion), and corporations in the settle category tended to fall in the middle range.

Industry Concentration. We used a measure of industry concentration as a proxy for market pressure, and it proved to be related to the corporation's choice of strategy. Corporations in less concentrated industries, which presumably face greater market pressure, tended to choose the prevent (or system) strategy, while corporations in more concentrated industries, facing less market pressure, tended to choose the contend (or traditional litigation) strategy. Corporations in the settle category once again tended to fall in the middle.

Industry. We found a pattern between choice of strategy and the industry in which the corporation operated (specifically, the two-digit SIC industry in which the corporation conducted its primary business). Corporations choosing the prevent strategy tended to cluster in financial services, insurance, construction, and non-durable manufacturing. Industry patterns in organizational strategy are harder to discern than Table 4.1 might suggest, however. As the PECO and Halliburton examples suggest, the variance within an industry can be very great. Construction, for instance, is listed in both the contend and prevent categories in Table 4.1, because

there are corporations, such as Halliburton and Zachry, in the construction industry that fall at either end of the spectrum.

ENVIRONMENTAL FACTORS

We hypothesize that the environmental factors shown in Figure 4.1
are independent variables influencing the organization's choice of
a conflict management strategy.

Market Competition

Our field research strongly suggests that one important environmental shift that has changed the approach of business to dispute resolution is the competitive pressure brought about by the globalization of
the economy. Over the past twenty years, increasing competition has
made organizations examine every facet of their operations in an
effort to minimize all costs and achieve every conceivable efficiency.
Internal counsel has not been immune to that pressure. Legal
expenses, once seen as a cost that was not necessarily controllable,
came to be managed much like the cost of materials, human
resources, and marketing. The resulting pressure forced general counsels to manage their internal costs, and their use of external counsel,
much more efficiently. Thus, litigation expenses have come to be
viewed as costs to be minimized whenever possible.

Government Regulation

In its 1994 report, the Dunlop Commission noted two related but
distinct problems in contemporary employment law: "The first is a
steep rise in administrative regulation of the workplace, whose
overlapping mandates (both federal and state) impose significant
costs on employers and employees. The second is the explosion of
litigation under laws that rely in whole or in part on individual lawsuits for enforcement."[4] Thus, coincidentally with employees' collective rights being weakened by the decline of unionization, their

individual rights were strengthened through a series of federal and state statutes. In the employment arena, as we noted in Chapter Three, Congress passed at least two dozen major statutes beginning in the early 1960s, starting with the Equal Pay Act of 1963, the Civil Rights Act of 1964, the Age Discrimination in Employment Act of 1967, and the Occupational Safety and Health Act of 1970. After a lull during the Reagan years, Congress passed the Americans with Disabilities Act in 1990, the Civil Rights Act of 1991, and the Family and Medical Leave Act in 1993.

As the Dunlop Commission recognized, statutory regulations impose costs on employers independent of their litigation potential, that is, overhead or fixed costs. A new employment statute almost always has staffing and organizational consequences for major employers. Corporate counsel's in-house attorneys and human resource managers must understand the implications of the new statute for their organization, whether new staff needs to be added or the organization needs to lean more heavily on outside counsel, consultants, trainers, and educators, or both. The fact that regulations impose costs on employers is a truism that does not need elaboration here, although the magnitude of those costs and the scale of potential benefits are always matters of serious debate. It is sufficient to note for our purposes that the steep rise in statutory employment regulations prompted employers to seek methods of minimizing the effect of these regulations on their cost of doing business. For many employers, ADR seemed to be one obvious solution.

Litigation Trend and Tort Reform

The real or perceived growth of litigation, especially in the 1970s and 1980s, was a significant factor leading to the adoption of pro-ADR policies by many organizations. We hypothesize in our model that the growth of ADR is closely related to the movement for tort reform.

The business interest in both ADR and tort reform is motivated by the same set of factors: the belief that there has been a dramatic growth in litigation, resulting in an ever-increasing burden of legal costs borne by business in the United States. In the corporate mind, tort reform and ADR are linked to the perception of excessive government regulation and a need to strip away this excess. Arguably, ADR, tort reform, and deregulation are complementary efforts by the U.S. corporate world. One can hypothesize that if the business community had achieved the comprehensive tort reform it sought, accompanied by the thorough elimination of objectionable regulations, the corporate interest in ADR would be much less intense. That is, ADR and tort reform are to some degree substitutes for one another, and the inability of the business community to achieve its objectives on tort reform has probably intensified corporate interest in ADR.

Nevertheless, it would be a mistake to believe that the various interests supporting tort reform are identical to those supporting ADR. Our research suggests that many corporate managers and lawyers believe there is a crisis in our legal system and yet do not favor ADR. The most conservative spokespersons, who are typically allied with the business community, are often staunch advocates of tort reform but oppose the use of ADR. Conservatives believe systemic change in the legal system is required and ADR is merely a palliative. By contrast, more moderate elements of the business community may support tort reform but believe it is even more important to develop effective means of managing disputes.

Statutory Requirements and Court Mandates

Congress and most state legislatures have a long history of encouraging, and occasionally mandating, the use of negotiation, mediation, arbitration, and other private methods of resolving disputes. Key landmarks of that history include the Federal Arbitration Act of 1925, as well as the Railway Labor Act, the National Labor Relations Act, and other federal statutes regulating labor-management relations.[5] Federal and state courts have usually supported statutory measures designed to promote the private resolution of disputes. After World War II, the courts increasingly deferred to arbitration as a means of settling disputes in labor relations.

When the ADR movement gained momentum in the 1970s, the courts proved to be equally supportive. The Supreme Court has supported the use of mandatory arbitration in employment disputes, allowing employers to require their employees to use arbitration instead of litigation as a means of resolving their statutory claims. (In Chapter Six, we discuss the Supreme Court's seminal decisions.)

Over time, both federal and state courts have adopted so-called court-annexed ADR procedures designed to expedite the litigation process. Early neutral evaluation, summary jury trial, arbitration, fact finding, and mediation are some of the most common ADR techniques they have adopted. As FitzGibbon notes, "Court-annexed ADR is a simple and predictable response to the increased use of litigation to resolve disputes and to solve societal problems. It builds on proven and traditional methods of extra judicial settlement; it reflects the fact that parties frequently settle their original differences even after they [have] resorted to court and commenced litigation."[6] The court systems in more than half the states now encourage or even mandate the use of court-annexed ADR procedures to reduce backlogs and speed up the handling of disputes. In many states, the use of these procedures originally took root in the management of family disputes, spreading more recently to most types of civil cases.

The support that ADR has received in the courts has been buttressed by federal and state statutes designed to promote or require its use. Although the effort to achieve federal tort reform has not yet succeeded, legislators and policymakers have not been oblivious to the stresses being felt in the U.S. legal system. In 1990, for example, Congress passed the Civil Justice Reform Act, which required federal district courts to experiment with case management systems.[7] The net effect of this statute was to encourage the courts to institute various forms of ADR. In 1998, Congress took the next step, requiring federal district courts to use ADR.[8] In recent years, Congress has frequently added ADR provisions to statutes it has passed, usually allowing claimants the option of using mediation before turning to the appropriate regulatory agency or courts for resolution. Administrative agencies such as the federal Equal Employment Opportunity Commission have begun to require the use of ADR (usually mediation) to resolve complaints.[9] The U.S. Department of Labor recently established a pilot program to test the efficacy of using mediation to resolve enforcement cases arising under the many statutes administered by the department.[10] Many state administrative agencies have also experimented with ADR as a response to the costs and delays inherent in their systems.

In sum, judicial and legislative support of the use of ADR has contributed to the permissive environment in which U.S. businesses have developed their ADR policies over the past two decades.

Unionization

The long-term decline of unionism in the United States has generally been welcomed by corporations. Nevertheless, the lack of a formal method of dispute resolution for day-to-day employment problems has led some companies to conclude that unresolved conflicts have their price as well. Many unionized employers became accustomed to relying on these formal procedures for resolving employment disputes and even came to see the advantages of their use. Without these grievance and arbitration procedures, employees alleging either statutory or contractual violations by their employers need to bring suit against their employer. The simultaneous decline of unionization and rise of ADR, we maintain, was more than a coincidence. Many nonunion employers came to realize that the use of some form of employment ADR provided a faster and cheaper means of resolving disputes than conventional litigation.[11]

Unions have viewed the use of ADR in employment relations with some skepticism. Many suspect that employers often institute workplace dispute resolution systems as a means of avoiding unionization. Because most employers will not freely admit to antiunion motives, hard evidence on this concern is not available. In the course of our field research, however, several corporate respondents readily admitted that union avoidance was a principal motive for their use of ADR in employment relations.

Although labor's suspicions are thus justified in some cases, many unions have also supported the development of workplace dispute resolution systems that extend beyond the traditional grievance procedure. Employee concerns ranging from the quality of their relations with supervisors and fellow employees to the adequacy of their computers and office equipment are not usually matters that are easily handled through the grievance procedure. Unions have discovered that employee complaints that fall outside the purview of the mandatory topics of bargaining can be addressed effectively through a dispute resolution system designed jointly by the parties. Indeed, some unions have embraced ADR with enthusiasm, not only valuing its potential benefits for its members but also recognizing that ADR systems can extend the authority and influence of a union into areas normally considered management prerogatives.[12] In the next chapter, we describe the unions' embrace of a systems approach for the handling of quality-of-working-life disputes.

ORGANIZATIONAL MOTIVATIONS

Continuing with our explication of the model depicted in Figure 4.1, we now turn to the role of organizational factors in determining the organization's choice of a conflict management strategy.

Organizational Culture

Organizational cultures, which play an important role in determining conflict management strategies, "provide organizational members with more or less articulated sets of ideas that help them individually and collectively to cope with all of [the organization's] uncertainties and ambiguities. People in organizations, as in social life generally, generate ideologies that tell them what is, how it got that way, and what ought to be. Such ideologies form the *substance* of cultures."[13] In conducting our field studies, we were struck by the differences in the cultures and ideologies of the organizations we visited. Many other researchers, of course, have observed the same phenomenon.[14] It seems obvious to us that there is a close relationship between the culture of an organization and the nature of its choice of conflict management strategy.

Here, we briefly examine one aspect of culture and its relation to strategy: the extent to which authority relationships in an organization are hierarchical and authoritarian versus the extent to which they are nonhierarchical and egalitarian.[15] We hypothesize that conflict management systems are more likely to emerge in egalitarian organizations than in hierarchical ones. We discovered in our case studies that the widespread adoption by employers of team-based production has created a substantial need for effective conflict resolution as well. In traditional hierarchical work organizations, employers can usually (but admittedly not always) rely on their authority to minimize and resolve conflicts. When employers reorganize their workers into teams—and particularly when they introduce the use of high-performance work systems—they give up a considerable amount of their authority and control over their own employees. In organizations in which there are authentic work teams, the employees themselves assume major responsibility for preventing, negotiating, and resolving conflicts. Some organizations that use teams, however, have realized that the creation of more formal dispute resolution systems strengthens the effectiveness of their teams.[16]

Management Commitment

During the course of our research, it became clear that the role of top management in shaping the organization's conflict management strategy cannot be overestimated. We heard several stories about CEOs who usually paid little attention to conflict management but focused intently on the topic after the organization experienced a major, expensive lawsuit or a crisis involving the legal function. In some cases, we also heard stories about CEOs who became concerned about the ongoing costs of the organization's legal affairs and directed a significant budget cut for the counsel's function. In one case, a CEO ordered the downsizing of several staff functions, including the counsel's office, and the counsel reacted by adopting strongly pro-ADR policies, which he believed would help him stay within the bounds of his smaller budget. In some organizations, the chief financial officer, concerned about the organization's litigation costs, became the organization's most ardent ADR champion.

It should be clear that management commitment is a two-sided variable, as are the others in our model. That is, management can be committed to either a pro-ADR or a pro-litigation strategy. In some cases, experience with mediation or arbitration helped shape management's attitudes. Some of our interviewees revealed that they had become interested in conflict management through a single or small number of ADR experiences. Often, they were exposed to mediation or arbitration as an experiment in dealings with another company. They were satisfied with the result and attempted to replicate it in their own company. Such experiences do not always work to create an atmosphere in which ADR flourishes, however. A small number of companies told us that their past experiences with ADR had been negative or not good enough to cause them to seek to manage conflict in this manner.

In a handful of cases, we could not fathom why management had a pro-ADR or a pro-litigation attitude. We visited two companies that were very similar in many respects but the CEO of the one company was strongly committed to ADR while the CEO of the other company was strongly opposed to ADR. We suspect that ideology and personality differences helped to shape these contrasting attitudes.

The Role of the Champion

Another key feature of the organizations that were developing integrated conflict management systems was the role of a key internal champion. In virtually all of our interviews with companies with conflict management systems, the interviewees would point to a single individual or a very small group as responsible for initiating and maintaining the system in its early stages of development. As Ulrich notes, a champion is a change agent, that is, a person within an organization dedicated to the "cultural transformation" of the organization.[17] Champions, Ulrich says, play four roles: they are sponsors of the change they advocate; help facilitate the change by obtaining internal support, external support, and management ownership; help design the change; and demonstrate, by example, experiments, and pilot efforts, the superiority of the change they advocate.[18]

The ACR report on integrated conflict management systems also discussed the important role played by champions:

> Champions communicate and implement the goals of the integrated conflict management system, often led by one person who is the acknowledged "keeper of the flame." At least one senior person must be a visionary who champions the cause of creating a conflict-competent culture through developing and maintaining an integrated conflict management system. The champion's passion inspires others to act. It is this ability to connect others to a vision that often drives the success of a program. Champions are trailblazers, who build an integrated conflict management system piece by piece—never losing sight of the difficulty of creating change. They are able to "grow" programs that work, abandon programs that are struggling, and, perhaps most important, identify areas of new opportunity. Champions must be great innovators and good marketers of their ideas, for without effective communication, the "flame" dies.[19]

The role of the champion underscores the potential fragility of system development in this arena, however. A champion is often faced with powerful opponents. In one of the organizations we studied, the ADR champion in the counsel's office was opposed by the anti-ADR director of human resources. The ADR champion lost the battle and left the organization. When the champion leaves his or her position or moves to another organization, the entire ADR effort may be thwarted if no one steps into this role.

Exposure Profile

One of the factors that lead to a more aggressive business response to the litigation explosion is the amount of potential litigation exposure faced by an individual firm. This exposure profile of a particular organization is a function of the industry in which it operates, the firm's history, the nature of employment in the firm (particularly whether the jobs it offers are high risk or low risk), and its relationships with other businesses and consumers. Some firms are in industries that make inherently dangerous products, for example, or products that have been associated with class actions in the recent past. Other firms have been accused of, and sometimes found liable for, business practices that have led to widespread litigation. Firms vary by size of employment and unionization, which leaves some very large nonunion firms with significant potential litigation exposure. Some firms have a large number of business relationships that simply cannot be allowed to result in costly and time-consuming litigation because of the pressure of time. Finally, some firms have so many business transactions that could sour and lead to litigation (consumer transactions involving relatively expensive goods, for example) that they are highly exposed to litigation. We hypothesize that the higher the organization's exposure profile, the more likely it is, all other things being equal, that the organization will adopt a conflict management system.

The Precipitating Event

In many of the organizations we studied, we found that the company was motivated to consider adopting an ADR strategy because of a precipitating event—a multimillion dollar lawsuit, a series of lawsuits, or a crisis or catastrophe that led to lawsuits and a public relations problem for the organization. Companies such as PECO

Energy and Prudential, for example, adopted sophisticated conflict management systems largely because they had been the objects of lawsuits causing them considerable embarrassment. Alcoa moved in the direction of a conflict management system after downsizing its workforce resulted in a series of expensive lawsuits. Top management does not usually interfere with counsel's day-to-day management of the legal function, but an expensive lawsuit will definitely attract its attention. Major lawsuits are often the occasion for top management to review the organization's conflict management strategies and policies. Such reviews frequently reveal the costly and time-consuming nature of litigation and prompt top managers to seek alternatives. The counsel's office may have been promoting the use of ADR for many years, but may have been able to adopt the use of a conflict management system only after the organization faced a major crisis. Still, an expensive lawsuit does not always lead to the organization's adoption of pro-ADR policies.

If our hypothesis about the relationship between precipitating events and conflict management strategies is correct, it constitutes yet another example of how organizational policy is often based on managers' experience with—and desire to avoid—worst-case scenarios, rather than policy being based on the organization's normal (or median) experience.

THE ORGANIZATION'S CHOICE: SOME EXAMPLES

Examples that draw on our fieldwork and case studies illuminate how organizations choose their conflict management strategy.

Contend Strategy

In our organizational survey and field studies, we discovered that some organizations—albeit a shrinking minority—have chosen to reject almost any use of ADR and instead have decided to contend any claim or charge brought against them. The contend group in

Figure 4.1 consists of those organizations that, in the light of their own environmental setting and organizational characteristics, have chosen to continue their traditional approach to litigation. In our 1997 survey, these corporations responded that when their organization is either a defendant or plaintiff in a lawsuit, they prefer to "litigate always." We categorize them as *contenders* because the top managers and lawyers in these corporations, as a matter of conscious policy, rigorously defend their interests in virtually every lawsuit or proceeding in which they are involved. Decision makers in these organizations pursue zero-sum strategies, putting a heavy premium on winning legal contests. They often dislike negotiation because they understand that negotiators usually need to compromise and therefore they cannot win all the time.

We talked to the senior vice chairman and chief administrative officer of the Emerson Electric Corporation, a successful multibillion dollar international organization headquartered in St. Louis, Missouri, and later invited him to participate in a session we were asked to organize for the 1998 *Forbes Magazine* superconference on ADR. He began his presentation on that occasion by showing a slide that reproduced the American Revolutionary War flag with a rendering of a coiled snake and the warning, "Don't Tread on Me." He used the flag as a symbol of Emerson's strategy on litigation management. On any given claim, the vice chairman explained, Emerson would decide whether the company was right or wrong. In the relatively rare case that it believed it was wrong, it would readily concede the issue and attempt to settle. When the company decided it was right, however, it would make every effort to defend its position and be unwilling to make compromises or concessions to an opposing party. It has been important to Emerson to establish a reputation as a company that will fight all claims that in its view lack merit. The use of mediation, arbitration, or any other form of ADR, in Emerson's view, undercuts the company's conflict management strategy. Over time, the vice chairman maintained, this policy of contending almost every claim has had the effect of deterring lawsuits and reducing the company's legal costs.

Not every organization that we place in the contend category has adopted such a stringent, if principled, approach to conflict management. Some contenders are somewhat more pragmatic and flexible. For example, the Schering-Plough corporation, one of the largest pharmaceutical companies in the world, produces the best-selling allergy medication Claritin. Like other manufacturers of pharmaceuticals, Schering-Plough is often sued by users of its products who claim the drugs they used did not have the intended effects. Schering-Plough has also been the defendant in several expensive lawsuits involving claims by current or former employees. The corporation's litigation experience led it to undertake a comprehensive study of the use of ADR as a substitute for the company's strategy of contending. The vice president of human resources and the company's deputy counsel conducted a thorough year-long study and concluded that the systematic use of ADR might indeed save the corporation time and money. Nevertheless, they did not recommend that the corporation adopt the use of ADR as a matter of policy because they had discovered in the course of their study that their middle managers thought any use of ADR threatened their authority. Middle managers and supervisors are responsible for making decisions that are the source of many employment disputes, and it is important to them that their decisions be supported by the corporation. If top management uses ADR to arrive at negotiated agreements that compromise these decisions, middle managers may feel their authority is undermined, as at Schering-Plough. Thus, Schering-Plough's decision not to adopt the use of ADR as a matter of policy (although it will use mediation in selected cases) was based on its middle managers' firm belief that such a policy would undercut their authority.[20]

Hewlett Packard, another firm we studied, also belongs in the contend category. We believe Hewlett Packard is typical of the high-tech firms in Silicon Valley. Their success depends in part on their ability to innovate new technologies, and they attempt to retain control of their innovations through the use of patents and copyrights. Because intellectual property is in many ways the lifeblood of these corporations, they are prepared to fight any threat to their intellectual property rights. For Hewlett Packard and many other Silicon Valley firms, the stakes in many lawsuits are so high that the idea of negotiating or mediating a compromise settlement cannot be considered. The use of ADR in the Silicon Valley also seems to run counter to the entrepreneurial culture prevalent there. Bill Gates was reluctant to negotiate a settlement of the government's antitrust case against Microsoft, and the effort by federal judge Richard Posner to mediate a settlement failed.[21]

The firms we examined in the contend category have little interest in ADR, formally or informally. They may express some discontent with the U.S. legal system, but in general they are quite prepared to litigate when they believe it is necessary. In some cases, they even relish the opportunity.

Settle Strategy

Based on our research, we believe that the overwhelming majority of U.S. corporations routinely attempt to settle almost all complaints and claims against them. Some corporations may do this as a matter of conscious policy and some as a matter of established practice. These corporations have neither wholeheartedly adopted nor categorically rejected the use of ADR. Instead, they usually approach conflict management in a pragmatic and flexible fashion (while adhering to their own core values and principles). They tend to view conflict management less in strategic terms and more in terms of tactical choice. The tactics and techniques they use in a particular case normally depend on the specific circumstances of the case. They view the techniques of ADR as part of a tool kit that includes other options, including contending.

To the extent that a corporation in this category pursues a deliberate litigation or conflict management strategy, it is ordinarily driven by counsel's office, often working collaboratively with outside counsel, the chief financial officer, the human resource function, or another appropriate part of the corporation. The counsel's office seldom needs to involve top management directly in its day-to-day handling of claims and complaints, unless the company's lawyers find themselves in a situation that potentially represents a significant financial liability for the corporation or a critical matter of principle and precedent.

Corporations in the settle category can choose to use ADR on a postdispute or a predispute basis. A corporation that chooses ADR on a postdispute basis will attempt to use mediation or arbitration, or one of their variants, after a dispute between the organization and another party has arisen. These corporations are prepared to pursue litigation in a particular case when they believe the stakes involved, either in terms of money or principle, dictate that choice. In the majority of cases, however, they are prepared to negotiate a settlement of a dispute. In a typical corporation, the counsel's office, frequently relying on the advice of outside counsel, decides at each stage of a case whether negotiating an agreement or proceeding to the next stage of the case is the wise course of action. In these corporations, the use of ADR is simply part of the litigation manager's tool kit. At some point in the processing of a particular case, the lawyers representing the corporation and the other party (or parties) in the dispute come to believe that the use of mediation or arbitration is a desirable alternative to pursuing the next stage of litigation.

The other approach a corporation can choose is to use ADR on a predispute basis. When a corporation uses ADR on a predispute basis, it identifies certain types of transactions as prone to disputes and decides as a matter of policy to use ADR to resolve such disputes. Typically, corporations using predispute ADR seek to include an ADR provision in contracts covering the transactions in question. A corporation may insert an ADR provision in all of its construction contracts, product warranties, or executive salary agreements. Almost all automobile manufacturers include an arbitration provision in the leases signed by their customers, for example. Computer manufacturers routinely include arbitration provisions in their warranties; customers who sign these warranties may or may not realize that if they have a product liability claim against the manufacturer, they are required to have the claim arbitrated and cannot pursue a lawsuit. A growing number of employers require their employees to sign mandatory predispute arbitration agreements, a practice that the U.S. Supreme Court has sanctioned.[22]

In our 1997 survey, many of the corporate lawyers we interviewed told us that their organization had adopted a pro-ADR policy; however, in our fieldwork, we discovered that counsel's view of the corporation's conflict management strategy was not always shared by other key members of the organization. Indeed, in a few cases, corporate managers had very little awareness of, or no knowledge at all about, counsel's pro-ADR policies. In fact, we might have categorized a corporation as strongly pro-ADR on the basis of our survey of the Fortune 1000 in situations where the counsel's view of the corporation's conflict management strategy had not penetrated other parts of the organization. The results we obtained in our survey might have been somewhat misleading in this respect. In that survey, we interviewed only one respondent in each corporation, usually the counsel or one of the counsel's deputies. We did not fully realize until we conducted our field research that the respondent we had interviewed in the counsel's office did not always speak for his or her colleagues. With hindsight, this is not a surprising situation.

We conducted several interviews in a large midwestern corporation, for example, that on the basis of our earlier survey we had classified as strongly pro-ADR. When we arrived, however, we found that the respondent we had interviewed was the corporation's staunchest ADR champion. His colleagues, both inside and outside the counsel's office, did not share his views and did not agree that the corporation had adopted ADR as a matter of policy. This corporation clearly did use ADR, but ADR was less a matter of corporate policy and more a matter of tactical choice made within the counsel's office. We thus recategorized that corporation in our database. We were obviously not able to do this exercise for all the corporations in our survey, so the presence of respondent bias, a common problem in survey research, needs to be considered in interpreting our survey findings.

In the settle category, corporate conflict management is reactive and contingent. In many of the corporations we studied, counsel's office viewed the use of ADR in certain classes of disputes as an experiment. The corporate representatives we interviewed often had an open mind about ADR and wanted to let their experience with its use guide them on the possibility of adopting ADR as a corporate policy. We began to call some of the corporations in the settle category *incrementalists*. Their mode of operation was to experiment with ADR in some types of disputes (say, employment cases) and, if they were satisfied with its use in those cases, to extend its use to other types of disputes.

For example, we conducted interviews at Kaufman and Broad, one of the nation's largest home builders. (In 1999, Kaufman and Broad built twenty-one thousand homes.) Kaufman and Broad routinely includes mediation and arbitration clauses in the home-building contracts it signs with customers. Customer claims of defects in the homes they have purchased are submitted to mediation and, in some cases, to arbitration. Customers waive their right to sue Kaufman and Broad when a claim is deemed suitable for arbitration. Over the years, Kaufman and Broad developed a very favorable view of the use of ADR in its home-building contracts and eventually decided to adopt mandatory predispute arbitration for its sales staff, whose disputes over commissions were frequent.

We found this pattern of incrementalism in several of the corporations we studied. ADR was initially an innovation adopted for limited use in one class of disputes, subsequently proved to be successful, and then diffused into other arenas. We entered the field phase of our research with a tentative hypothesis that proved to be incorrect, however. We expected to find that most corporations would use what we began to call an *integrated conflict management strategy*, by which we meant a more or less standard corporatewide approach to conflict management. (Later, after the publication of the ACR report, we dropped this definition of an integrated conflict management strategy.) We found in fact that most organizations do not have a common conflict management strategy, but instead use a patchwork (more kindly, a pragmatic and flexible) approach to conflict management, choosing one strategy in one class of disputes and a totally different strategy in other classes.

We have formed a revised hypothesis regarding the integration of an organization's conflict management strategy across classes of disputes. We now believe that corporate structure strongly influences the choice of conflict management strategies. In particular, the degree of centralization of authority within the corporation is a significant determinant. All other things equal, a highly centralized corporation tends to have a standard approach for conflict management, while a highly decentralized corporation does not. As an example, consider both Warner Bros. and Universal Studios in Los Angeles. Warner Bros. is a subsidiary of AOL Time Warner; at the time of our interviews, Universal was owned by the Seagram Company. Both studios, however, had considerable autonomy, and both had an approach to ADR that was distinctly different from that of their parent organizations. Warner Bros. and Universal had similar conflict management strategies because both studios operated in the same culture: motion picture and television production. The culture had more influence on their approach to conflict resolution than did the culture of their parent companies.

It is a truism that the culture—the traditions, norms, and standards of behavior—of motion picture and television production differs from the culture of publishing magazines or providing Internet services. The vast majority of studio employees, including actors, directors, writers, and musicians, are unionized and have a long history of craft bargaining.[23] These traditions have strongly influenced the studios' attitudes toward ADR—and not necessarily in a positive direction. In common with other unionized employers, the experience that Warner Bros. and Universal have had with the use of mediation and arbitration in collective bargaining has colored their view of the use of ADR in other types of disputes. Arbitration clauses are routinely included in executive contracts and in many construction contracts in the motion picture industry. But we would characterize the studios' attitude toward ADR as cautious and even wary; by no means has the experience in Hollywood spilled over into other business units in the parent corporations.

The perception of a negative experience with ADR can deter its diffusion to other parts of an organization. For example, we conducted interviews at Kaiser Permanente at its headquarters in Oakland, California. Kaiser Permanente, the largest not-for-profit health maintenance organization in the United States, serves nearly nine million members in seventeen states. It requires patients treated by its doctors and medical facilities to sign mandatory arbitration agreements. Such agreements require patients with medical claims, including allegations of malpractice, to waive their right to sue and submit their complaints to arbitration.

Kaiser was highly embarrassed by a couple of arbitration cases, reported extensively by the *San Francisco Chronicle*, that allegedly demonstrated the problems of mandatory arbitration.[24] As a consequence of its experience in arbitration, including the negative publicity, Kaiser revised but did not abandon its mandatory arbitration policy. In 1999, it decided to turn over the administration of the arbitration procedure to the American Arbitration Association instead of managing the procedure itself. By doing so, Kaiser clearly hoped to reassure the public that its arbitration procedure was impartial and fair. Kaiser's difficulties in this regard have limited the diffusion of ADR to other types of disputes within the organization, though.

Our respondents at the USX Corporation told us the corporation had a "tradition of litigation," but in recent years, it had become more open-minded about the use of ADR. USX is apparently one of many corporations experimenting with alternatives to litigation. It has been motivated by the growing burden of statutory employment cases and its potential liability in asbestos lawsuits.

Another organization we studied is Mirage Resorts, one of the largest hotel and casino operators in the country. It owns the Bellagio, Golden Nugget, and Treasure Island hotels in Las Vegas and the

Beau Rivage in Biloxi, Mississippi, and was developing a large hotel and casino in Atlantic City at the time we conducted our interviews. Mirage was owned by Steve Wynn for many years, until he sold the corporation to MGM Grand in 2000.[25] We were impressed with the apparent extent to which Wynn directed policy in every corner of the corporation. In the gaming industry, lawsuits are an everyday occurrence, and under Wynn, Mirage had had more than its fair share. Wynn's legal battles with Donald Trump were an ongoing saga in the late 1990s.[26] But Wynn, in many ways the quintessential pragmatist, was always prepared to experiment with alternative means of settling disputes. Consequently, Mirage attorneys were disposed to use mediation, particularly in cases where the stakes were not very high. In our view, Mirage was a classic example of how top management ultimately drives the choice of a conflict management strategy.

Each corporation is a story unto itself. A diverse set of circumstances and motivations influences the choice of a conflict management strategy in each of the companies we studied. Nevertheless, we think a careful observer can discern clear patterns in the evidence. In the settle category are a very large number of corporations pursuing a variety of specific strategies. All of them, however, use ADR regularly, if not routinely, as a means of managing disputes.

Prevent Strategy

As we have previously noted in this book, companies that we have classified as having a prevent strategy have either adopted a full-blown conflict management system or have adopted a policy of using ADR in all types of disputes and have implemented many of the features of a full-blown system. As our analytical model in Figure 4.1 shows, we believe companies adopting a prevent strategy do so as a consequence of a combination of environmental factors and organizational motivations. We remind the reader here that environmental (or exogenous) factors, such as the growing pressure of global competition, the increasing level of government regulation of the workplace, and the decline of unionization in some industries, are conditions that we believe are necessary but not sufficient for a corporation to adopt a prevent strategy. Based on our field research, we concluded that it was essential for a set of permissive organizational factors to be present to cause a corporation to move in the direction of having a conflict management system. In the list of organizational motivations in Figure 4.1, we particularly emphasize the critical importance of a supportive organizational culture and strong commitment from top management as elements critical to the development of a system. In addition, as noted earlier, we have not yet visited an organization that has a comprehensive conflict management system that did not have a champion who was largely responsible for spearheading the effort to adopt such a system. Finally, it may not be essential for a corporation to have a certain type of exposure profile (or vulnerability to certain types of disputes) or to have suffered a precipitating event (such as a major lawsuit or crisis), but we discovered that typically corporations with systems were also motivated by these factors.

Some organizations are well known for their development and use of conflict management systems: General Electric, Nestle USA, the U.S. Postal Service, Johnson and Johnson, and the Bureau of National Affairs come quickly to mind.[27] Included in our study are several corporations that have all or most of the essential elements of an authentic conflict management system: Alcoa, Chevron, PECO, An Exelon Company, and Prudential. Alcoa's Resolve It program incorporates multiple options and multiple access points, voluntary participation, the right to representation, protection against retaliation, and an ongoing commitment to training. In our interviews at Alcoa, we learned that the development of this system was triggered in large part by the corporation's downsizing in the 1980s, which was accompanied by a rash of lawsuits. Alcoa's success with the use of ADR in employment disputes has led to the corporation's exploring ways to incorporate ADR provisions into its commercial contracts. In addition, Alcoa has pioneered the use of a fixed-price contract with its outside counsel: Alcoa and its principal outside law firm negotiate a yearly fee for the firm's services that covers all cases handled by the firm. This arrangement clearly strengthens the law firm's incentive to resolve cases as quickly as possible and, accordingly, predisposes the firm's attorneys to favor ADR.

Chevron has a comprehensive program similar to Alcoa's but also gives employees access to an ombudsperson. A precipitating event—a large class-action sex discrimination case—was one of the factors motivating Chevron to adopt an employment conflict management system. PECO parent Exelon Corporation (formerly PECO Energy Company) is a utility company heavily committed to the use of nuclear power.[28] A shutdown at one of the corporation's nuclear facilities, followed by several major lawsuits and a considerable amount of unwanted publicity, was one event that helped to precipitate that corporation's adoption of ADR.

PECO's conflict management system, PEOPLE*SOLVE, is described in Figure 4.2. As the figure shows, the corporation divides employment disputes into two categories: those that involve statutory claims ("legal disputes") and those that do not involve such claims ("nonlegal disputes"). Ultimately, the principal techniques used to resolve disputes involving statutory claims are mediation and voluntary arbitration. For nonlegal disputes, the corporation ultimately relies on a peer review process. A special feature of the PECO conflict management system is its use of so-called resolution facilitators: employees located in every unit of the corporation who are specially trained to give advice and guidance to employees with nonlegal complaints. In the next chapter, we discuss the use of resolution facilitators in the design of conflict management systems.

Prudential was also the object of a series of embarrassing lawsuits and SEC investigations in the 1990s. One lawsuit resulted in Prudential's agreeing to pay $2 billion to over 1 million policyholders who sought restitution for abuses in the company's life insurance sales practices.[29] Top management responded to this crisis by resolving that the company would adhere strictly to a code of ethics. It established an independent ethics office in the early 1990s. To improve employment relations, the company came to believe that a comprehensive and fair dispute resolution system was needed, and it viewed such a system as an expression of its renewed

**Figure 4.2. The PECO Conflict Management System,
PEOPLE*SOLVE**

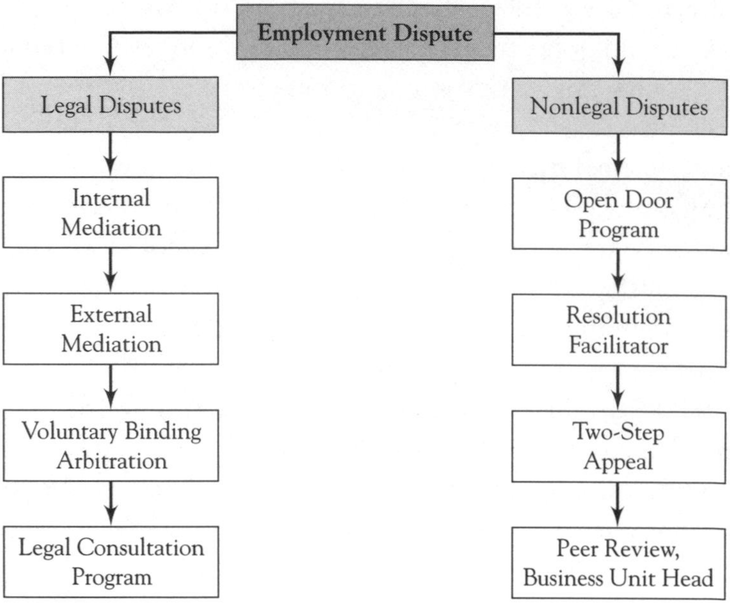

Source: Used by permission of PECO, An Exelon Company.

commitment to ethical behavior. It hired Ernst & Young to conduct a benchmarking study of dispute resolution systems in other
organizations. After a year's work, the consulting firm submitted its
report and recommendations to Prudential, which the company
adopted and implemented in 1999. Prudential's system, called
Roads to Resolution®, is illustrated in Figure 4.3. The system contains almost all the elements recommended by the ACR committee. Noteworthy is the fact that the system is operated by an
autonomous office within the corporation headed by an experienced and respected attorney.

CONCLUSION

In our research, we discovered that in most U.S. corporations,
managing conflict is a reactive rather than a strategic choice. We
also found, however, that a growing number of companies are

Figure 4.3. The Prudential Conflict Management System, Roads to Resolution

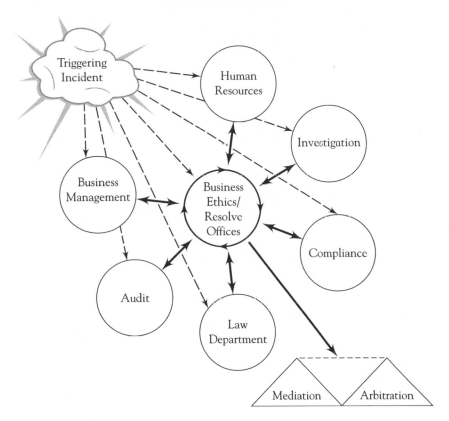

adopting a strategic approach to conflict management. They are doing so as a consequence of dramatic changes in the corporate environment, particularly growing global competition and government regulation. Managers in these organizations have concluded that they can no longer afford a reactive or passive approach to managing disputes and litigation but must shift to a more proactive approach to conflict in the same fashion that they manage marketing, sales, finance, and other corporate functions.

We discovered that not all corporations that have adopted a conscious conflict management strategy have embraced a systems approach, or what we have termed a prevent strategy. A small, and possibly shrinking, proportion of U.S. corporations have rejected ADR and deliberately adopted a pro-litigation strategy. The vast majority of U.S. corporations, we believe, are experimenting with ADR and the systems approach. They tend to use ADR techniques on an ad hoc and contingent basis. Many of them have experimented with pilot programs and have introduced elements of the systems approach but not a full-blown system. We have characterized these companies as incrementalists and believe they have what we have termed a settle strategy.

A relatively small proportion of corporations have adopted an authentic conflict management system. The emergence of these systems in American corporations is so recent that it is difficult, if not impossible, to gauge the ultimate success of such initiatives. In Chapter Eight, we will discuss methods of evaluating ADR programs and workplace systems, and we will note that only a handful of careful evaluations of programs and systems have been conducted to date. Nevertheless, we are encouraged by the fact that the managers and lawyers we have interviewed at corporations that have systems have told us, without exception, that their experience with the systems they have implemented has been very favorable.

They also report that participants in these systems, including supervisors and employees, have been well satisfied with their operation. The companies using systems report that most employee complaints are resolved early in the procedures and, in fact, few end up being resolved by outside neutrals. Moreover, contrary to the expectations of some skeptics, making elaborate procedures available for employees does not promote the filing of complaints. Finally, it is highly significant that no company or other organization that has adopted a workplace conflict management system, to the best of our knowledge, has yet abandoned that system in favor of more traditional methods of managing conflict.

Part Two

The Establishment of Conflict Management Systems

Chapter Five

Design of Conflict Management Systems

Internal Features

Substantive and procedural decisions that need to be made as part of the design process include determining who is eligible to participate in the system, the scope of disputes that can be raised within it, the options available to employees to resolve their conflicts, and the procedural rules governing the use of these options. A complete workplace system has two sets of conflict resolution options: those that involve internal processes and resources and those that involve external processes and resources.

These options can be interest based or rights based in nature. Internal processes, which are generally considered more cost-effective, are used in the early resolution phase of a dispute. External processes, which are often more expensive, involve experts who are outsiders to the organization and are used in the later phases of the resolution process. Conceptually, these options create a spectrum from those being less invasive on the parties to those literally imposing solutions.[1]

An excerpt from the Halliburton Company's Dispute Resolution Program describes the spectrum as follows:

> If you have a work-related problem you can't resolve on your own, Halliburton has a program that may be of help. Its purpose is to give you an improved process and flexible options for airing and settling almost every kind of workplace disputes . . . from minor, everyday misunderstandings to violations of your legally protected

rights. It offers many advantages. It allows us to settle our differences among ourselves:

- *Constructively*—without destroying careers, relationships and reputations
- *Swiftly*—in weeks and months, rather than in years
- *Confidentially*—with respect for your privacy
- *Simply*—at the lowest possible level, as preferred by both employees and managers
- *Inexpensively*—with few if any attorneys' fees or legal expenses, and
- *Fairly*—with the help of trained mediators and independent neutral third parties, if needed

SCOPE OF WORKPLACE ISSUES

One initial step in designing a workplace system is to determine the scope of issues to be resolved within the system. Generally, workplace systems are designed for a very broad range of employee issues that include work assignments, compensation, peer or supervisory conflicts, promotions, training, policies, and terminations. In most organizations, these issues are separated into statutory and nonstatutory claims. *Statutory claims* refer to conflicts alleging violation of some state or federal law, such as age discrimination, whereas *nonstatutory claims* refer to conflicts alleging violation of a company policy or practice but not any state or federal law.

In some organizations, such as the Boeing Company, for example, the issues are separated into three categories: claims alleging unfairness of a manager's decision, claims alleging incorrect application of a company policy, and claims alleging that management's action was motivated by an illegal bias or violated other employment laws. This approach has proved valuable in modeling how employees should view their conflicts.

There is a good deal of variety in the scope of issues actually included in workplace systems. Many systems, for example, exclude statutory issues covered by another internal policy, such as claims under the Employee Retirement Income Security Act of 1974. Some systems do not include statutory issues that are covered by external appeal systems, such as workers' compensation claims. Other systems do not include nonstatutory performance evaluation or pay system issues. Some workplace systems accept an unlimited scope of issues into the initial steps but exclude some from the final arbitration step. For example, some systems allow performance evaluations or benefit policies to be mediated but not arbitrated. Almost all systems provide for the resolution of statutory conflicts alleging employment discrimination (age, race, gender, and so forth), while not preventing the employee from simultaneously filing a discrimination charge with the Equal Employment Opportunity Commission.

Limiting the scope of issues covered is controversial. Some design consultants believe that broad exclusions of claims eligible for resolution in the workplace system (such as with performance evaluations or benefit disputes) are a mistake because they raise questions about the credibility of the process. They question why any broad categories of claims should be excluded and see no problem in some duplication of conflict resolution avenues for employees.

Proponents of covering a broad scope of issues voice two additional reasons for doing so. One is to allow an issue to be raised without framing it as a violation of rights. Because the underlying purpose of workplace systems is early resolution of conflict, we believe it is preferable to address a claim prior to the employee's declaring his or her dispute a statutory violation. The second reason is to allow a claim to be raised without associating it with a specific person. Since an employee may be reluctant to go on the record against his or her own supervisor, and many conflicts involve groups of employees anyway, making a broad scope of issues and avenues available in a workplace conflict resolution system encourages concerns to be raised early that would otherwise fester in the workplace.[2] For example, an excerpt from the Boeing Company's *Alternative Dispute Resolution Process* manual for its Mesa, Arizona, facility states:

ADR is a way to address some of the more serious issues that occur in the workplace. It is not designed for challenging the content of existing policies or procedures or for implementing new ones. While there is an unlimited range of issues that can be addressed by ADR, there are essentially three types of disputes.

1. *Fairness:* an employee's concern about the fairness of a manager's decision

2. *Misapplication of policy/procedure:* disputes as to whether a company policy or procedure has been correctly applied

3. *Legal claims:* employee's concern that a management decision/action was motivated by an illegal bias or it violated other employment laws

Issues Excluded from ADR

A complete list of issues that cannot be addressed through ADR can be found on the ADR web site. Examples of excluded issues include:

- Contractual disputes (e.g., pension, health, and life insurance benefits)

- Disputes governed by laws and regulations (e.g., unemployment and workers' compensation)

- Serious violations of company policy (e.g., termination for criminal conviction violation of drug- and alcohol-free workplace rules)

ELIGIBILITY TO USE THE WORKPLACE SYSTEM

Another initial step in designing a workplace system is to determine who is eligible to use it. On the surface, the answer seems apparent: all employees. However, questions quickly arise as the rights of current applicants, rejected applicants, retirees, subcontractors, terminated employees, executives, and independent contractors are considered. These are complex questions that can ultimately determine the success or failure of the workplace system.

Employees currently covered by a collective bargaining agreement and certain senior executives covered by employment agreements are typically excluded from eligibility. Furthermore, some programs include only employees hired after the program became effective. The American Arbitration Association, for example, has created the Smart Solution method of resolving employment disputes. It covers all full-time and part-time employees on the payroll as of a specific date but excludes employees covered by a collective bargaining agreement providing for another means of resolving disputes.

Other systems define eligibility by exempt or nonexempt status or geographical location. Some programs exempt employees hired before the program was implemented. Most current systems exclude independent contractors, applicants, subcontractors, retirees, and terminated employees. Each of these broad exclusions may be unwise, though, because claims raised by these groups will remain unresolved and may lead to litigation.

Some design consultants argue that eligibility to use the workplace system should be as broad and inclusive as possible, not restricted to certain "active" employee groups within a site, but covering everyone who has a potential dispute with the organization, even retirees, terminated employees, and job applicants. Their logic is as follows: if the workplace system is intended to channel conflicts in the workplace and reduce litigation, excluding any categories of people who have an independent right to sue the organization is counterproductive. Large organizations have thousands of applicants per year, for example, who never become employees. Some are interviewed, and some are not. Regardless, each applicant has standing to sue the employer under state and federal laws for failure to hire. Why not include applicants within the system and attempt to resolve these disputes without forcing the claims directly to litigation?

SYSTEM STAKEHOLDERS

In designing a workplace system, the organization should determine who the stakeholders of the system are, that is, the distinct groups with interests in the design and effectiveness of the system who may be direct players in its application.

Organizations typically view current or active employees as their primary stakeholders. In reality, though, numerous other key stakeholders are involved in a workplace system: first-line supervisors, managers, individuals serving the in-house legal and human resource functions, senior leadership, retirees, and even members of the board of directors. Each of these groups has unique interests in the system that need to be examined during the design phase. Some of these stakeholders will embrace the new system, some will be neutral, and some will resist its application in the workplace. Considering these differences as early as possible in the design of the workplace system is important to the design effort.

UNION PARTICIPATION

For several reasons, workplace systems are generally viewed as applicable only to work environments without organized labor or a recognized labor union. One reason is the belief that unions are satisfied with their traditional grievance procedures for all disputes. Another is the notion that union leaders will feel threatened with the flexibility and employee ownership of conflict inherent in workplace systems. A third reason is the fear that union leaders will view workplace systems as a means of undermining their authority and a mechanism to serve employers as a union-busting vehicle. The view that these systems are not appropriate for unionized organizations is not necessarily valid. In fact, increasingly it has been rejected by public sector organizations that are collaborating with their labor unions and inviting their participation in workplace systems.

The primary motivation for labor unions to join in workplace systems is to resolve quality-of-work-life disputes. These are highly interpersonal conflicts that often involve peer conflicts, supervisory relationships, and other individual issues and have less to do with official terms and conditions of employment. These disputes are by definition without major consequence to the bargaining unit. The unions are far more likely to value the potential of the system's features in these disputes if an employer includes its unions early in the design process. Acceptance of the system is also more likely to occur if a champion of the idea is found in the union leadership—one who embraces the concept and socializes the idea throughout the union leadership structure. In practice, union involvement in workplace systems is centered on mediation. In organizations with more than one union, it is not uncommon for some unions to accept the system and its mediation process and others to refuse to do so. The Department of the Interior's program is an example of such an arrangement. CORE: Conflict Resolution Program, one of the features of its workplace system for all Interior employees, covers all levels of employees and managers including union representatives and union members from unions that elect to participate. Cases in the program are mediated by CORE specialists who are experienced and trained in informal workplace mediation.

Another program that includes unionized employees and is based on mediation is a pilot offered by the Unified Court System of New York. This program specifically includes "interpersonal conflicts or disputes that arise between any two employees or within work groups or teams affecting the workplace" and "matters referred to the MAPP [Mediation Alternative Pilot Program] Dispute Resolution System by the Office of the Special Inspector General for Bias Matters or the authorized union and management representatives to the grievance procedure." It specifically excludes "any matter subject to the grievance and arbitration procedure contained in any collective bargaining agreement (CBA) with the State of New York, Unified Court System, unless all authorized union and management representatives mutually agree otherwise."

ELEMENTS OF A FAIR SYSTEM

Over the past ten years, several national organizations, including the Society of Professionals in Dispute Resolution (now the Association for Conflict Resolution), have established committees to define the elements of fairness of a workplace conflict management system.[3] The committees have agreed on the elements and parameters set out here.

Voluntariness

Every individual with a conflict has a unique interest in how to settle the issue. This principle requires that the choice to use any option available be voluntary. The use of the system or of any path offered in it—or outside it—must remain an option to be chosen voluntarily. Individuals should be informed about their options, should feel empowered to select from among them, and should find themselves free to make a choice, without pressure, regarding how to resolve their conflict.

Protection of Privacy and Confidentiality

Individuals in conflict have a right to expect that their issues will be held in confidence by their organizations and by those working with them to resolve their issues. Without this protection, most individuals would be reluctant to use the system. Thus, any credible workplace system must guarantee that every use of the system, along with the substantive issue involved, will be treated as confidential. This protection must be reinforced continuously by the organization. Permission for limited disclosure only may be requested from participants for use in specific research or data keeping.

Impartiality of Neutrals

In a workplace system, neutrals can include ADR advisers, ombudspersons, mediators, and arbitrators. It is essential that these people be viewed as, and in fact be, neutral. They cannot have any interest in the outcome of the process. If participants perceive that any neutral is biased, the very credibility of the system is put at risk. The easiest way to foster the perception of neutrality is to use only outside neutrals from an independent roster.

Trained and Qualified Neutrals

Neutrals must be trained and qualified to perform their duties. Each neutral must have the qualifications and experience required to deliver quality services to the system. There are many types of neutrals, so many sets of qualifications and experience are needed. The skill sets of a mediator, for example, are totally different from those of an arbitrator. The simplest way for an organization to ensure the quality of the neutrals it uses is to choose them only from established, professional, independent rosters. If an employer uses any in-house neutrals, it is responsible for ensuring that they have adequate training.

Prohibition of Retaliation

An essential but often overlooked element of a fair workplace system is a prohibition against retaliation. In general, retaliation refers to any negative consequence against an employee, a witness, or an adviser from use of the system. Participants who think that they could be the targets of retaliation put the very credibility of the system at risk. Therefore, any workplace system must assure its users that retaliation will not occur, and it must provide a vehicle for complaints if an act of retaliation appears.

Protection of Collective Bargaining Rights

Respect for existing collective bargaining rights is a key element of a fair workplace system. The system cannot be designed or used in a way to diminish legitimate collective bargaining rights. That does not mean that the two systems cannot work together, however. A mediation element can be integrated effectively into a traditional grievance procedure, but the design and approval of such blended systems require extensive communication between the system designer and the leaders of the union. The City of Phoenix, Arizona, for example, has successfully implemented a peer mediation program that is embraced by its police and firefighter unions.

Diversity and Accessibility

The core credibility of a workplace system requires that its internal and external neutrals comprise a diverse group of people. Historically, though, workplace neutrals have not been a diverse group. Recently, there has been some outreach for women and minorities to become qualified and serve as workplace neutrals in an attempt to rectify this situation. It is also essential that the system ensure accessibility to disabled participants.

Preclusion of Statutory Rights

An ongoing controversy concerns whether a fair workplace system can preclude rights to statutory forums. The basic question is whether a fair system can insist that individuals give up their right to file suit in court against their employer in return for the right to an arbitration forum that has the ability to grant full remedial powers. ADR organizations and government commissions that have examined this issue have not reached a consensus.[4] As a practical matter, the federal courts have increasingly given employers the right to insist on a preclusion of statutory rights.[5] As an ethical matter, however, the issue continues to divide the workplace system community.

OTHER FACTORS INFLUENCING SYSTEM DESIGN

There is a natural and inherent resistance to change in all organizations. This includes change resulting from the adoption of a workplace system. Experience has demonstrated that this resistance can be overcome through initial buy-in, extensive communication, and use of an organizational change model. Therefore, stakeholder resistance must be anticipated in the design process.

Anticipating Resistance to the System

Resistance to the system may come from unexpected sources. In almost all cases, there is an initial lack of comfort with an interest-based approach toward settling employee conflict. Sometimes the strongest resistance comes from first-line supervisors who feel that the system's values and flexibility interfere with traditional paths of communication and give too many rights to those with meritless claims. Sometimes the strongest resistance comes from human resource personnel who feel that the new system changes the power structure, diminishes their role in conflict resolution, and decreases the emphasis on rights-based determination of employee disputes.

The in-house law department may be resistant because they believe a workplace system encourages frivolous claims without the presumptive use of a rights-based forum. Most lawyers were never exposed to dispute resolution in law school and are unclear about its value or outright hostile to its use. In-house lawyers fear that workplace systems diminish their role in employee dispute resolution; furthermore, they do not fully understand the benefits of mediation. Even senior management may be a source of resistance because they fear that implementing such a system will motivate a flood of complaints.

Right of Employees to Select Access Options

Another core element in designing a workplace system involves whether employees should have the right to select options in the continuum when and as they wish or should instead be forced to access the system in a sequential, step-by-step manner.[6] Senior leaders often prefer that employees be required to use the system sequentially, while design consultants prefer the benefit of a more flexible approach.

The concept behind system design suggests that employees should be able to move back and forward to resolve their issues, a procedure often referred to as *looping back and looping forward*. The theory behind this preference is that employees have different innate styles in resolving conflict and that their needs may change as resolution of their conflict is addressed by the organization. For example, an employee may attend a dispute resolution conference to evaluate her options and find out that she needs an important bit of information before proceeding to mediation. So she "loops back-ward" to talk to her supervisor and obtain the information. She may stop there, pursuing the process no further, or she may continue.

System designers often recommend that employees be encour-aged to move forward and back as needed to resolve their conflicts, with workplace systems viewed as a flexible, not linear, process.

Who Pays for the Use of the Internal System Features?

Controversy and debate over whether the claimant should pay to use various higher-end features of the workplace system are on the increase. Traditionally, in the union environment, there is no cost to the individual employee, but there is a cost to the union. In grievance arbitration and grievance mediation, management and union equally share the fees of the arbitrator. In the nonunion environment, though, the tradition in workplace systems has been not to charge the employee for the initial steps or for any internal feature, such as peer review, advisers, hot lines, or internal media-tion. Senior leaders often believe that their workplace system should impose some financial charge in order to prevent wide-spread use or even abuse of the system. They believe that imposing a charge will screen out the meritless claims.

In practice, employees do not abuse the system, and so these fears are unwarranted. The vast majority of employees use the upper-end internal features (such as peer review or internal medi-ation) only after careful consideration. Because the purpose of a workplace system is to encourage early conflict resolution and avoid litigation, it seems foolish to impose financial barriers that discourage its use.

In fact, it is very uncommon for employers to impose costs for an employee to use an internal feature of a workplace system. Nevertheless, employers often impose costs for an employee to use an external feature, such as external mediation or arbitration, a subject we take up in the next chapter.

Criteria to Evaluate Options Within the System

There is no one ideal model for designing an effective workplace system because each must fit the goals, resources, and culture of its organization. Nevertheless, several criteria can be used to evaluate the appropriateness of any design option or feature:

- What will be the transaction costs of this option? How much time, money, and emotional energy will be needed to implement it?

- Does this option encourage the claimant to own the resolution?

- How does this option affect internal relationships within the organization? Does it facilitate understanding of the relational dimensions of the conflict?

- What will be the expected durability of the anticipated outcome of this option? (It is commonly assumed that decisions made in mediation are more durable than decisions imposed in arbitration.) Should the outcome last and not be rejected over time by a party?

- What will be the anticipated satisfaction with outcomes?

- Will the option typically lead to a satisfactory result between the disputants?

- How does this option align with the existing corporate culture? Does it reinforce the desired culture or run in the opposite direction?

One company that made its choices and designed a program is the Sears Corporation. It recently rolled out a pilot ADR program for two of its businesses—hardware stores and the Great Indoors home decor stores—that will be available for nearly sixteen thousand employees. The program will be mandatory for new applicants and existing employees, except those already working at the Great Indoors stores, who will have the option not to use it. Employees who do agree to participate give up their right to sue.

The process begins with a step called "Let's Talk," in which employees are encouraged to settle their differences with local management or human resources. An employee who fails to find a solution can take the case to a peer committee that the employees help select. Mediation comes next. If the employee is still unhappy, he or she can advance to arbitration, the last stage, in which a professional arbitrator's decision is final and binding.

With more than 300,000 employees and a high turnover rate, Sears spends more legal dollars on battling its own people than anything else, according to general counsel Anastasia Kelly, who estimates that each litigated case with an employee costs between $50,000 and $75,000. That is powerful motivation for creating a conflict resolution system that may cut litigation costs.[7]

COMMON DESIGN FEATURES

Although there is no single ideal combination of design features because the system must be crafted to achieve specific goals, work with a particular level of resources, and be aligned with the organization's mission and culture, there are nevertheless some common design features that use resources internal to the organization. Here, we examine the open door, ombudspersons, hot lines, managerial mediation, resolution facilitators, conferences, internal peer mediation, trained employee advisers, peer review, and executive panels.

The Open Door

The open door is the most common feature in all organizational workplace systems. In fact, the term *open door* has almost become trite in many organizational cultures. An open door philosophy implies that the supervisor believes in open dialogue and encourages employees to come into his or her office and talk through differences or questions that may arise. Some organizations communicate this openness in a broad-based manner, while others feel that it does not require reinforcement because it is such a core element of their culture.

Experience with the effectiveness of the open door model has mixed outcomes. Some observers suggest that it is highly overrated as an accepted vehicle of conflict resolution for several reasons: supervisors are not trained to problem-solve with employees, supervisors are too busy to accept the role, and employees feel there is a high risk of retaliation for using the open door. Opposing observers suggest that despite the obvious barriers, the open door model still resolves over 90 percent of all employee problems. This view also concludes that most employees believe the open door process is a desired step, despite its faults and the acknowledged fact that it does not always work. The open door feature is the first step in the vast majority of workplace systems.

Wells Fargo, for example, lists talking to the supervisor as the first step in its dispute resolution process:

> Any work-related problem should be brought to the attention of the employees' supervisor. In most cases, problems can be solved easily by the supervisor because he or she is in the best position to handle the problem. If the employee feels that he or she is uncomfortable talking with the supervisor, the employee can contact a Human Resource consultant with any work-related problem and the HR Consultant will work to resolve the matter.

The Halliburton Company also relies on an open door policy and pushes for its use. Its workplace system provides what it refers to as "Ten Good Reasons to use the Open Door Policy":

- Management is committed to it.
- It makes early on-site problem-solving more likely.
- It encourages you to give feedback to management.
- You get your questions answered and learn about your options.
- You have instant support.
- It's free.
- It's flexible.
- You can contact an adviser in confidence.
- Retaliation is forbidden.
- It helps you help yourself.

Ombudspersons

Another popular option in system design, particularly for larger organizations, is the ombudsperson. There are numerous forms and roles of ombudspersons, but according to Mary Rowe, special assistant to the president of MIT, *ombudsperson* generally refers to "a neutral or impartial manager within an organization who may provide informal and confidential assistance to managers and employees in resolving work-related concerns; who may serve as a counselor, informal mediator, informal fact-finder, upward feedback mechanism, consultant, problem prevention device and change agent; and whose office is located outside ordinary line management structures."[8]

The ombudsperson feature has been widely adopted by federal and state governments to provide alternative channels of conflict resolutions for external customers. It is viewed as a highly successful means to counter governmental bureaucracy; for example, the U.S. Internal Revenue Service has an ombudsperson for taxpayer disputes. The Ombudsman Association estimates are that there are over ten thousand ombudspeople working in a variety of roles in the United States and Canada.

Shell Oil, Eastman Kodak, American Express, and Lucent Technologies are among the private sector organizations that use ombudspersons. In private sector organizations, the most commonly voiced objections to the ombudsperson are the cultural statement that employees should have options other than directly discussing their issues with a member of management, the potential conflicts with human resource policy and practices, and the cost of creating another function with staff. Although it may not be stated outright, another objection among senior leaders is the creation of a function to investigate issues that some would prefer be ignored. Countering the concern about cost, however, is research sponsored by the Ombudsman Association, which concluded that the ombudsperson process is cost-effective for organizations when considering the accompanying decrease in employee litigation, violence, and turnover.[9]

Most universities have an ombudsperson for student and faculty disputes. Stanford University, for example, has an active ombudsperson office that provides the following services:

What Services Does the Ombuds Office Provide?

- Hearing and discussing your concerns
- Identifying and evaluating options to resolve problems
- Opening avenues of communication with all parties and gathering information
- Striving for fairness, equitable solutions, and adherence to university policies

Providing Information

- Providing you with information about university services
- Referring you to other university services and programs
- Working with other university offices, when needed, including the Sexual Harassment Coordinating Adviser and the Office for Multicultural Development
- Helping university officials understand general problems faced by faculty, staff and students and, at times, suggesting revisions to policies and procedures

- Serving as a channel to communicate information about health, safety or ethical concerns

- Informing the community of trends and issues by publishing a statistical report

The Ombudsman Association code of ethics, developed to guide its members in their tasks, lays out the importance of confidentiality and the steps to be taken to safeguard it:

> The ombudsman, as a designated neutral, has the responsibility of maintaining strict confidentiality concerning matters that are brought to his/her attention unless given permission to do otherwise. The only exceptions, at the sole discretion of the ombudsman, are where there appears to be imminent threat of serious harm. The ombudsman must take all reasonable steps to protect any records and files pertaining to confidential discussions from inspection by all other persons, including management.
>
> The ombudsman should not testify in any formal judicial or administrative hearing about concerns brought to his/her attention.
>
> When making recommendations, the ombudsman has the responsibility to suggest actions or policies that will be equitable to all parties.[10]

Hot Lines

The philosophy of workplace system design is to provide employees with a variety of choices for resolving their conflicts. One choice that some organizations offer is the hot line, a telephone service available to employees to voice issues with upper management. Almost all hot lines allow anonymous messages to be left and taken seriously; they are investigated by the hot-line coordinator. The assumption behind the hot line is that some employees have legitimate issues that they will not raise directly with their supervisor due to fear of retaliation, the employee's preferred style, or the fact that the issue involves or implicates that supervisor. A key benefit to a hot line is that it allows employees in a distributed organization (that is, at various locations) to connect with experts easily to discuss their conflicts.

There are two types of hot lines. One model is staffed during the workday with a professional who is trained on collecting information and asking questions. The second model is unstaffed; all calls are left as messages.

In the private sector, federal defense contractors have used the hot-line feature for many years. The original purpose for its use there was to facilitate whistle-blowers in raising concerns about waste or other federal contracting violations. This remains an important value of hot lines, but the vast majority of telephone messages concern personal workplace issues involving a supervisor.[11]

Two objections are commonly voiced against the hot line as a design feature. One is the cost of assigning someone to collect and investigate the messages. This requires a lot of work, particularly in returning calls and attempting to understand the messages. The second objection concerns the anonymous nature of many of the calls. The anonymity means there is no one to call back to clarify the message, and thus a great deal of time is spent exploring the meaning of some of the calls. There is also a philosophical objection to allowing anonymous calls to the hot line in a culture embracing openness and direct dealing. Nevertheless, most system design consultants believe that the hot line is a legitimate vehicle within a system model.

The hot line is a standard tool used by ombudspersons. Shell Oil Corporation, for example, uses a hot line as a conduit to its ombudsperson. It describes its corporate system, Shell RESOLVE, in the following way: "Although Shell RESOLVE is designed to help you help yourself, the program recognizes that you may need advice or assistance in this regard. When you do, you may call the Shell Ombuds office via a toll-free hotline. The Ombuds are skilled conflict resolution professionals who will offer independent, confidential help at any time during the resolution process. The Ombuds act under a professional code of ethics to ensure confidentiality, independence and neutrality."

Managerial Mediation

Progressive organizations are increasingly providing basic mediation training to line managers, and a few have designated conflict resolution as a key supervisory competency. This approach recognizes that a supervisor is the first line of contact with the vast number of interpersonal conflicts that occur among employees in the workplace. In managerial mediation, the supervisor uses his or her authority to convene disputing employees and explore mutually acceptable solutions. If no resolution is achieved, the parties can move forward through the workplace system.

Supervisory training for this task can take a variety of forms. Its duration is typically much less than the standard forty-hour program for persons desiring to become accomplished mediators. The curriculum includes evaluating which employee conflicts are appropriate for managerial mediation, convening the parties, using listening skills, exploring underlying issues, and closing the mediation. This training can be given by internal or external providers.

An organization that provides supervisors with skills training for mediation makes a significant statement about the role its supervisors are to play and the way it wants employee conflict to be resolved in its workplace. Some managers feel this process imposes an undue burden on supervisors, who are already overworked. Some human resource managers feel that giving supervisors this new skill diminishes their own role. However, an increasing minority of progressive organizations are providing basic conflict resolution training to first-line supervisors as part of their tool kit and the organization's workplace system.[12]

Resolution Facilitators

Many organizations observe that employees would be able to resolve their own conflicts if they simply knew their options and could get together with the disputing party. Researchers sometimes refer to this process as *convening the parties*.[13] "Convenors," write Slaikeu and Hasson, "are independent and impartial third parties

(often ADR vendors) who assist those in conflict in picking a dispute resolution process and in selecting an individual or group to
provide the services required. The role of the convenor is to assist
the parties in selecting the most appropriate dispute resolution
mechanism in light of their interests, important facts, the alternative procedures available (inside and outside the organization or
organizations in question), and the key solutions the parties seek."

To convene the disputing parties, these organizations create
what is sometimes called a resolution facilitator function. Such a
facilitator is one or a group of trained peers whose role is to facilitate the employee's needs through the system. The resolution facilitators are typically selected to represent a range of employees, but
do not typically come from the corporate staff.

There are numerous advantages to this design feature. One is
that no full-time incremental staff is required. Another is that facilitators are credible because they come from employee ranks. Still
other advantages are that the training is less complex than for
other options, such as mediation, and this approach aligns with the
existing culture and receptiveness for employee problem solving
that permeates the progressive organization.

The resolution facilitator feature has a few disadvantages, however. One is that employee issues are often more complex than this
feature assumes, and because facilitators are employees and not full-
time dispute resolution experts, they are not fully prepared to handle the complexity. Another is that regular turnover requires
frequent training of new facilitators.

Conferences with an Employee to Discuss Options

The purpose of a conference with a complainant is to facilitate
selection of a process for resolving an issue. Not a meeting to
resolve the issue directly, it is an attempt to evaluate the employee's
options and help the employee decide which option best fits his or
her needs. Such a conference usually results in the employee's
choosing one of three options: returning to the prior level for more

dialogue, selecting informal mediation, or moving forward to a higher level of the system, which is often a rights-based option.

The major difference between the resolution facilitator model and the conference model is the skill required of the consultant who is meeting with the employee. In the facilitator model, the person is a trained peer of the employee but not an expert on conflict resolution. In the conference model, the person hosting the conference is a staff professional, such as a human resource executive or an ombudsperson.

In the Halliburton Dispute Resolution Program (DRP), an employee or supervisor contacts the DRP office and participates in a conference. This meeting explores all the options available to suit the particular dispute.[14] Halliburton has this to say about the DRP:

> The Conference provides an opportunity to meet with a Company representative and a program facilitator to discuss your issue and choose one of the following options for resolving it.
>
> • Go back to the Open Door
> • Seek assistance through the Adviser process
> • Try an informal mediation process within the company
> • Go directly to an independent outside mediator and arbitrator, if your dispute concerns your legally protected rights

Internal Peer Mediation

There is an increasing trend toward the use of internal employees as mediators of workplace conflict. As an interest-based feature, this trend is generally limited to the public sector and includes claims of a nonstatutory basis, such as unfairness or violation of a policy. Internal mediators do not typically mediate statutory claims, such as race or age discrimination. A crucial element of this feature is the selection of employees with the capabilities to become effective mediators. Established mediation programs have written criteria for prospective trainees, which are used to weed out those who do not have the basic skills. There is significant debate as to the benefits of internal peer mediation.

Many assumptions lie behind the use of this design feature. One is that employees can be capably trained in the mediation process, typically by using the standard forty-hour training model. Another is that trained employees can maintain their mediation skills over time. A third is that peer mediation is a cost-effective feature that saves money that would otherwise be paid out to external professional mediators. A fourth assumption is that using internal peer employees as mediators provides significant credibility to the disputing parties, and a fifth is that the volume of internal claims going to mediation justifies the initial and ongoing expense.

Numerous problems nevertheless plague internal peer mediation. One is that a forty-hour training program is insufficient to build skills for workplace disputes, yet few organizations are willing to provide more time to build capability. Another is that employee mediators do not usually maintain their skills due to the lack of ongoing practice.

Several administrative concerns also surround internal peer mediators. One administrative problem is that the scheduling of employee mediators is cumbersome due to their lack of availability (they are too busy in their job) or conflicts with the parties. It is common for the supervisor of a peer mediator to refuse the mediator time off until an important project is completed, which could be weeks. Another administrative issue is the normal turnover of trained mediators, which shrinks the qualified pool and requires continual training of additional mediators. A final administrative problem is that peer mediation requires dedicated staff support to convene the parties, select the mediators, and maintain the metrics. In light of these disadvantages, many organizations that consider selecting internal peer mediators as a design feature instead choose to use external professional mediators who specialize in employment issues.

Organizations that have used peer mediation for many years, however, report significant satisfaction with its effectiveness. Two examples are the City of Phoenix and the U.S. Department of the

Interior. The City of Phoenix described the aims of its mediation program, called Resolve, and its choice of mediators in a memorandum distributed in August 2001:

> Resolve can help with situations involving co-workers, supervisors and employees. It is a confidential and informal way to help resolve problems from broken agreements or promises, personality conflicts, lack of communication, personal issues, miscommunications, or other issues that may interfere with job satisfaction and productivity. Mediators are other city employees who are specially trained and carefully selected in each situation to ensure neutrality. Mediators do not handle cases in their own departments.

The U.S. Department of the Interior's CORE Program is described as follows:

Who and What Are CORE Services About?

The CORE program is a new means for Interior employees and managers to protect against abuse, bias and other improper treatment or unfairness. The CORE program is for everyone—all levels of employees and managers, union representatives and union members whose union elects to participate. Core cases are mediated by CORE Specialists who are experienced and trained in informal workplace mediation. All CORE Specialists are neutral and have no stake in the outcome of the mediation cases. Each bureau in Interior has CORE Specialists.

The CORE program identifies roles any Interior employee may face—conflicts between co-workers, conflicts between supervisors, and supervisors and management, and more. CORE is not a top-down management versus employees program—there is no determination of guilt and no punishment. CORE specialists are trained to help people discuss the cause of conflicts and develop reasonable and responsible options.

Trained Employee Advisers

A well-established premise of conflict resolution is that claimants have a right to an adviser during the process. In a labor union setting, the adviser is a union representative or shop steward. In litigation, the adviser is an attorney. In these two settings, the right of an employee to a professional adviser is inviolate and never limited in scope. Advisers are viewed as helpful in achieving settlement.

In a workplace system, the adviser serves several roles, including providing substantive advice, process coaching, and moral support. The adviser is an advocate, not someone neutral to the system. Typically, the adviser is not an external attorney but a fellow employee. In a few organizations, the adviser can be a family member who is not even an employee. Current workplace systems generally allow for some form of advisers but limit their roles. In some systems, in fact, advisers are not even allowed to speak.

In organizations that provide employee advisers for claimants, the advisers are typically peer employees who have volunteered or have been selected for the role. They are never members of management. They have been trained in conflict resolution processes and are assigned to work with claimants. Their role is to provide information and coaching and to assist with case preparation for an upcoming ADR process, such as mediation, peer review, or arbitration. The key assumptions behind this model are that trained advisers can be effective, claimants will accept trained advisers selected from a pool or a list of names, and claimants will see these advisers as providing a useful service.

The Problem Resolution Option (PRO) is a former Phoenix-based pilot project of Honeywell Corporation. The program describes the adviser feature: "What is PRO? The letters stand for the Problem Resolution Option, a new method for settling problems in the workplace. PRO is a further option for those who have already been unsuccessful in trying to resolve their disputes through the usual process. The program provides alternative resources as well as a fair and impartial hearing of the employee's dispute. It is designed to handle employee disputes in a structured and non-threatening manner." Individuals chosen to hear a Honeywell employee's case—whether an employee adviser, ombudsperson, or review panelist—are selected from a pool of volunteers by a committee of employees and managers. Before hearing their first cases, these volunteers go through more than forty hours of training on conflict resolution, ethics, confidentiality, company policies, and other relevant topics.

Peer Review and Employee Appeals

One rights-based feature sometimes found in workplace systems is peer review. Similar to an adjudicatory approach to conflict resolution, this process has been used by blue-collar manufacturing organizations for many years, often for union-avoidance purposes. In some organizations, decisions of the peer tribunal are final and binding, while in others, decisions are only advisory on the employee or management. For most peer review models, employees are preselected and trained by human resource personnel or an outside consultant. Typically these models have no mediation option. In the 1970s, peer review was sold as a credible alternative to labor arbitration in the union environment, and there were several national consultants selling and installing the process. In fact, it became common in the aerospace industry. Some peer review programs include only peers, while other programs include peers and managers.

The core assumptions behind the peer review process begin with the notion that employee disputes should be resolved through internal mechanisms, not litigation. A second assumption is that resolution of claims by peers is credible and acceptable to the claimant. A third is that allowing each adversary to present its claims to a peer tribunal is a valid problem-solving model. A fourth is that peers can be capably trained as fact finders and decision makers, and a fifth is that the model is both practical and cost-effective. Opponents of the peer review process argue that its time as a useful approach has passed because of the increased complexity of workplace disputes. They view it as administratively difficult for three reasons: employee turnover requires constant retraining, the feature is no longer credible to claimants who now want an external forum, and it is not cost-effective because of the staff resources required to manage the process. Today peer review is found mainly in manufacturing industries.

An approach related to the peer review process is an employee appeals board. In some organizations, in fact, the two terms mean the same thing. Generally, though, they differ in that an employee appeals board always includes members of management as part of the process and is more often found in nonmanufacturing organizations. An appeals board hears employee complaints and renders a decision that is binding on the company but not necessarily on the employee. An employee appeals board could be made up of only members of management, while a peer review panel always has peers as well.

The Boeing ADR Process includes the possible use of a five-member peer review panel as an option once internal mediation has failed. It is described as follows:

Eligibility for Step 3 Peer Panel

- If the ADR manager determines that a dispute involves the possible misapplication of a company policy or procedure, the employee has the option of presenting the issue to a peer panel when internal mediation is not successful.

- A peer panel reviews the documents, questions witnesses, and then determines whether the company policies and procedures were correctly applied.

- A peer panel decision [based on a majority vote of the panelists] is mutually binding if the employee accepts the decision and any award granted by the peer panel.

Assembling the Peer Panel

- A peer panel has five members. A peer panel decision is based on a majority vote of the panelists (minimum of three of five). The decision is recorded in a Peer Panel Decision Record.

Executive Panels

Executive panels in a workplace system generally represent the opportunity for employees to present their claims to a panel of the organization's senior executives.[15] The concept behind an executive panel assumes that employees feel that upper executives would be objective and potentially sympathetic to their claims. Panels typically have three to five executives, usually at the vice-presidential level, who are not related to the employee whose claim is being presented. This feature works in a variety of settings, but is most common in paternalistic or smaller organizations with a legacy of accessible executives.

We are unaware of any research conducted on the effectiveness and credibility of executive panels. Despite the lack of research, our experience is that a surprising number of employees prefer this option and feel no hesitation in raising certain issues to senior management. Executives also often feel comfortable with this option, although these panels are not as common as they were in the 1980s.

CONCLUSION

We believe there is no single ideal workplace system for all organizations. Each workplace system must be customized according to organizational mission, needs, available resources, and culture. The internal options described in this chapter may be effective in some organizations and ineffective in others. Ultimately, the design of the system must provide the elements of fairness described in this chapter and encourage personal ownership of the conflict.

Chapter Six

Design of Conflict Management Systems

External Features

In contrast to internal options, which attempt to instill ownership of the creation of the solution to a conflict in the employee, external options take ownership away from the employee and give it to the outside neutral.

Despite the slow-growing trend toward the use of internal employees as workplace neutrals described in Chapter Five, the vast majority of workplace systems today primarily use the services of external, ad hoc neutrals, usually selected from panels of local or national ADR providers. External mediators and arbitrators have certain advantages over internal ones: as specialists, they presumably have greater knowledge of such pertinent information as employment discrimination law and workplace torts and have demonstrated experience as a mediator or an arbitrator. Using external mediators and arbitrators is cost-effective in that they need be hired only on an ad hoc basis and are generally available to serve in a reasonably short time. Their presumed objectivity from being an outsider often provides them with greater credibility with the claimant. The preference for using external neutrals as a design feature in workplace systems is expected to continue.

Using external neutrals has been a long-established practice in labor-management relations. For example, almost all grievance arbitration provisions in collective bargaining contracts provide for the use of arbitrators chosen from sources external to the organization. These external arbitrators are often employed on an ad hoc (case-by-case) basis. In some industries, such as apparel, steel, and agricultural implements, the arbitrators—usually called "permanent umpires"—are retained by the parties to hear and decide all cases that arise under the collective bargaining agreement. In collective bargaining, external mediators are frequently used to resolve interest disputes and are typically assigned by either the Federal Mediation and Conciliation Service or a state agency. In labor relations, a handful of sectors, such as trucking and other jurisdictions organized by the Teamsters, have a tradition of using internal means to resolve grievance disputes. Generally, however, the parties in collective bargaining rely on external neutrals to resolve their disputes.

In the nonunion setting, the practice of using external neutrals is not as well entrenched as it is in labor relations.[1] An examination of whether internal employees could be trained effectively and could serve credibly as resolvers of conflict has begun and continues to expand. Internal employees are being used to resolve conflicts, most commonly in peer review and internal employee mediation. The advantages for using internal employees as neutrals are company knowledge, availability, and credibility. For most organizations, internal employees are no added cost (they are already on the payroll), so there is an opportunity to save money. Because internal employees work in the organization, they are assumed to be credible and respected by their fellow employees. In addition, they have in-depth substantive knowledge of the company's policies and practices and therefore have some advantage over external neutrals that lack this knowledge.

EXTERNAL DESIGN OPTIONS WITH WORKPLACE SYSTEMS

Because each workplace system is unique, there is no single ideal combination of design features. This holds true for external as well as internal features. The scope of external features that can be considered includes external mediation, advisory arbitration or hearings, fact finding, and final and binding arbitration. These features pass ownership for creating the solution to the outside neutral.

External Mediation

Workplace mediation is a well-established and proven ADR process. It can involve disputes of a nonstatutory nature, such as interpersonal conflicts or contentions over company policies, or disputes alleging some violation of a statute, normally employment discrimination.[2] Mediation of workplace disputes offers the advantages of privacy because the press and outsiders are not allowed in the mediation room and generally are not allowed to inspect the final settlement. It also offers the benefit of speed: the mediation session can typically be arranged within sixty days of the request.

Another benefit is that mediation is interest based, as opposed to litigation, which is rights based. Settlements arising from interest-based negotiations are assumed to be more creative and have greater buy-in from the parties. Other advantages to mediation often mentioned are that the mediator is a workplace subject matter expert and may be creative and persuasive because of this knowledge, the process provides the potential to focus on ongoing relationships, and the disputants (not a judge or jury) maintain control of the outcome. A major advantage of mediation over litigation, of course, is cost (primarily in attorney fees and court costs), because most mediation cases are settled within a day.

There are obstacles, though, to selecting external mediation as a design feature. Some counsel (even management counsel) are reluctant to be the first to propose mediation because of the risk of being seen as having a weaker case. Many plaintiff attorneys are still skeptical of mediation. A few rare employment disputes may need to set a precedent and so are not appropriate for mediation. Finally, there is an issue of timing: mediation may not be effective until one or both sides have conducted some degree of discovery. If discovery reveals clear evidence of liability, then the employer's motivation to mediate may be greater.

The vast majority of workplace systems provide that mediators will be selected from an external panel. The remaining programs provide for ad hoc selection of mediators or for selection from a panel that has been already created by the employer (this latter approach may be considered unethical but not unlawful). Many programs allow the employee to select the mediator, while others allow the parties to strike names off a list on an alternating basis. The name that remains is chosen.

A minority of workplace systems require specific qualifications of mediators acceptable to the process. For example, the Anheuser-Busch Dispute Resolution Program Policy Statement provides: "In addition to not having any financial or personal interest in the result of the mediation, mediators shall have a minimum of five years experience in the practice of employment law or in the mediation of employment claims or comparable experience."

The Chevron Corporation plan provides a rather elaborate explanation of the step toward using an outside mediator:

In Step Three, you can submit the problem to an objective, outside mediator selected by you and the company from American Arbitration Association, JAMS, Endispute or similar organizations. To begin this step, you describe your concern and desired outcome in writing.

During mediation, you can informally explain your position. The mediator's role is to listen, offer suggestions, and try to help reach a solution. There are no witnesses, testimony, depositions, or subpoenas. However, you may be represented by your own attorney if you so desire. The step is designed to be cooperative and problem-solving. Only individual complaints are eligible for this step.

Neither you nor the company are required to reach an agreement. If you do reach an agreement, it will be final and binding. The company will pay the cost of the mediator. If the complaint is resolved, the company will pay for any reasonable attorney fees you incur up to $1500. If the matter is not resolved at mediation, you are responsible for your attorney's fees. If the issue is not resolved, you can go to Step Four.

Advisory (Nonbinding) Arbitration or Hearings

Advisory arbitration (nonbinding on both parties) is a common ADR process in the public sector. It is a rights-based process. The term *advisory arbitration* is commonly used but is really a misnomer, because arbitration, by definition, is always final and binding on the parties. Advisory arbitration is really a hearing process, such as in administrative law proceedings.

Organizations often select advisory arbitration because enabling legislation prevents the public entity (commonly educational organizations) from delegating the final decision to outside neutrals. The process often provides a full evidentiary hearing for the claimant, but provides for a nonbinding decision that serves in essence as a recommendation to the senior leadership of the organization. State colleges and universities often offer advisory arbitration as part of their due process system. Attorneys are typically allowed to represent their clients in the forum, and the losing party has the right to appeal the decision. The prime advantage to advisory (nonbinding) arbitration for both parties is that it provides a significant degree of due process, a full evidentiary hearing, and a recommendation that can be appealed to a higher level or to a court.

In the private sector, advisory arbitration is occasionally offered as an option for employees who are required to arbitrate their claims as part of their workplace's system. In these systems, to encourage the employee to proceed to arbitration, the arbitrator's decision can be binding on the employer but not on the employee. Advisory arbitration is mandatory in this model and is a prerequisite to going to court, but the decision is not binding on the employee. Law firms are increasingly suggesting this option to their clients as an alternative to the growing controversy of mandatory, final, and binding arbitration of statutory disputes.

Fact Finding with a Recommendation

Another common ADR process sometimes chosen as a workplace system feature is fact finding with a recommendation. This is not to be confused with fact finding as historically applied in collective bargaining, in which a person is asked to hear evidence of wages and terms of employment. This fact-finding process is much more informal than advisory arbitration. The fact finder's role is to receive and uncover the facts and then to write a recommendation to the senior leader of the organization. The fact-finding process is not an evidentiary hearing, and the fact finder has the right to pursue his or her own leads and to receive testimony and facts outside of the presence of the opposing party. Attorneys are allowed but not commonly used in the fact-finding process.

Using the fact-finding report serves three purposes: to use the report as the basis of further negotiations, to use the report as the basis for a management response or an offer of settlement, or to have the report serve as information for the senior leader (such as the university president) to reach a final decision. A small minority of workplace systems use this feature, generally in the public sector.

Final and Binding Arbitration

Workplace arbitration is an established and proven ADR process.[3] In this phrase, *workplace* refers not to a location but to a variety of disputes involving nonstatutory policy and practice issues (such as work assignments and claims of general unfairness), statutory disputes involving employment discrimination, and disputes involving workplace contract claims and workplace torts (such as invasion of privacy or defamation). For years, breach-of-contract disputes involving employment agreements have been arbitrated in private forums while all other claims have been resolved in courts before a judge or a jury.

The term *final and binding* is a term of art as it applies to arbitration. It means that the award is not generally intended to be appealed to a higher forum. This concept implies that the parties value the finality of the process: once the award is rendered, the parties plan to move on with their lives and not seek to overturn it. Historically, workplace grievance arbitration under collective bargaining agreements has been final and binding, with few exceptions. This is partially true because the Federal Arbitration Act of 1925 provides few grounds to overturn an award. The primary reasons are fraud and duress. Awards from labor arbitration have long enjoyed a strong deference by federal courts. It is too early to determine the degree of deference the courts will provide to awards arising out of statutory employment arbitration, however.

In the majority of workplace systems, only statutory or contract claims are allowed to proceed to arbitration. In other words, employees are allowed to proceed to arbitration in employment discrimination disputes only if they allege race, age, or gender discrimination, for example. In most other organizations, all other claims alleging violations of company policies or other nonstatutory discrimination must be resolved earlier in the process or must be withdrawn by the employee.

There are some exceptions. At Boeing Company, employees have the option of referring their nonstatutory claims to peer review, another rights-based process. Phelps-Dodge Corporation allows nonunion employee discharges to be arbitrated in a final and binding forum without an allegation of a statutory violation.

Some design consultants view this general prohibition against raising nonstatutory claims to arbitration as a mistake. They argue that if the underlying goal of the workplace system is to resolve employee conflict, the company should allow a rights-based process to resolve all disputes. The primary reasons most employers limit the claims allowed to arbitration are potential cost and fear of employee abuse. But experience has demonstrated that employees do not abuse the options provided in workplace systems.

Most workplace arbitration programs have one of three design features. One is a voluntary postdispute feature that does not obligate the employee to agree to arbitrate prior to the dispute. Under this option, when the claim arises, the employee can move directly to court or use the arbitration procedure in the workplace system.

This is not controversial and is endorsed by the EEOC and by plaintiff groups.

A second option is a mandatory predispute feature that does obligate the employee to arbitrate the dispute, but the decision is not final and binding. In this case, the employee can reject the decision of the arbitrator. This option is not particularly controversial and is not common.

A third option is a mandatory predispute feature that does obligate the employee to arbitrate the dispute and the decision would be final and binding. In other words, the employee would give up his or her opportunity to proceed to a court for a trial. In most cases, this agreement is made a condition of employment for the employee. This option, which is highly controversial to certain groups, is the focus of a great deal of recent litigation.[4] It is also becoming increasingly common with larger corporations.

There are numerous advantages to the arbitration of workplace disputes for both the employer and the employee. One benefit is privacy and confidentiality, because the hearing is closed to the public and press and the decision is kept private among the parties. Another benefit is speed to hearing, because an arbitration hearing can typically be conducted within six months of the demand, as compared to the years a case would take to go through a state or federal court.

A third benefit concerns selection of the arbitrator. The parties control the selection and can thus choose a workplace expert with subject matter knowledge as their arbitrator. A fourth benefit is the conclusive and binding nature of the decision, which provides finality to the process. The last commonly accepted advantage to arbitration over litigation is cost. While some observers dispute this view, the majority believes that arbitration is more cost-effective for both plaintiffs and defendants in employment litigation.

Concerns About Arbitration

One of the numerous concerns about workplace and employment arbitration is the increasing legalism of the process, which creates delays and increases costs if the parties are not committed to a timely hearing. Another concern is the lack of available counsel for the claimant who does not have a highly lucrative case. Because of the wide variation in the potential financial values of cases, typically only one case out of twenty brought to an employment plaintiff attorney is accepted. Other concerns cited include the lack of qualified neutrals, and the threat to the finality of a "final and binding" decision in some statutory claims, particularly in view of the rights given to the EEOC to pursue litigation after the *Waffle House* decision by the Supreme Court.[5] *Waffle House* held that the EEOC can pursue independent litigation against employers even when the claimant has signed a binding arbitration agreement.

Our research revealed that about half of current workplace systems use some form of workplace arbitration. Of those arbitration systems, the vast majority require mandatory, predispute arbitration. Given recent legal history, the number of employers choosing this feature is expected to increase.

Another key design element is the selection of the arbitrator. In the past, the employer selected the pool of neutrals. With mandatory arbitration of statutory claims, the courts have declared that practice unfair and overreaching for employers. Thus, today it is unethical and unlawful in the statutory context. The method currently used to select a neutral is for the parties to strike the neutrals they do not like from the roster of qualified neutrals one at a time or to negotiate the preferred person informally.

Shell Oil Corporation describes its arbitration alternative in this way:

> Arbitration is also an effective way to resolve employment-related conflict that involves a legally protected right. If you do not achieve satisfactory resolution and agreement through External Mediation, you may request Arbitration. Arbitrators are selected in a way similar to mediators. However, in Arbitration, a neutral third-party arbitrator will issue a written decision after a review of the facts as presented by both parties. The Arbitrator may award any remedy

available to an individual under applicable law. Unlike External Mediation, Arbitration is optional. The Company will agree to be bound by the arbitrator's decision if that decision is acceptable to you. If you're dissatisfied with the arbitrator's decision, you're free to take your case to court, and the arbitrator's decision will not be binding on any of the parties.

Mercy Healthcare Arizona has a different arbitration and termination dispute resolution policy:

> It is the policy of Mercy Healthcare Arizona to provide an exclusive (unless stated otherwise within this policy) final, binding, speedy, fair, inexpensive, and impartial method for employees to bring employment claims to the attention of management without fear of reprisal and to resolve claims and disputes arising out of alleged unlawful employment discrimination, termination by breach of alleged contract or policy, violations of federal or state discrimination statutes, or employment tort, not covered by worker's compensation. . . .
>
> All disputes . . . shall be resolved pursuant to this policy and there shall be no recourse to court, with or without a jury trial.
>
> This policy does not prevent, prohibit or discourage the employee from filing a charge, participating in an investigation, or giving testimony before or otherwise seeking redress from the NLRB, EEOC, ACRD, or other state or federal agency.

As another example, here is the American Arbitration Association's arbitration policy description:

> If agreement is not reached through mediation, the parties may next turn to final and binding arbitration of disputes involving termination or legally-protected rights. . . .
>
> For AAA employees, arbitration is optional or voluntary. If an employee requests arbitration, the AAA is required to do so. If, on the other hand, an employee decides not to arbitrate, he or she is

free to pursue any available legal remedies through the courts or administrative agencies.

Legal Consultation Benefits

A controversial but increasingly common feature of workplace system design is the financial incentive for employees to obtain legal advice. The incentive is offered as another employee benefit, which has an annual cap and is a reimbursement paid on submission of legal bills. Typically, it applies only to claims of a statutory nature, such as employment discrimination or workplace torts. Many employers and their outside law firms find this a surprising proposition: that the employer would pay for the employee to sue the employer. However, employers who have adopted this feature have found it to be a highly successful benefit in resolving disputes. The general concept behind providing a legal consultation benefit is that these statutory disputes will be more quickly resolved if the employee has a legal adviser who will be candid about the merits of the employee's claim. Employers who select this feature have no fear that offering an employee this incentive to meet with an attorney will make matters worse.[6]

This employee benefit generally has several steps. First, the benefit is available to any employee using the mediation or arbitration steps of the workplace system. Second, there is an annual cap, often at $2,500. Third, the system is a reimbursement, not an advance, and the benefit must be issued directly to the attorney, who must be legally trained or licensed in the state. Finally, payment must be preapproved by the benefits manager. One employer who provides a $2,500 legal benefit is Shell Oil Corporation. After several years of experience, they have found that only about 20 percent of eligible employees use the benefit for mediation or arbitration, and most employees do not use the entire amount.

Shell describes its legal assistance plan as part of its conflict management system:

The Company recognizes that you may need legal advice at some point in the process of resolving a conflict. To that end, Shell RESOLVE includes a Legal Assistance Plan, where you will pay a deductible and co-payment and Shell will pay the balance of your fees for legal counsel, up to an annual limit. You pay no premiums to be covered by this plan.

Here's how it generally works:

- You pay a deductible of $50 per conflict situation
- After the deductible, you pay 10% of the balance
- The Company pays 90% of the balance
- The maximum annual benefit is $2,500 per employee

The American Arbitration Association has a similar feature, which it describes as part of its Smart Solution program:

Who Pays Attorney's Fees?

While each party is responsible for its own attorney's fees, the American Arbitration Association will provide a one-time $1000 reimbursement of employee's or former employee's attorney's fees for the mediation or arbitration of each matter. The attorney must be licensed to practice law. . . . The reimbursement is paid once for each dispute filed under The Smart Solution.

Employee Costs for Mediation and Arbitration by External Neutrals

The employer must determine whether, as a design feature, employees should be required to pay to use an external mediator or arbitrator. Where the feature provides voluntary postdispute arbitration, employers should consider how best to create incentives for its use. In these cases, where the employee can go directly to court, fees are typically minor so as not to discourage the employee from choosing to use arbitration. Where the use of arbitration is mandatory for the employee, the philosophical debate about charges centers on two issues: Should the system impose a charge that is potentially greater than if the claimant hired a contingency attorney and went to court, and how does the employer prevent abuse (the proverbial floodgate of claims) if some charge is not imposed?

The American Arbitration Association made the following decisions for its system:

What Are the Costs Associated with Mediation and Arbitration?

There are two types of costs associated with mediation and arbitration—administrative costs and the compensation and expenses of the neutral.

Unless the law provides to the contrary, all administrative costs will be paid by the American Arbitration Association, except that the employee shall pay a one-time $100 contribution toward administrative costs when the Request for Mediation/Arbitration is filed.

All mediator and arbitrator compensation and expenses—unless the law provides to the contrary—will be paid by the American Arbitration Association. An employee may elect, however, to pay up to one-half of the neutral's compensation and expenses.

Employee Costs to Initiate Mediation or Arbitration

The majority of workplace systems offering mediation by an external neutral do not impose any charges for simply filing the demand for mediation. A minority do require some charge, however, typically a token fee of fifty dollars per case.

The vast majority of systems offering arbitration by an external neutral do impose a charge to initiate the demand for arbitration. This payment is commonly paid to the ADR provider. Most systems require a token fee of fifty dollars, but some require the claimant to pay the full cost, which is hundreds of dollars. Some systems use the employee's salary as a guide, imposing a greater fee on executives. Plaintiff attorneys argue that the employer should assume any expenses above the $150 filing fee the employee would assume in federal court. Employers in increasing numbers are agreeing to pay the filing fee because they do not want it to become an appealable issue if they initiate a subsequent motion to compel arbitration against the employee who desires to proceed to court.

Caesars World's mediation and arbitration policy is to pay a large percentage of the costs of external mediation and arbitration:

> Caesars will pay ninety percent of the American Arbitration Association's mediation administrative fees and expenses and the fees and expenses of the mediator and the employee shall pay ten per cent. Caesars will pay seventy-five per cent of the American Arbitration Association's arbitration administrative fees and expenses and the fees and expenses of the mediator and the employee shall pay twenty-five per cent.

Cost Sharing in Fees of the Mediator or Arbitrator

An external mediator or arbitrator commonly charges by the hour. A one-day mediation, with no preparation costs, can easily cost sixteen hundred dollars at two hundred dollars per hour. A two-day arbitration, with normal prehearing conferences and prehearing briefs, can easily cost six thousand dollars at two hundred dollars per hour. The system design question is, Who pays these expenses, and should they be shared between the parties?

In the vast majority of workplace arbitrations, the employee is required to pay a substantial share. A few years ago, employees were expected to share the costs of the neutral's time equally. Today, most systems limit employee costs with a cap, such as one or two days' income.[7] Another pattern provides that the employer pay the first two days of the arbitrator's fees; after that, the cost is shared equally with the employee. The majority of courts have found it unethical and unlawful for employers to impose significant expenses on arbitration if the system is predispute and mandatory.

Boeing Company has structured its fee schedule to encourage reasonable use of mediation and peer review. It describes its arrangement as follows.

Step 2—External Mediation

Fees—the Company will pay all AAA charges for professional services and any administrative fees. . . .

Step 3—Peer Panel Review

Fees—For Peer Panel Review, the employee must pay a fee equal to two days (16 hours) by check. If the panel grants the employee's requested remedy, the fee will be returned to the employee.

Anheuser-Busch has established a different fee set-up:

The Company will pay 1) the Association's filing and other administrative fees, 2) the arbitrator's fee and reasonable travel expenses, 3) the cost of renting an arbitration hearing room, and 4) the employee's salary, if still employed by the Company, for the time spent at the arbitration hearing up to a maximum of seven hearing days. The employee will pay a $250.00 arbitration fee to the Company.

In October 2002, the American Arbitration Association announced that as a result of recent case law developments, it will implement changes to its rules to provide additional safeguards for employees involved in the arbitration process. The primary changes require the employer to deposit the full amount of the anticipated compensation for the arbitrator, unless the employee chooses to pay a portion, and cap the filing fee for the employee at $125 for employer-promulgated plans.

THE LEGAL ENVIRONMENT FOR MANDATORY ARBITRATION

Since issuing the landmark *Gilmer* case in 1991, which we discuss later in this chapter, the U.S. Supreme Court has revolutionized the options available to litigants in resolving statutory claims of employment discrimination. Early cases focused on the applicability of the Federal Arbitration Act of 1925 and whether the Civil Rights Act of 1964 (and its amendments in 1991) precluded such arbitration agreements. More recently, the focus has been on the circumstances under which an employer may require an employee, as a condition of employment, to agree to submit any disputes that arise to arbitration and to give up a right to a jury trial. The heart of this controversy involves the fairness of the employer-imposed rules for mandatory arbitration.

One federal district court judge recently observed in his decision:

Access to the courts now is neither affordable nor expeditious. In many federal district courts and state courts, years pass before an aggrieved party can even have the proverbial day in court. In the meantime, the process grinds along, inflicting staggering legal expenses on the parties. Except for the very rich (and the very poor, in some circumstances) we have simply priced the court system beyond the reach of most citizens, because the cost of litigation far exceeds the value of the decision itself. Indeed, even the most resourceful parties often decline to pursue legal rights, simply because quickly accepting or paying a sum of money in settlement of any claim often costs far less than determining in court the merit of that claim. In short, our current legal system for resolving disputes is losing the respect of the public and is rapidly approaching failure.

The arbitral process, for instance, nearly always exceeds the judicial process in speed, efficiency and in expense. We should view arbitration not with suspicion but with relief. Arbitration and other alternative methods of dispute resolution provide for ordinary citizens and businesses what the court system no longer produces with any regularity: affordable, speedy justice. Until we resolve the ills besieging our courts, I urge the United States Supreme Court, the Fourth Circuit, and all other federal courts to favor arbitration of disputes. For the record, this Court surely does.

RECENT EVOLUTION OF CASE LAW ON EMPLOYMENT ARBITRATION

Since passage of the landmark Civil Rights Act of 1964, there has been controversy as to whether employment discrimination claims could be referred to predispute final and binding arbitration. Beginning in the 1980s, a few industries required employees to sign predispute agreements to arbitrate future claims alleging employment discrimination, and there was a debate as to whether this practice would be upheld by the courts. The securities industry was a forerunner in this use of predispute agreements.

The Gilmer Case: Extending the Reach of Arbitration

In 1991, the U.S. Supreme Court stunned the human resource and legal communities by holding in the case of *Gilmer v. Interstate/Johnson Lane Corp.* that a claim of employment discrimination under the Age Discrimination in Employment Act (ADEA) was subject to predispute binding arbitration in the securities industry. The Court determined that an arbitration agreement would apply to statutory claims unless the party seeking to avoid the agreement demonstrates that the statute reveals that Congress intended to preclude the waiver of a judicial forum. Comments in the opinion were very supportive of arbitration and encouraged employers to expand the practice of predispute agreements to arbitrate claims.[8]

Excerpts from the majority opinion clarified the Supreme Court's stance:

Statutory claims may be the subject of an arbitration agreement enforceable pursuant to the Federal Arbitration Act. . . .

By agreeing to arbitrate a statutory claim, a party does not forego the substantive rights afforded by the statute; it only submits to their resolution in an arbitral, rather than a judicial forum.

There is no inconsistency between the important social policies furthered by the ADEA and enforcing agreements to arbitrate age discrimination claims. . . . Nor will arbitration undermine the EEOC's role in ADEA enforcement, since an ADEA claimant is free to file an EEOC charge even if he is precluded from instituting suit. . . . The mere involvement of an administrative agency in the enforcement of a statute is not sufficient to preclude arbitration. . . .

Moreover, compulsory arbitration does not improperly deprive claimants of a judicial forum provided for by the ADEA; Congress did not explicitly preclude arbitration or other nonjudicial claims resolutions. . . .

The unequal bargaining power between employers and employees is not sufficient reason to hold that arbitration agreements are never enforceable in the employment context.

Gilmer's challenges to the adequacy of arbitration procedures are insufficient to preclude arbitration. This Court declines to indulge his speculation that the parties and the arbitral body will not retain competent, conscientious and impartial arbitrators, especially when both the NYSE [New York Stock Exchange] rules and the FAA protect against biased panels.

Although this decision was technically limited to the securities industry and pre-hire agreements to arbitrate claims, it was a revolutionary direction for ADR and employment arbitration. Because the ADEA is a distinct federal law with a separate legislative history, the resulting questions included the decision's applicability to claims under the Civil Rights Act of 1964, as amended. Ultimately, Gilmer raised as many questions as it resolved for the first generation of arbitration agreements.

The Circuit City Case: Upholding Arbitration Agreements Under the Federal Arbitration Act

Opponents of mandatory predispute arbitration and the *Gilmer* case quickly focused on ways to limit the reach of the *Gilmer* holding. One approach was to find a legal theory that would limit *Gilmer's* application to the ADEA but not the Civil Rights Act of 1964. That approach was to argue that these predispute arbitration agreements were violative of the Federal Arbitration Act (FAA) of 1925.

In *Circuit City Stores, Inc. v. Adams*, the employee applied for a job as a sales clerk at a Circuit City store in California. He was subsequently hired and signed a predispute agreement to arbitrate any future claims. In 1997, he sued the electronics retailer in state court for discriminating against him. Circuit City asked a federal court to stop the lawsuit and require arbitration. The federal district court issued an order compelling arbitration, and the order was reversed on appeal by the Ninth Circuit, which held that the FAA prohibited such mandatory arbitration agreements.

In 2001, the U.S. Supreme Court rejected the Ninth Circuit's position and upheld the enforceability of predispute mandatory arbitration agreements contained in private sector employment agreements. Addressing the FAA of 1925, the Court expanded its application to the vast majority of employment agreements, holding that the FAA exempts only employment agreements that involve transportation workers. The Court refused to accept the position of the EEOC, which argued that mandatory arbitration was contrary to the remedial purposes of antidiscrimination statutes. Judicial comments in the opinion were pro-arbitration and served to encourage employers to expand the practice of predispute agreements to arbitrate claims.[9]

On a practical level, *Circuit City* put to rest the question of whether arbitration is a judicially accepted forum for the resolution of employment discrimination cases. It did not serve to settle the entire area of law, however. The debate has now turned to the circumstances of the arbitration agreement that would be considered fair by the courts. In response to the *Circuit City* decision, several federal legislative bills have been submitted in the House and Senate. House Bill H.R. 815 (2001), for example, would amend the FAA to allow employees to accept or reject arbitration of their disputes. There has been no movement toward passage of this or similar bills in Congress.

The Waffle House Case: Allowing Independent Prosecution by the EEOC

Throughout this period of evolving acceptance of arbitration to resolve statutory discrimination claims, the EEOC asserted that its authority to prosecute claims was independent of arbitration agreements. In essence, it desired to limit the binding nature of *Gilmer* and *Circuit City* by proclaiming that employees could, in fact, receive two bites of the apple. It wanted to establish the pattern that even if the employee lost the arbitration, the EEOC could still litigate and achieve a satisfactory remedy against the employer.

In *EEOC v. Waffle House* (2001), the employee was a restaurant grill operator who had signed a predispute agreement to arbitrate any future claims. After working sixteen days, he suffered a seizure at work and was eventually terminated. He did not seek to arbitrate the claim, but filed an EEOC charge alleging violation of the Americans with Disabilities Act (ADA). The EEOC filed an enforcement action in federal court, and the restaurant insisted that the EEOC claim should wait until the arbitration. In 2002, the U.S. Supreme Court agreed that the EEOC is not bound by a private arbitration agreement between the charging employee and the employer in prosecuting a claim in its own name.[10]

Some observers view *Waffle House* as a step back in the desirability of arbitration agreements because the decision creates the possibility of defending in two arenas and losing the finality and lower costs associated with ADR. But *Waffle House* is not an anti-ADR decision by the Supreme Court. It merely upholds the statutory prerogative of a federal agency. On a practical level, though, it has served to reduce the rush toward implementation of predispute arbitration plans. The EEOC has insufficient resources to allow it to pursue more than a few hundred cases per year. In addition, any settlement with the EEOC after an arbitration agreement would not provide double payments. Given this outcome, some commentators feel that the EEOC should announce guidelines for deferral to arbitration similar to the action taken by the NLRB.

The Minority Duffield Case Is Reversed

In *Gilmer*, the Supreme Court held that an arbitration agreement would apply to statutory claims unless the party seeking to avoid the arbitration agreement demonstrates that the statute in question reflects Congress's intent to preclude the waiver of a judicial forum. Opponents to *Gilmer* quickly argued that claims under the Civil Rights Act of 1964 in fact were precluded by congressional intent. In 1998, the Ninth Circuit Court of Appeals agreed in *Duffield* v. *Robertson Stephens and Co.* and held that a claimant cannot be compelled to arbitrate if a Title VII claim of the Civil Rights Act of 1964, as amended, is alleged in the case. In another stockbroker discharge case, the Ninth Circuit refused to enforce the agreement to arbitrate because the judges found that Congress intended to preclude mandatory arbitration of such employment discrimination claims.[11] In September 2002, the Ninth Circuit finally reversed itself and declared that *Duffield* was not the law of the circuit.

STAKEHOLDER VIEWS OF MANDATORY EMPLOYMENT ARBITRATION

For the past five years, there has been a raging debate around the ethics, fairness, and legality of mandatory predispute arbitration of statutory claims. From the plaintiff's perspective, this form of arbitration is an unfair, twisted interpretation of the law by federal judges who are overturning the intent of Congress and the legislative history of the Civil Rights Act of 1964, as amended. From the management perspective, this form of arbitration is an effective and fair solution to a national public policy that is consistent with legislative intent.

View from the Plaintiff Bar

The plaintiff employment bar in this country refers to a broad group of employment discrimination attorneys who serve the interests of employees in vindication of their rights. The national organization of plaintiff employment attorneys, the National Employment Lawyers Association (NELA), publishes journals, sponsors training workshops, and lobbies for changes in the civil rights arena. NELA has articulated a strong policy against mandatory arbitration programs.[12]

View of the EEOC

The EEOC has a clearly articulated hostility to mandatory arbitration clauses. In 1997, it published a "policy statement on mandatory binding arbitration of employment disputes as a condition of employment." The statement alleges that making the arbitration of statutory disputes a condition of employment is contrary to the core principles of civil rights laws. This assertion has been argued in numerous amicus briefs filed in past years, and some EEOC offices will issue a "for cause" decision on any charge involving a mandatory arbitration program. This position has not been successful in federal court, however, particularly after *Circuit City*. Some observers believe that the EEOC policy may be ready for change and that the Bush administration will make that change soon.[13]

Although the EEOC is clearly against mandatory predispute agreements to arbitrate, it has become increasingly in favor of voluntary postdispute mediation of statutory claims. This policy is best found in the EEOC's mediation program for new charges, which started as a pilot program in 1992. Thousands of EEO cases have been successfully resolved under this program, which is administered by the EEOC regional offices. The program uses two types of mediators: in-house EEOC employees and external mediators, who are normally paid a flat per diem fee.

Here are some pertinent excerpts from the EEOC Policy Statement on Mandatory Binding Arbitration:

2.   The federal Civil Rights laws are squarely based in this nation's history and constitutional framework and are of a singular national importance.

3.   The federal government has the primary responsibility for the enforcement of the federal employment discrimination laws.

4.   Within this framework, the federal courts are charged with the ultimate responsibility for enforcing the discrimination laws.

4a. The courts are responsible for the development and interpretation of the law. . . .

4d. The private right of action with its guarantees of individual access to the courts is essential to the statutory enforcement scheme.

5.   Mandatory arbitration of employment discrimination disputes "privatizes" enforcement of the federal employment discrimination laws, thus undermining public enforcement of the laws.

5a. Mandatory arbitration has limitations that are inherent and therefore cannot be cured by the improvement of arbitration systems.

6.   Voluntary, post-dispute agreements to arbitrate appropriately balance the legitimate goals of alternative dispute resolution and the need to preserve the enforcement framework of the civil rights laws.

View of the National Academy of Arbitrators

The National Academy of Arbitrators has also issued a public statement regarding mandatory employment arbitration clauses, which it clearly opposes. The statement provides:

The National Academy of Arbitrators opposes mandatory employment arbitration as a condition of employment when it requires
waiver of direct access to either a judicial or administrative forum
for the pursuit of statutory rights.

The Academy recognizes that, given current case law, Academy
members may serve as arbitrators in such cases. However, members
should consider and evaluate the fairness of any employment arbitration procedures in light of the Academy's "Guidelines on Arbitration of Statutory Claims under Employer-Promulgated Systems."

The Dunlop Commission on Worker-Management Relations

In 1993, the secretaries of labor and commerce created the Commission on the Future of Worker-Management Relations consisting of thirteen prominent individuals and chaired by John
Dunlop, a former secretary of labor. The Dunlop Commission, as
it became known, was charged with reviewing several employment issues, including how the parties can resolve disputes without resorting to the courts and federal agencies. In its final report,
the commission recommended that private parties be encouraged
to adopt in-house ADR systems appropriate to the particular
workplace and ideally created with employee involvement. The
report further noted that government officials accustomed to litigating or even settling lawsuits are often not well equipped to
mediate or settle claims rapidly. Furthermore, the report observed,
a substantial reinvention and retraining would be needed to transform agencies into organizations that could play a more effective
role in dispute resolution. Finally, the report emphasized that private arbitration systems are a good thing but must meet quality
standards for fairness. The commission concluded that at the time
it was writing, predispute arbitration agreements should not be
enforceable as a condition of employment, although at some time
in the future (as fairness becomes ensured) it may be appropriate
to reevaluate that conclusion.[14]

The Due Process Protocol on Employment Arbitration

After *Gilmer*, a significant wave of employers adopted workplace polices and systems requiring arbitration of disputes. Some observers perceived that many of these policies or so-called systems were one-sided and not fair to the employee or the arbitration process. As a result, several ADR organizations joined together to issue a detailed set of rules for employment arbitration.

The Due Process Protocol was developed by a group of national ADR organizations such as the National Academy of Arbitrators, the American Bar Association, the American Arbitration Association, the Society of Professionals in Dispute Resolution, the Federal Mediation and Conciliation Services, and the National Employment Lawyers Association. The task force debated the issue of predispute mandatory arbitration but failed to reach a consensus. The task force did agree, however, on a set of due process standards that included the right to representation, adequate discovery, employer reimbursement for partial attorney fees, and the use of qualified and impartial neutrals. The American Arbitration Association declared that it would refuse to administer any cases whose procedural rules fell outside the protocol. This was a major change of policy for the American Arbitration Association and represented the seriousness of the ADR community toward unfair or overreaching arbitration policies.[15]

LEGAL CHALLENGES TO MANDATORY PREDISPUTE ARBITRATION

Despite the pro-arbitration policy set forth in *Circuit City* by the U.S. Supreme Court, employees still have numerous avenues available to them to challenge arbitration agreements as unenforceable contracts. As interpreted by the Court, generally applicable contract defenses can be applied to invalidate arbitration agreements without contravening the Federal Arbitration Act. These defenses are commonly fraud, duress, or unconscionability. Most recently, lower state and federal courts have been deeply troubled by arbitration procedures that deny due process and take away rights available in court. At this time, the most successful challenges to arbitration agreements involve adequacy of consideration to current employees, lack of knowing and voluntary waiver, allocation of expenses to the claimant, and the scope of remedies available to the arbitrator.

Challenges Based on Contract Defenses

The most basic challenge to an arbitration agreement is that it was not properly made between the parties and thus is unenforceable. The U.S. Supreme Court has held that courts should apply ordinary state law principles that govern the formation of contracts when deciding whether an arbitration agreement is enforceable.[16] As a result, employers implementing a nationwide workplace system should first review whether the arbitration terms of the proposed system are enforceable in each of the states in which the system will operate.

Adequate Consideration.   A basic element of contract formation in all states is adequate *consideration*, that is, the value, usually money, that is provided by one party to the other party in order to motivate the contract formation. Consideration does not need to be of equal value between the parties. Employers have argued that sufficient consideration can be found in new employment, continued employment after program adoption or linkage of program adoption with a salary increase, stock options, or bonus payments. For new employees, the offer of employment is typically considered adequate consideration. What constitutes sufficient consideration for existing employees is less clear.

In the arbitration context, courts have examined two forms of consideration: continued at-will employment and mutual obligations to arbitrate claims. (At-will employment is the common law for private employers that allows either side to end the relationship without penalty.) Many courts have concluded that an employee's continued at-will employment is sufficient consideration to enforce an arbitration agreement.[17] Courts have also held that the employer's agreement to take employee disputes to court creates the mutuality of obligation sufficient to find adequate consideration.[18]

Validity of Adhesion Contracts. Another challenge to contract formation is the concept of *adhesion*, or "take it or leave it" contracts of employment. Although adhesion contracts are presumed valid, there are two judicially imposed restrictions on enforcement of an adhesion contract. One is that if such a contract does not fall within the reasonable expectations of the weaker party, it will not be enforced against him. The second is that a contract will be denied enforcement even if consistent with the reasonable expectations of the weaker party, if it is unduly oppressive or unconscionable. Numerous pro-employer arbitration agreements have been denied enforcement by courts due to unconscionability. Over the past three years, this argument has become the most successful objection to employer-imposed arbitration agreements.

Caesars World has a strongly worded adhesion clause in its mediation and arbitration policy:

Acceptance

All employees who continue employment after August 31, 1997, will be deemed to have accepted this Policy as the exclusive method to resolve Claims not resolved through informal or internal dispute resolution procedures and therefore, will not litigate Claims in court or in judicial type proceedings before administrative agencies except Employees may file charges as provided above. Caesars will also use this Policy in lieu of litigation in court or in judicial type proceedings before administrative agencies. Any individual hired after August 1, 1997 shall be deemed to have accepted this Policy

Validity of Ambiguous Language. Another challenge to contract formation is ambiguous language. Generally, the test for determining if an ambiguity exists in a written contract is whether the disputed language, in the context of the entire agreement, is reasonably susceptible of more than one construction giving the words their plain meaning as understood by a reasonable average person. Increasingly, courts are finding that most agreements to arbitrate cannot be challenged for ambiguity, but workplace systems should be written in plain English, or a non-English language that is appropriate for the workplace.

Knowing and Voluntary Agreement to Arbitrate. Whether the employee enters into an agreement to arbitrate on a knowing and voluntary basis is another challenge to contract formation. Basic contract expectations include that the agreement is in written form, that the content is described in plain English, and that it fully defines the features and the rights being given up. Other expectations are that the employee signs the agreement and that it is a separate instrument plainly presented and not hidden or included in another document. Some employers are now using professional videos to explain the benefits of mandatory arbitration to employees.

There is a continuing question as to enforceability of an arbitration agreement embedded in an employee handbook rather than as a separate written agreement. An employer's distribution of an employee handbook that contained an arbitration agreement buried inside may not represent a knowing and voluntary waiver of rights. This can be true even though employees had signed a statement saying that they had read and understood the entire handbook.

Challenges Based on Unconscionability

Unconscionability may be applied to invalidate arbitration agreements without contravening the Federal Arbitration Act. Although the concept is difficult to define, *unconscionability* is generally accepted to mean "the absence of meaningful choice" together with "terms unreasonably advantageous" to one of the parties. Courts examine the process by which the agreement was made and whether it was the product of clear and voluntary consent. This concept has proved to be the most successful defense used by plaintiffs to argue that a mandatory arbitration agreement is unfair and should not be enforced against them. According to one court, the most infamous case of an unfair predispute arbitration agreement came from Hooters of America.[19]

In 1994, Hooters restaurants gave their employees the ultimatum to sign a predispute agreement to arbitrate future employment claims. By 1996, a female bartender in South Carolina claimed a company official was harassing her by grabbing and slapping her buttocks. In 1999, the U.S. Court of Appeals for the Fourth Circuit held that the former bartender did not have to arbitrate her sexual harassment claim against the restaurant chain. Finding that Hooters of America set up a dispute resolution process "utterly lacking in the rudiments of evenhandedness," the appeals court concluded that the company breached the arbitration agreement and violated its contractual duty of good faith. Under the rules, the employee had to provide notice of the nature of the claim and the specific acts or omissions involved, but the company had no reciprocal obligation to respond in writing or provide notice of its defenses. The employee, but not Hooters, had to provide a list of all fact witnesses and a brief summary of the facts known to each. Hooters had total control over the list of potential arbitrators. Finally, only the company could move for summary judgment (a legal motion to end the lawsuit) or even record the arbitration hearing.

Cost to Employee. An increasingly common challenge to a mandatory arbitration agreement is the fee-splitting clause. Although courts are not consistent on this issue, the majority trend is to strike down clauses that charge substantial costs to the employee. One test that the Third Circuit uses is to determine whether the arbitration costs are related directly to the litigant's ability to pursue a cause of action in that forum. If the costs are too high, then the arbitral forum fails to allow the litigant effectively to vindicate the cause of action. Other tests are being applied by other circuit courts. For example, the District of Columbia Circuit has held that an employee can never be required, as a condition of employment, to pay an arbitrator's compensation in order to secure the resolution of statutory claims. The court reasoned that paying more than a reasonable filing fee comparable to the cost to file in court could deter bringing statutory rights claims.

Restrictions on Discovery. Restrictions on the right of the claimant to obtain relevant information and to know what the defense will argue in the arbitration is another challenge to a mandatory arbitration agreement. *Discovery* is a legal term that refers to the process of obtaining information about the claims, witnesses, and documents to be presented by one's opponent. The theory behind discovery is that justice and the hearing will be better served if everyone knows what will be argued in advance. A court will strike down an agreement that prevents reasonable discovery.

Restrictions on Scope of Remedy. Restrictions on the available remedy create yet another challenge to mandatory arbitration agreements. The majority trend provides that there cannot be any limitations on the remedy, including attorney fees and punitive damages, for the agreement to be enforced.

Employer Control of the List of Arbitrators. An employer cannot select the pool or list of arbitrators alone, even if the employee has the right to select the final arbitrator.

Form of the Award. Another challenge to a mandatory arbitration agreement is the form of the award. In the past, some workplace arbitrators did not issue *reasoned awards;* that is, they did not explain the reasons and understanding of the facts and law. Today, courts disfavor unreasoned awards for statutory cases, requiring instead that opinions be written and explain the basis for the decision.

BEST PRACTICES IN DESIGN OF EMPLOYMENT ARBITRATION PROVISIONS

There is no single model for drafting an enforceable arbitration agreement. The law of each state is slightly different as it concerns contract formation, and the following comments do not represent our endorsement of any particular form of arbitration. In addition, we have not included every possible clause in an arbitration agreement.

Scope of Disputes Subject to Arbitration

Not all workplace issues are subject to arbitration. Most programs exclude certain subjects, either because they are covered elsewhere (ERISA or workers' compensation disputes) or because they represent highly subjective issues, such as performance evaluations.

Exclusivity

This clause in an arbitration agreement clarifies that there is no right to a trial by jury for either party and that both parties are precluded from bringing an action in a state or federal court.

Requirement to Attempt Mediation Prior to Filing a Demand

Many workplace systems impose a requirement that the employee attempt mediation as a mandatory prerequisite to filing the demand for arbitration. In such a situation, there should not be any cost to the employee. Given the voluntary nature of mediation, there is sometimes limited value to requiring mediation when the claimant refuses to settle at that point.

Shell Oil has such a requirement.

As a condition of employment, Shell RESOLVE requires that, before you file an individual or class-based lawsuit, you will attempt to resolve your differences with the help of an external, neutral third-party mediator, who will mediate each claim separately. If this external mediation does not achieve resolution and the conflict involves a legally protected right, you can proceed to arbitration or litigation.

If you file a lawsuit, either on an individual or class basis, without first participating in external mediation, Shell will ask the court to dismiss the case or refer it back to external mediation before considering it.

The spirit of this requirement is to underscore the company's commitment to resolving conflict quickly and equitably within the Shell RESOLVE program. The intent is not to take away any rights but to provide the parties every opportunity and incentive to resolve problems without costly and disruptive litigation.

Time Limit to Initiate Arbitration

Rules concerning when the claim can be filed to be "in a timely manner" must be specified in a clause in the agreement. Typically, the clause sets a time limit of fourteen days in cases of termination alleging breach of contract or employer policy. In other cases alleging employment discrimination or employment tort, the employee must initiate arbitration within the period required under state or federal statute that applies to that dispute.

Right to Representation

It is universally accepted that legal counsel or any individual of his or her choice may represent an employee. The employer has the same rights. The employee must often notify the employer if counsel is to be retained in the case, though.

Initiation of Arbitration

Every arbitration agreement requires a means to initiate a demand for arbitration, including the paperwork and submission. This provision explains how to complete the process.

Selection and Authority of the Arbitrator

Numerous court battles have been fought over clauses defining procedures to be used to select the arbitrator. There are two questions concerning this issue: How shall the pool of potential arbitrators be gathered in the process, and How should the parties select the final arbitrator? It is now universally established that the employer cannot impose a list of predetermined arbitrators on the claimant. Instead, the program must provide a roster of objective neutrals. The selection of arbitrators is normally conducted by the alternate striking method. Very few employers allow the claimant to select any arbitrator (from the list) he or she prefers without employer input.

Venue and Governing Law

The venue of a dispute is typically the county of the primary workplace of the claimant. Typically, it is unethical for the program to require the claimant to travel outside his or her county to participate in the case. Governing law is normally the law of the state in which the claimant resides. For the reason mentioned previously, state law is very important in interpreting arbitration agreements.

Prehearing Discovery

A well-drafted arbitration program provides an extensive set of expectations for discovery. The basic rules provide that discovery should be a voluntary exchange and that it should be expeditious and cost-effective. The rules also provide that parties shall be able to take depositions, that a discovery cut-off occurs within thirty days prior to the hearing, and that ongoing discovery disputes are referred to the arbitrator.

Sample language from Mercy Healthcare Arizona's arbitration and termination dispute resolution policy illustrates this point well:

Discovery

4.9.1   The parties shall cooperate in the voluntary exchange of such documents and information as will serve to expedite the arbitration. Each party shall list each witness to be called, a short summary of their testimony, and each document to be offered into evidence within thirty (30) days of the Employer's written statement as set forth in Paragraph 4.6.3. . . .

4.9.2   Discovery shall be conducted in the most expeditious and cost-effective manner possible, and shall be limited to that which is relevant and non-privileged.

4.9.4   The parties shall be entitled to take one (1) deposition each. Reporter and transcript cost are borne by the party noticing the deposition.

4.9.6   The arbitrator may grant, upon good cause shown, either party's request for additional discovery.

Subpoenas and Documents

A *subpoena* is a written request for action from the other party. There are two types of subpoenas. One type requests another party to locate and produce a desired document before the hearing. The second type requests the attendance of a specific person during the hearing. Unless disputed, subpoenas are issued by either a party or the arbitrator. They are not self-enforcing; the parties or the arbitrator cannot order the sheriff to enforce them. If they are disputed, the moving party must go to court to seek an order requiring the performance asked for in the subpoena. An effective arbitration program provides for counsel to issue subpoenas, the arbitrator to issue subpoenas, and the moving party to bear the cost of serving them.

Order of Presentation

The order-of-presentation clause clarifies that traditional rules of trial presentation shall apply to the hearing and that witnesses shall testify under oath. Witnesses are commonly sworn in by either the arbitrator or the court reporter.

Standard and Burden of Persuasion

Clauses clarifying that each party will have the burden of persuasion raised by that party, consistent with state and federal standards, are required in every agreement. The fact that the plaintiff typically has the burden of production and the burden of proof has been well established in federal employment law.

Evidence and Argument

The evidence and argument clause commonly has two parts. One part is to affirm that each party will be afforded a full and fair opportunity to present any relevant proof, to call and cross-examine witnesses, and to present its evidence. The second part concerns the rules of evidence. Some clauses provide that the Federal Rules of Evidence shall apply as far as practicable, whereas other clauses provide that the arbitrator shall not be bound by the federal rules.

Allocation of Arbitrator Expenses

The clauses covering the allocation of arbitrator expenses are very controversial and have been the subject of numerous court decisions. The expenses of arbitration can include the administrative filing fee, hearing room charges, and the arbitrator's hourly fees. The public policy issue is whether employees should be forced to pay these expenses when their costs would be far less if they had proceeded to court. The expenses can be allocated between the parties in numerous ways. The old approach was to split the costs. The more recent approach is to ask the claimant to pay only a sum up to a target, such as two days' pay, and thereafter have the employer pay the remainder.

Form of the Award

The form of the award is an increasingly important part of the arbitration program. In the past, some workplace arbitrators did not issue reasoned awards. Today, it is crucial that opinions be written and reasoned. This clause generally provides for a deadline of thirty or sixty days for the award to be prepared, for a written and signed award, and for a rationale for any grant of damages or relief.

Inland Container Corporation outlines its program requirement this way:

Time of the Award

The award shall be promptly made by the arbitrator and, unless otherwise agreed to by the parties or specified by applicable law, no later than thirty days from the date of the closing of the hearing or the closing of a reopened hearing, whichever is later.

Form of Award

The award shall be in writing, shall set forth the basis of and the reasons for his decision, and shall be signed by the arbitrator. If any party requests in its Notice or Answering statement, the arbitrator shall write a summary of reasons for the decision. The award shall be executed in any manner required by applicable law.

Record of Proceeding

A record-of-proceeding clause clarifies the official record of the hearing and provides a right of either party to have a court reporter, at its expense. This clause often states that the arbitrator shall retain the record of the proceeding, including all documents, for one or two years after the award is issued to the parties.

Damages and Relief

A clause dealing with damages and relief clarifies that the arbitrator shall have the same power and authority as would a judge in a non-jury trial to grant any relief that a court could grant. This authority includes injunctive relief and awards of damages where reinstatement is warranted but may not be reasonable or practicable. Setting any limitation on remedies, including punitive damages, is not advisable and would create an automatic route to appeal.

The Uncertainty of Predispute Mandatory Arbitration

Recently, we have seen much greater certainty about the future of mandatory arbitration than we have in the past. *Circuit City* and its progeny have clarified the legal foundation for mandatory arbitration. The Ninth Circuit has reversed its antimandatory arbitration decision in *Duffield*. The remaining focus is primarily on the fairness of the predispute mandatory arbitration clauses.

Other ongoing issues include the effect of agreements on class action litigation, the effects of the expiration of an arbitration contract, court review of awards for manifest disregard of law or facts, and the necessity of a reasoned award. These and many other legal questions will be resolved over time.

WORKPLACE NEUTRALS: QUALIFICATIONS AND STANDARDS

There has been an explosion of workplace mediators and arbitrators in the market. One reason is that numerous organizations and colleges across the country have been offering mediation and arbitration training. Most of these courses apply to any type of neutral and do not have a substantive focus, but a few are directed exclusively to employment mediation and arbitration. Some are conducted over an entire week, while others are conducted on weekends and evenings over time. Another reason for the increase in workplace neutrals is that many retired judges are entering the field.

The standard mediation course requires at least forty hours of instruction, although there is no empirical research to suggest that this length produces a quality mediator. On the contrary, most observers believe that mediator effectiveness reflects a combination of knowledge, instinct, and experience.[20] There is not yet a standard duration for an employment arbitration course.

The Employment Mediation Profession

The professional style of workplace mediators is highly disparate. Some apply a strictly transformative style, intended to help the disputants learn to help themselves in future conflicts. Some are strictly facilitative, intending to help the parties explore their underlying interests and develop their own solutions. Still others are strictly evaluative, intending to facilitate resolution through objective assessments of merit. Retired judges are generally evaluative mediators.

No national standards exist for employment as a workplace mediator. National ethical standards have been issued by the Association for Conflict Resolution, but they are not mandatory.[21] It is difficult for parties to evaluate the effectiveness of a mediator except from prior experience. If the mediator has been employed full time as a neutral for several years and is on a national ADR roster, it is likely that he or she has the skills for effective service.

The Employment Arbitration Profession

Arbitrators have various levels of quality and experience. Some new employment arbitrators come exclusively from a labor background, which historically does not have significant statutory implications.[22] Others are from a commercial law background and have minimal familiarity with the workplace. Others may have substantive knowledge but not extensive experience in holding hearings and writing awards. Some employment arbitrators are practicing attorneys, some are retired judges, and some do not have legal backgrounds at all, although a legal background is increasingly preferred to arbitrate statutory claims.

No national standards exist for employment as a workplace arbitrator either, although there are nonmandatory national ethical standards. California is increasingly imposing disclosure obligations on its arbitrators and ADR providers. As with mediation, it is difficult for the parties to evaluate the effectiveness of an emerging arbitrator except from prior experience. Similar to mediators, if the arbitrator has been employed full time as a neutral for several years and is on a national ADR roster, it is likely that he or she has the skills for effective service.

Research was conducted recently on the evolution of labor grievance arbitrators to statutory employment arbitrators. The research was conducted by the Cornell Institute on Conflict Resolution on behalf of the National Academy of Arbitrators, a national organization of labor grievance arbitrators.[23] Membership in the academy is a prestigious accomplishment for labor-oriented neutrals.

The Cornell study explored the extent to which academy members have moved into the mediation and arbitration of disputes outside the labor-management arena. The survey suggested that member experience was reasonably extensive but not very intensive. According to its results, published in 1998:

- 46 percent arbitrated one or more nonunion employment disputes

- 23 percent mediated one or more nonunion employment disputes

- 25 percent arbitrated one or more nonemployment disputes

- 16 percent mediated one or more nonemployment disputes

The study also surveyed the fee rates charged by academy neutrals for their work as arbitrators and mediators. The members who charged for mediation charged higher daily rates than is the norm for arbitration. The lowest daily rate charged for arbitration was $640 and the highest was $851. For mediation, the lowest rate was $854 and the highest was $1,158. These daily rates are much lower than similar work on workplace or statutory cases and reflect classic market forces.

The Cornell survey revealed that academy members are becoming increasingly active in both nonunion workplace and nonemployment adjudication. As noted above, 46 percent of academy members responding to the survey confirmed that they had arbitrated cases in the employment field over the three years surveyed. A further 33 percent said they would accept such cases. With the average age of academy members at a relatively high sixty-three, the report summarized the struggle the academy is experiencing in balancing the disparate interests of its members and deciding whether to accept employment arbitrators into its membership.

Ethical Expectations and Qualifications in Mandatory Employment Arbitration

The National Academy of Arbitrators has established ethical guidelines for members to use while arbitrating statutory claims under employer-promulgated systems. The guidelines provide a checklist of questions to be considered before accepting the case and during the hearing. They remind the arbitrator of his or her right to withdraw from the case "in the face of policies, rules, or procedures that are manifestly unfair or contrary to fundamental due process."[24]

The Society of Professionals in Dispute Resolution (now the Association for Conflict Resolution) issued a report in 1989 on qualifications of mediators and arbitrators that noted:

> The role of the SPIDR Commission on Qualifications is to examine the question of qualifications of mediators and arbitrators. While the recommendations may have general applicability, the primary focus of the Commission's inquiry has been on those areas of ADR in which legislatures and other public bodies are now

seeking to establish criteria that define who can serve as a mediator or arbitrator.

In determining how best to promote competence and quality in the practice of dispute resolution, the Commission considered several policy options. These included reliance on the free market, disclosure requirements, public and consumer education, "after the fact" controls such as malpractice actions, rosters, ethical codes, mandatory standards for neutrals and for programs, and improvements in training, including enhanced opportunities for apprenticeships.

After weighing these options, the Commission adopted three central principles:

A. That no single entity (rather, a variety of organizations) should establish qualifications for neutrals

B. That the greater the degree of choice the parties have over the dispute resolution process, program or neutral, the less mandatory the qualification should be

C. That qualification criteria should be based on performance, rather than paper credentials

Sources of Workplace Neutrals

Sources of qualified workplace mediators and arbitrators include national and local providers and word-of-mouth recommendations. National providers include organizations like the American Arbitration Association, JAMS, and the Alliance for Education in Dispute Resolution. Local providers include professional ADR organizations that function at the state or local level. Word-of-mouth recommendations have traditionally been a strong source of neutrals. Major employment defense law firms now employ a Web listing of employment mediators and arbitrators, for example, with comments on the experience by the attorney. As another example, employment plaintiff groups such as the National Employment Lawyers Association regularly discuss their experience with neutrals and maintain a short list of preferred individuals. For use in workplace systems, relying on a more established ADR provider is preferred because it brings a high-caliber roster of several neutrals from which to select.

CONCLUSION

This chapter has provided broad information about external processes and resources, including mediation and arbitration programs. There are several versions of arbitration procedures. Mandatory, predispute arbitration is not the only option in system design. The essential guidelines for preemployment arbitration agreements will be clarified in the next few years. We will also know if Congress will overturn *Circuit City* and its progeny. The Supreme Court will presumably wait for the right arbitration case to clarify the fairness and reach of arbitration agreements. As to the EEOC, some believe that it has permanently "lost the battle" in *Circuit City* and *Duffield*, and should now review its position on mandatory arbitration.

Our goal with this chapter was to explore the complexity of the subject. As general advice, it is crucial to focus on the credibility of the workplace system. If the employer designs an unfair or one-sided program, it will fail. If the employer designs a fair, principled system, it will be effective and, if needed, enforced in court. Credibility is essential in system design. There is a saying in the legal community about workplace systems: "Do it right or don't do it at all. You only get one chance to build it right."

Chapter Seven

Implementation of Conflict Management Systems

Implementing workplace systems requires a well-planned multistep process that takes place over several phases (see Exhibit 7.1):

Phase One: The organization creates the essential foundation on which a system can be built. It is both exploratory and creative in that it explores the state of the organization, locates an internal champion, convenes a and design team, obtains leadership support, and creates a plan.

Phase Two: The organization gathers information with which to build. It researches and analyzes workplace systems in other organizations as well as its own and then explores the data with employees and management to get beyond the myths regarding such systems.

Phase Three: The organization builds on the two prior phases and develops a preliminary structure. This is the meat of the design process. This preliminary plan is tested and refined through employee focus groups and presented to the organization's leadership for approval.

Phase Four: The organization finishes the system design, deciding critical issues such as the inclusion of mandatory arbitration. Changes requested by senior leadership are incorporated into the design and a summary plan description is completed.

Phase Five: The organization launches and markets the system, clarifies the roles of the various participants, and trains supervisors to support the system

Phase Six: The organization gives the system long life. It enables the system to become embedded in the organization by instilling incentives, maintaining credibility, reinforcing activity, analyzing results, and readjusting the system over time to ensure long-term success.

We believe that there is a significant distinction between a truly integrated conflict management system and a few fragmented dispute resolution policies thrown into an existing organization. This distinction is crucial to recognize when implementing a system. Our field research observed that many employers failed to recognize the difference, intentionally chose to take a fragmented approach, or simply took the easy way out. These employers failed to achieve the benefits of a true workplace system.

PHASE ONE: ASSESSMENT, INQUIRY, AND INITIAL COMMITMENT

In Phase One, the organization creates the essential foundation on which a system can be built. It is both exploratory and creative in that it explores the state of the organization, locates an internal champion, convenes a design team, obtains leadership support, and creates a plan.

Exhibit 7.1. How to Implement Workplace Systems

Phase One: Assessment, Inquiry, and Initial Commitment

- Embrace the impetus for change
- Define the business case
- Align with an internal champion
- Obtain senior leadership commitment

- Outline the design contract
- Select and build the design team
- Determine whether to retain an external design consultant
- Create a work plan
- Diagnose current organizational conflict
- Decide whether to move ahead with the project

Phase Two: Research, Analysis, and Internal Alignment

- Conduct research on employee dispute systems
- Benchmark other organizations and define best practices
- Define the data and metrics
- Conduct employee and management focus groups
- Respond to myths of workplace systems

Phase Three: System Design and Support

- Draft the system
- Calibrate the proposed design
- Build the support structure
- Consider a pilot project prior to full implementation
- Present the plan to senior leadership for final approval

Phase Four: Finalizing the Design

- Finalize the system design
- Encourage adversaries to embrace the new workplace system
- Determine whether to include a mandatory arbitration agreement
- Draft the summary plan description

Phase Five: Implementation and Training

- Launch and market the system
- Clarify the role and responsibilities of all players in the system
- Train supervisors to support the system

Phase Six: Institutionalization

- Build incentives to use the workplace system
- Maintain credibility through ongoing education and reinforcing communications
- Conduct an ongoing assessment of outcomes
- Readjust the workplace system over time

Embrace the Impetus for Change

Organizations typically require some impetus to initiate planning for a workplace ADR system. Researchers call this the "presenting problem."[1] This impetus commonly arises from one of three sources: a precipitating crisis, settlement of litigation, or a visionary executive. For many organizations, a crisis initiates the focus on workplace ADR systems—perhaps a public scandal, a large-scale resignation of employees, serious employee unrest, or resolution of expensive litigation. The settlement of class action litigation, typically alleging employment discrimination, can also formally require the establishment of a workplace system. In the past years, several corporations resolving litigation based on racial discrimination have agreed to implement workplace systems as part of their agreements.

An interview by Peter Phillips of the CPR Institute for Dispute Resolution with Donna Malin, assistant general counsel with Johnson and Johnson, highlights this example. When asked if there was a particular incident that prompted the creation of her organization's ADR program, Malin responded:

> Several incidents. First, we were historically seeing the number of lawsuits in the employment area going up. We were spending a significant amount of money on outside counsel. And then we had a large and disappointing jury verdict in a discrimination and retaliation case in which the jury awarded the plaintiff approximately $411 million in compensatory and punitive damages. So that really got us more aggressive in pursuing alternative dispute resolution for employment matters.[2]

In other organizations, a visionary executive creates the impetus for change. CEOs have led many efforts due to their desire for workplace systems to be an enabling tool in a cultural transformation. This was the case at Shell Oil Corporation. Sometimes the visionary executive is the human resource executive or in-house general counsel. In other cases, the impetus can come from the quality movement within an organization. This was the case at Chevron Corporation. All of the major writers on quality stress that employee motivation and satisfaction are essential elements of the quality process.

In this description, Shell Oil outlines the initial goals of and hope for its conflict management system:

> Using Shell RESOLVE, we can transform our culture from conflict-adverse to conflict-aware and create an environment that allows us to approach disagreements as opportunities to learn, gather information and ideas and find solutions. Further, dealing with conflict in an open, constructive way can strengthen understanding and commitment to the larger purpose of the organization and free us to focus on our goal of becoming the premier company in the U.S.

Define the Business Case

The initial active step in creating a system is to define the strategic opportunity and build a business case. Defining the strategic opportunity means offering reasons to change the status quo—reasons like increasing productivity, reducing legal exposure, modeling conflict resolution, enhancing employee morale, and reducing staff turnover. Building a business case means taking the strategic opportunity and molding it into a framework of numbers and metrics by establishing current costs, risks, and financial opportunities. Some authors have framed this in terms of the "presenting opportunity."[3] Formally, a business case is not a recommendation, but a planning tool to coalesce support to launch an effort. As an initial active step in implementing a workplace system, the business case is typically used to mold a consensus that there is reason to change organizational practices.

To be most effective, the business case should be linked to the organization's mission statement, which sets out the organization's reason for existing, including how it provides value to its customers.

Sometimes it includes the management's vision statement as well.[4] A vision statement is aspirational and depicts a future state. Whenever possible, the business case should refer to the collaborative language already used in the mission statement.

Align with an Internal Champion

The majority of workplace system efforts have one internal champion, typically a senior executive. If a crisis initiated the effort, the champion is often the leader in whose function the crisis occurred. If there was no precipitating crisis, the champion is not necessarily the original visionary, however. It could be the general counsel, a staff vice president, the human resource executive, or even the quality control executive.

The internal champion is important because he or she will lead the effort to embellish the business case and start socializing the proposal to the executive team. Aligning the process with an internal champion is important because in many cases this individual plays a continuing role in the implementation process, including ensuring financial support. The champion usually requires education as to the scope of the effort and anticipated obstacles in the organization. The champion is rarely a subject matter expert on workplace systems; rather, his or her passion often derives from solid business intuition. The first key role for the internal champion is to focus on the business case and gain its acceptance by the senior leadership.

Chevron Corporation credits its internal champion, Ken Derr, in its description of the philosophy behind STEPS, its conflict management system:

STEPS Was Developed by Chevron People

Ken Derr sponsored an employee team to develop STEPS. He stated, "It is apparent that it would be beneficial if we could find a better way than litigation to deal with employee disputes. In that spirit, Chevron is undertaking a comprehensive and meaningful review of its dispute resolution processes to ensure that employee concerns can be resolved in an expeditious and objective manner."

The team based the design of STEPS on the Chevron Way, focusing on the principles of open communications, teamwork, trust and mutual respect. STEPS also supports Chevron's renewed efforts to value diversity by providing another avenue of recourse to handle problems concerning discrimination.

Obtain Senior Leadership Commitment

Leadership commitment is the threshold step for implementing workplace ADR systems. Most planning efforts will not succeed unless there is some tangible level of senior executive support for the effort. At the strategic level, senior leadership must understand the business issue, the current costs of conflict, the concept for change, and the cost-saving opportunity. At an operating level, they must understand the essential steps, time frame, and anticipated expense. Support among the senior leadership does not have to be unanimous, but it must be broad enough to warrant the allocation of initial resources. It is often the role of the internal champion to present the business case to senior leadership and obtain their conceptual and financial commitment.

Outline a Design Contract

A design contract is a written or verbal road map for the design team to use to achieve its goals. Creating the contract that outlines the scope of the design process is the next step. Some organizations use a formal design contract with their senior leadership: a written document (often used by consultants in organizational development) that outlines the goals, expectations, steps, and costs. Use of a design contract often leads to greater buy-in and more funding by the senior leadership, because it generally enhances the perceived professionalism of the project.

A major advantage of the design contract is its assistance in avoiding different expectations and deliverables between organizational leadership and design team members. In the end, the goal of a design contract is to calibrate expectations and a timetable and to get senior leadership to allocate resources of people and money.[5]

As part of an ADR system design effort, the U.S. Department of the Interior created a design contract with the following components:

> Goal: The team is charged to build a comprehensive, integrated workplace dispute resolution system that provides all employees easy access through multiple entry points and clear options for addressing any concern.

> Product/Result: The team will design a blueprint and transition plan for presentation to the Executive Committee.

> Level of Authority: The Executive Committee will review the final product of the design team and is responsible for approval.

> Time Frame: 6 month goal—blueprint ready for implementation.

> Membership: CADR [the office of Collaborative Action and Dispute Resolution] attempted to identify and invite all key constituencies to participate in this effort. Additional constituencies may be represented as determined by the team. Team members will have no alternates, and will make every effort to participate in all meetings.

> Champions: [Specific names are provided here.]

Select and Build the Design Team

Although a single individual can adequately perform some system design, it is strongly recommended that a team be created to lead the effort. The core design team should include representatives of the various stakeholders who will interact in the workplace system: human resources, in-house counsel, management, and employees from the organization's workforce. A design team provides increased technical and political capability, adequate resources to move the process and delegate work as required, and enhanced buy-in during subsequent launch. Staffing the design team from just one function, such as human resources or the law department, is unwise. Rather, the team should represent the range of constituencies and demographics that will be using the ultimate ADR system yet be small enough to be responsive. Building this team is the next step in successful implementation of a workplace management process.

In addition to the core design team members, it is common for other resources to be deployed to the team from time to time. The employee communications function, the supervisory training function, and an outside law firm, for example, will be key players later in the design effort. It is important for those playing the extra roles to be fully aware of the business case and their part in the design effort.

Similar to any other new team, there is a life cycle to the core design group. They cannot long remain a group of individuals thrown together. Instead, they must meld into a high-performing work team with clear roles and responsibilities. To accomplish this goal, professional facilitation is recommended at the beginning of the team's efforts to ensure understanding of their mission and alignment of the members' skills. A design team will often be together for several months and will likely have its share of internal conflict. It is not expected to disband until effective implementation of the workplace system.

Determine Whether to Retain an External Design Consultant

During the planning process, a decision must be made as to whether an organization needs to retain a consultant to assist the design team. Large organizations universally retain consultants for an extended engagement, whereas small organizations commonly attempt to build workplace systems by themselves or retain a consultant only on an ad hoc basis, depending on the needs of the design team. The organization can ask itself the following questions as it considers its need for a consultant:

- *Do we need a design consultant?* A competent system design consultant brings knowledge, expertise, process skills, and an understanding of the political barriers to effective implementation of a workplace system. These are crucial competencies that can save the design team money and time. Large corporations almost always retain a credible design consultant. In fact, most large design projects require several consultants. Organizations retain a design consultant because the design team wants to work with a person with demonstrated prior experience, there is some urgency in establishing the system, and they prefer a full-service consulting model to serve all their needs.
- *What kind of design consultant do we need?* A variety of consultants with varying degrees of capability offer services in system design. Law firm attorneys, human resource experts, organization development experts, college professors, and sometimes mediators serve as consultants. In reality, there are very few true system design professionals. It is recommended that any design team seek a person who has highly substantive knowledge of ADR, organizational savvy, project planning expertise, and an understanding of an organizational change process model. Workplace system design has become highly complex and has many serious legal implications. Other authors have commented, "The first interventions into an ongoing system by an external consultant, particularly around the issue of conflict, cast a long shadow on the ultimate outcome."[6]
- *What role should the design consultant play in our effort?* A consultant is often involved in diagnosing current conflict levels and costs. He or she often provides general education to the team, sets up visits to other organizations with workplace systems, and may facilitate employee focus groups. All of these contributions save the design team significant time in getting up to speed and achieving results.

A design consultant is retained at least through the initial draft of the system. Some organizations stop using a consultant at this point. Often the consultant is brought back for the evaluation phase. Other design teams ask the consultant to review their work on a quarterly basis. This kind of relationship can be effective, or it can be a mistake, depending on the capabilities of the design team. For example, design teams that prematurely cancel their relationship with a competent design consultant often find that they lose momentum and lose their focus. Finally, many organizations with an existing workplace system are now retaining consultants solely to evaluate their system and make recommendations for change over time.

Create a Work Plan

At this point, a design team of several capable individuals with a relatively clear vision of the project has been established. The team understands the expectations of senior leadership, it has a design contract, and it has had a preliminary team-building session. Furthermore, it is being motivated by the internal champion.

The next step in the design process is the establishment of a project or work plan. A project plan is a detailed schedule of the work to be accomplished over a set period of time. The timetable is often placed onto project planning software, and one member of the team is asked to keep it up-to-date and to identify any shortfalls along the way.

The project plan is merely a planning tool, but it is important for several reasons: it serves to focus the efforts of the team members, motivates the team and identifies slackers, and informs senior leadership as to the team's progress. The design of a workplace system is a major organizational commitment that is complicated and a lot of work. To maximize the opportunity for success, the design team should use a formal project planning process.

Diagnose Current Organizational Conflict

This is a data-gathering and data assessment step. The core objectives of this step are to define current and anticipated sources of workplace conflict, current and anticipated costs of workplace conflict, trends of workplace conflict, and the ability of the existing conflict resolution practices to handle workplace disputes.

The data needed are commonly collected from the employees and managers, the in-house law and human resource functions, and employment liability insurance carriers. The data include softer analysis of employee turnover, loss of productivity, time spent by managers in conflict resolution, and costs arising from employee unrest, as well as information related to litigation costs. The collection of data arises from both interviews and document review. For this step, it is important to request as extensive a documentation of employment and litigation costs as possible.[7]

Once collected, these data must be analyzed for their implications and then formatted into a formal presentation. The data can be used to quantify the original business case and clarify where conflict is currently most significant. For example, the majority of workplace conflict incidents in an organization may arise in the manufacturing function or may concern performance evaluations. Ultimately, the data reveal whether the current organization's practices are likely to be capable of channeling conflict in the future. If they are, its existing practices may require only minor modifications. If not, however, a full workplace system may be the preferred solution.

When one of the coauthors of this book, Richard Fincher, consults with a systems design team, he recommends that the team undertake an analysis of the organization's cost of conflict based on data usually in the possession of the organization's human resource and legal functions. He suggests that the team request the following data:

Selected Data from the Human Resource Function

- Organization chart of the human resource function and the organization's mission statement

- How the organization measures its success and the metrics it uses
- Type of human resource function (consultative or transactional)
- Number of employees
- Classifications of employees
- Voluntary turnover per year by classification
- Number of new employees hired annually
- Description of the current culture of conflict
- Copy of the current employee grievance procedure
- Volume of employee grievances per year
- Volume of employee claims and litigation per year
- Types and sources of employee claims
- Estimated productivity losses from unresolved conflict
- Any anticipated changes to current practices and costs
- Any dispute resolution clauses that are in employment handbooks or contracts

Selected Data from the Legal Function

- Annual legal report to the CEO, if any, and the organization's mission statement
- Type of legal function (consultative or transactional)
- Organizational chart of attorneys
- Volume of transactional versus counseling versus litigation work, in hours billed
- Which departments generate the most billings per year
- The function's assessment of current culture of conflict
- Total employment litigation billing per year for the past five years

- Total equal employment opportunity claims in the past five years

- Any history of using ADR

- Any restrictions on using ADR

- Whether employment contracts include any dispute resolution clauses

- Any anticipated changes to current practices and costs

Decide Whether to Move Ahead with the Project

The collection of organizational data is an essential step in the process, because it provides the foundation for deciding whether the organization needs to move ahead with the project. By this time, the hard and soft data should convey the costs of conflict and the opportunities for savings. They should also show whether existing conflict resolution channels are performing their roles and will likely be able to handle future conflicts.

At this juncture, there are three choices for the design team: move ahead with the project, stop moving ahead and declare the project unnecessary, or paralysis, in which the team makes no decision. In the case of no decision, intervention by the design consultant or senior leadership is required to move the decision making. Whatever the situation, this is a critical decision in the implementation process.[8]

PHASE TWO: RESEARCH, ANALYSIS, AND INTERNAL ALIGNMENT

In this phase, the organization gathers information with which to build. It researches and analyzes workplace systems in other organizations as well as its own and then explores the data with employees and management to get beyond the myths regarding such systems.

Conduct Research on Employee Dispute Systems

A design team should spend sufficient resources gathering research and information on the application and effectiveness of employment dispute systems. The purpose of this effort is to understand the philosophy and options inherent in such systems. Numerous sources can be of help in doing such research. The Association for Conflict Resolution in Washington, D.C., has guidelines on core principles of system design.[9] The CPR Institute for Dispute Resolution in New York City, a nonprofit organization that promotes the use of ADR in corporations, has published reference materials concerning workplace systems.[10] A number of books and ADR journals also include information on workplace systems.

Benchmark Other Organizations and Define Best Practices

Benchmarking is related to but distinct from research. Whereas research refers to reviewing written articles and texts, benchmarking involves on-site visits to organizations that have implemented workplace systems. The purpose of benchmarking is to learn the conceptual context for the system being observed and to understand the obstacles that arose during its implementation. Benchmarking also compares the design features considered and selected by the organization being observed with those features the design team is considering. It also collects successful practices in system design discovered by the organizations being observed.

Benchmarking is not simply visiting another organization and listening to its story. The term, originally used in process or continuous improvement, refers to the formal process of objectively comparing one organization's structure and requirements against another's. It often leads to identifying best practices, or processes that have been observed to produce favorable results over time. When benchmarking an organization, it is crucial to compare the corporate culture of the organization against your own corporate culture.

Workplace systems cannot be effectively implemented in cultures that do not support the core values of workplace systems. Of course, these core values include employee choice, encouragement of raising issues, rights to advisers, and overall system flexibility.

A design team should visit at least three organizations with existing workplace systems. Documents from the targeted organizations should be collected and studied by the design team before the visit. The team should follow an established protocol during the visit and maintain a common spreadsheet of findings. Typically, these benchmarking trips have proved to be a highly valuable step in the design process.

Define the Data and Metrics

Most design teams do not focus on data (information that reveals how participants are using the system) and metrics (information that reveals how effective the system is in achieving its goals) until near the end of the design process. This is a mistake. Numerous metrics can be used to measure the effectiveness of a workplace system. Some are data oriented, while others require significant work to quantify. A design team's selection of specific metrics serves to focus the process and highly influences which features are chosen for the organization's system.

The most common data collected from workplace systems are the nature of cases (such as termination, salary discrimination, or policy violation), the basis of alleged discrimination (age, gender, or race, for example), whom the conflict is with (peer or supervisor), which department the conflict is in (marketing, sales, or manufacturing), and the process of resolution selected (mediation, arbitration, or peer review). The most common metrics used in evaluating workplace ADR systems are elapsed time to close a case (in weeks), outcomes (agreement, impasse, or withdrawal), cost in legal expense (dollars), and historical changes in case-volume filed over time (numbers). In Chapter Eight, we discuss the data and metrics required for an effective workplace system in much greater detail.

A report issued in 1998 by Shell Oil included some information pertinent to our discussion of this step:

> The design of Shell RESOLVE is based upon employee feedback and a review of best practices. It must respond directly to what employees requested—namely, better ways to ensure that problems get addressed early (rather than being avoided) and in ways that preserve workplace relationships.
>
> An average of 15 cases per month were brought to Shell RESOLVE during the first 18 months for a total of 277 cases. The most frequent cases centered on performance or discipline issues, accounting for a total of 47 cases, whereas the number of cases dealing with potential violence numbered fewer than five.

Conduct Employee and Management Focus Groups

Asking for the opinion of internal stakeholders is often neglected in the system design process. Some design teams feel it requires too much effort or suspect that the employees will not provide valuable input. Some fear that a focus group will be openly hostile to any idea other than the traditional grievance procedure. But the purpose of conducting focus groups with employees and managers is to expose them to the general field of conflict resolution, gather candid data on their observations, and initiate a process of subsequent buy-in to the concept. Clearly, it is very valuable.

Focus groups can be conducted at several points during the design process. Some design teams conduct focus groups in the very beginning, before drafting their model or straw design. Others wait until their straw design is completed and present the basic model proposed in the focus groups. Others wait until the very end, when the model is almost finished. Generally, employee focus groups should be conducted earlier in the process design, with at least one follow-up meeting.

There are several prerequisites for these focus groups to work smoothly:

1. Select the participants carefully so as to represent a range of stakeholders.

2. Define clear goals for the sessions ahead of time.

3. Carefully plan the meeting, with predetermined questions and a clear time line.

4. Analyze the collected information carefully.

5. Keep the focus group participants informed about the progress of the design effort.

In the end, organizations that use focus groups report a greater incorporation of employee sensitivities, an enhanced workforce buy-in, and a quicker acceptance of the new system.

Respond to Myths of Workplace Systems

During the course of conducting managerial and employee focus groups, there will be numerous objections raised against workplace systems. The objections will come from employees, supervisors, senior executives, and staff functions. Many of these objections will be myths about workplace systems; nevertheless, they need to be responded to carefully or they will block the ultimate acceptance of the workplace system created:

- *Myth: Introducing a workplace system will open the floodgates of litigation.* This is the most common objection raised by senior leadership, yet we are not aware of any workplace system that has created this effect.[11] Organizations with a history of workplace systems report no increase in employee litigation.
- *Myth: The workplace system will offend employees who are used to the traditional grievance procedure.* In fact, most nonunion employees prefer the flexibility of workplace systems to grievance procedures.
- *Myth: The organization will lose control of its business to outside mediators and arbitrators.* Mediators do not impose decisions on par-

ties, and arbitrators can only impose decisions within the arbitration agreement. This perception misreads the role of both processes.

- Myth: *The outcomes of mediation or arbitration will create binding precedents on the organization that will hinder its effectiveness.* In fact, mediation settlements and arbitration awards are not necessarily precedent setting.
- Myth: *Employees will refuse to sign agreements to arbitrate their claims instead of going to court.* Experience has demonstrated that employees will sign such agreements.
- Myth: *The workplace system will be unduly expensive to manage and will not produce reciprocal benefits.* Our research has concluded that workplace systems are not unduly expensive.

These myths are so common they are almost universal. Nevertheless, each should be treated seriously and be responded to directly in a helpful, informative manner. The design team should not become defensive when others raise these common myths of dispute resolution.

PHASE THREE: SYSTEM DESIGN AND SUPPORT

In this phase, the organization builds on the two prior phases and develops a preliminary structure. This is the meat of the design process. This preliminary plan is tested and refined through employee focus groups and presented to the organization's leadership for approval.

Draft the System

By this time, the design team has accumulated significant information and knowledge about system design. Its members have studied their own organizational costs of conflict and considered each of the internal and external design features that might be appropriate for their purposes. They may have conducted employee and managerial focus groups.

This step moves the design process into the creation phase. It involves integrating the data and developing a straw design. This step often requires facilitation by an internal resource or the system design consultant. Drafting a straw design results in a written document that outlines the initial direction of the proposed system. It includes philosophy, scope of issues, eligibility, steps, features, and other unique elements such as legal consultation benefits (described in Chapter Six). Although a great deal of effort has been invested in coming up with this outline, it is still a draft.

One question commonly raised during straw design is whether there are ever too many options made available to employees to resolve their conflicts. The general answer to this question is no. Although employees value choices in the system, we have found that the vast majority of issues are handled through a few lower-level options. Very few conflicts, for example, are ever raised to peer review, external mediation, or arbitration. Although the presence of these options leads some executives to believe that greater options will increase the volume of issues raised in the system, this has not proved to be the case. The key limitation over the number of options in a workplace system is therefore the skills and resources that would be required to implement the options.

The proposed system or straw design must be aligned with the organization's culture, mission, and values. (The hope is that the organization has already defined its values and mission.) If the philosophy underlying the workplace system is radically different from the status quo within the organization, much work will be needed before the system can be successfully implemented.

Calibrate the Proposed Design

The straw design must be calibrated with organizational needs, employee and leadership expectations, and the existing culture. The purpose of this step is to receive feedback on the value and practicality of the proposal, continue the buy-in process, and gain insight into the potential obstacles or barriers to the system. If the design team conducted focus groups earlier in the process, the straw design should be presented to the same focus groups. If no focus groups were used, these meetings should be held now and be carefully scripted and facilitated to ensure value. In summary, the straw design must be calibrated with organizational needs, employee and leadership expectations, and the existing culture.

Build the Support Structure

By this time, the straw design has been converted into a final recommendation that will be shortly presented to senior leadership for their final approval and funding. But before that occurs, the design team must decide how the workplace system will be implemented and supported over time. This step is a complex decision. Some organizations simply delegate ownership of the system to the human resource function or the law department and think nothing more of it. They view the workplace system as akin to just another human resource or legal policy. A cavalier attitude toward this decision is a mistake, however.

Successful implementation of the workplace system as designed requires a complex support structure. The financial costs of this dedicated support must be quantified for presentation to the senior leadership. One part of this initial implementation is communication and training. A second part is the ongoing reinforcement of and communication about the system. A third part is the tracking of data and metrics. A fourth part is periodic review of the system for minor changes.

Experience has demonstrated that dedicated resources must be allocated to a person or function to manage the system and monitor its effectiveness. The person who performs this function is often referred to as the system coordinator. In large organizations, this function may be assigned to the ombudsman, who typically reports directly to the CEO.

When Anheuser-Busch Corporation set up its dispute resolution program in early 1997, its policy statement included a description of its administrator's tasks:

The DRP Administrator will:

- Coordinate the receipt of employees' disputes with managers and with HR representatives

- Answer questions about DRP [Dispute Resolution Program, the name of its dispute resolution program]

- Monitor compliance with all time requirements

- Schedule mediation meetings and arbitration hearings

- Schedule training sessions for employees and managers

- Schedule the Company's participation in pre-arbitration communications with arbitrators and with employees regarding specific discovery issues

- Administer the terms and conditions of the DRP

Consider a Pilot Project Prior to Full Implementation

Every organization about to launch a workplace system has a choice as to whether to launch a pilot project first or to implement on an organization-wide basis. Launching on a pilot basis generally means that the workplace system is implemented in one location or one division within the company and is considered an experiment until its effectiveness has been established over time. The pilot typically lasts for twelve to eighteen months.

The Unified Court System of New York launched a pilot program of its Mediation Alternative Pilot Program (MAPP) in January 2002 with this description:

A Pilot Program

Initially, the MAPP Dispute Resolution System is a pilot effort by the Unified Court System, its unions and its employees. This program will take effect January 1, 2002 statewide for a period of two years. After one year or the completion of twenty (20) cases, whichever is first, Cornell ILR will begin an evaluation and make recommendations to the Labor-Management Design Team on or before October 1, 2003. The criteria for evaluation of the program and the benchmarks for success will be determined in consultation with the labor-management design team. The design team will approve the plan for evaluation and the data collection process will be in place prior to the commencement of the pilot program.

Only a minority of organizations adopt workplace systems on a pilot project basis, although it can provide advantages involving both cost and predictability. Organizations that pilot a workplace system can learn from the experience at a reduced expense without obligating themselves to a particular overall system design that may not prove effective. A pilot basis, which is sometimes the result of a political compromise, allows actual experience to help decide if the concept has value and should be implemented throughout the organization. At the end of the pilot project, the organization can either cancel the system as a failure or implement it—as is or in a refined version.

An interview by CPR's Peter Phillips with Geoffrey Drucker, chief counsel for dispute resolution and prevention in the U.S. Postal Service's Law Department, highlights the value of a pilot model. When asked if there were changes to the workplace system after it was piloted, Drucker responded:

> One involved the decision to use exclusively outside mediators. Because of the cost of outside mediators, we needed to be able to determine if hiring them was cost-effective. And we found in the pilot locations that although the success rate with other mediation models was good, it was significantly better with outside mediators. Levels of satisfaction and perception of neutrality were significantly higher, too. So we decided, on the national roll-out, to go forward exclusively with outside mediators trained in the transformative process.[12]

There are also disadvantages to launching a workplace system on a pilot basis. One problem is the loss of synergy in implementing with a limited population of employees. A second is that it is more expensive to launch the system twice and incur the additional transactional and managerial costs. A third is gaining sufficient data on which to base the assessment at the end of the pilot period. If the original population used is not large, there may not be enough quantitative experience to evaluate the pilot.

In addition, all workplace systems are expected to evolve through annual assessment. If the first design has problems, the system is expected to modify itself.[13] An organization that effectively follows the steps in this chapter and conducts employee focus groups should have the knowledge to launch a credible system. Thus, a pilot project launch should not be necessary.

Present the Plan to Senior Leadership for Final Approval

This step completes the loop of communication with senior leadership. Several months earlier, the leadership team was briefed about the strategic opportunity. A detailed design contract may have been negotiated between the design team and senior leadership, outlining expectations and a schedule. Since that time, individual members of senior leadership should have been briefed as to the progress of the design, with the internal champion staying close to the work of the design team. This formal presentation of the recommended system sets out its goals and planned process, members of the design team, key research findings, and results from focus groups. It also includes metrics and the support structure.

At the presentation meeting, ample time should be scheduled for questions and answers. In the end, the design team will request approval and funding of the new system. If the team has kept in close contact with individual members of senior leadership, this formal presentation will go smoothly and approval will be given. To be successful, the design team must anticipate any obstacles and use the help of the internal champion to ensure getting approval of the final recommendation.

PHASE FOUR: FINALIZING THE DESIGN

In this phase, the organization finishes the system design. The design team must decide, for example, whether mandatory arbitration should be included in the system. The team also needs to prepare a summary plan description.

Complete the System Design

This step incorporates any changes arising from the presentation to senior leadership. Even in the best of circumstances, there will often be some minor changes suggested in the presentation meetings that are acceptable to the design team. If there are significant design changes, however, the team may wish to communicate the changes to the focus groups and other stakeholders who have detailed knowledge of the project. The goal, in the end, is to have one written workplace system ready to be implemented in the near future.

Encourage Adversaries to Embrace the New Workplace System

People resist change for numerous reasons, including negative prior experience, lack of participation in creating the new model, suspicion of the motives for change, and a perception of future loss under the new model. Implementing a workplace system is no different. Many employees, supervisors, and members of various staff functions will be hostile to the idea and will seek the new system's failure. These adversaries can sometimes have enough influence to bring it down. Normally, they have enough influence to make it controversial and to challenge its credibility among the workforce.

An organization has several means to change the negative attitude of these people toward the new workplace system.[14] The first is to anticipate who these adversaries are, individually and perhaps as a group. Employees in the manufacturing function, for example, are often more negative toward workplace systems than employees in a staff function, such as finance or marketing. The reason is often that manufacturing employees are used to having the traditional grievance system to resolve their issues.

A second means to win over negative employees is to invite them to participate in the design of the system. Some organizations choose instead to exclude them, a move that can be a major mistake in the long term. Still another means is to listen carefully to ensure a complete understanding of their objections and to launch an interest-based dialogue with the objectors. Many organizations that have successfully launched workplace systems report that they were able to listen to and address the concerns of system adversaries, ultimately converting these employees into major supporters.

Determine Whether to Include a Mandatory Arbitration Option

Chapter Six outlined the issues involved in the design and implementation of a predispute agreement to arbitrate statutory claims. This is a highly complex and controversial feature and must be addressed before meeting with senior leadership. If it is incorporated, members of the in-house legal function must provide a close review. Be warned that the feature may also conflict with the existing corporate culture.

There are three common forms of employment arbitration, only one of which is highly controversial: the model that requires acceptance of arbitration as a condition of employment, well before any discrimination claim is raised by the employee. As a second alternative, the system may provide arbitration on a postdispute basis in a feature that allows the employee to decide whether to proceed to arbitration or go to court. As a third alternative, the system may require arbitration but allow the employee to reject the arbitrator's decision and proceed to court.

For several reasons, the system design team should be careful when evaluating the option of mandatory predispute arbitration. Consideration of the option can divide an otherwise effectively working team and cause a lot of time to be spent on an issue that they will not be able to resolve at their level.

Draft the Summary Plan Description

When all decisions regarding content have been made, the next step is to create a summary plan description (SPD), which provides a detailed procedural outline of the workplace design features. Organizations most likely to use an SPD are those that provide for workplace arbitration. SPDs are common and often mandatory under federal law for organizations that offer other corporate benefits such as pension and 401K plans. SPDs are typically drafted by the organization's law department.

There are many advantages to using an SPD:

- The act of drafting the SPD ensures that the broad scope of procedural details is considered, and decisions reached regarding them, before employee conflicts enter the system.

- The SPD can serve as the single-source document for the entire workplace system, giving employees and managers the same booklet to refer to when responding to questions.

- The SPD can provide an alternative to the organization's marketing materials. Marketing materials for workplace systems should be informational, multicolored, pictorial, and easy to read. They should not be a textbook or a legal manual. The SPD, however, should be designed as a secondary reference source, written in a more legalistic manner.

Note the legalistic tone of this excerpt from the SPD of the Inland Container Corporation's dispute resolution plan:

Purpose and Construction

This Plan is designed to provide for the quick, fair and accessible and inexpensive resolution of legal disputes between the Company and its present and former employees. The Plan is intended to create an exclusive procedural mechanism for the final resolution of all disputes falling within its terms. It is not intended either to abridge or enlarge substantive rights available under existing law. The Plan contractually obligates the Company and Employee to its terms, but does not otherwise change the employment-at-will relationship between the Company and its employees. The Plan should be interpreted in accordance with these purposes. The Inland Container Corporation Dispute Resolution Rules and the Plan Description brochure are a part of the Plan and are incorporated by reference into this document.

PHASE FIVE: IMPLEMENTATION AND TRAINING

In this phase, the organization launches and markets the system, clarifies the roles of the various participants, and trains supervisors to support the system

Launch and Market the System

Launching the workplace system refers to the integrated actions required to implement the system in a professional manner. Launching is a multilayered organization development intervention into a complex social structure. Certainly, the entire design initiative has been an organization development effort. Yet the launch is even more so. It assumes that approvals, rewards, incentives, and education can be effectively blended at one time.

There are numerous ways to launch a workplace system, but all include marketing, communications, and training plans. Some organizations downplay the importance of this step, but that is a serious mistake. Experience has demonstrated that the best work-place system will not achieve its goals if the launch is poorly handled by the organization.

The following questions are important considerations for any launch:

- *Who owns the system launch?* This is the threshold question. Should the design team continue ownership of this step, or should the team disband and delegate the launch to human resources or the law function or to whoever is ordinarily responsible for employee communications? We recommend that the design team continue intact and assume ownership of this phase because its members best understand the issues and obstacles in launching the system.

- *How do you develop the marketing plan?* Using a project planning approach, the more common model is to focus on the benefits of the system and design clear informational materials. This approach includes conducting a survey of current awareness of both the old dispute resolution approach and the new system, and surveying the skills required to use the new effectively. Other elements are prelaunch education, creating a clear time line of communications, using a variety of communication vehicles (print, video, and meetings, for example), and allowing for follow-up activities. As time goes on, the design team should not forget employees who missed the initial rollout. Periodic information sessions should be held for these persons.

- *Should you create colorful and clever brochures?* There is no one answer as to whether the organization should develop a sophisticated multicolor brochure with charts, employee quotes, and encouraging information, but we do recommend that organizations launch the system in a manner worthy of the value being placed on the initiative. A workplace ADR system is not just another policy. It can easily be lost in the shuffle of other organizational initiatives. So, generally, launching a workplace system is worthy of a sophisticated brochure and marketing plan.

In this step, the employee communications function (if there is one) is the primary adviser to the design team. Commonly, an external designer and print shop are hired to design and print the informational materials. The best practice recommends that the design team remain intact and own the launch, while using the professional resources of other staff functions and outside experts.

Another important part of the launching of a workplace system involves documentation other than the SPD. There are two levels to this effort. One level refers to creating the basic documents by which to administer the options within the system. A new system may, for example, require a written demand for mediation, a demand for arbitration, and a legal benefits reimbursement form.

The second level of documentation involves the drafting of dispute resolution clauses. These clauses could be inserted into the offer letters, written disciplinary warnings, and employee handbooks and videos. The primary intent of these clauses is to encourage the resolution of conflicts at the earliest possible level. All documents and clauses need to be reviewed for clarity by the legal department.[15]

Excerpts from REDRESS, the mediation program of the U.S. Postal Service, describe the benefits of mediation as follows:

Why Choose Mediation Under the REDRESS Program?

- Mediation Is Fast. It gives you a chance to meet face to face with your supervisor soon after the dispute arises.

- Mediation Is Informal. No witnesses are called, nobody testifies under oath, and no complicated procedures and technicalities get in your way.

- Mediation Allows Representatives. You are entitled to bring a representative of your choice to the mediation; however, the process is designed for people who are handling the problem themselves.

- Mediators Do Not Make Decisions or Force Decisions on You. Mediators are trained to work with all parties to help them find solutions to their dispute. An agreement crafted by the people involved is almost always more satisfying and more lasting than one dictated by an outside third party.

- Mediators Are Impartial. They are trained, experienced, third-party neutrals.

- Mediation Is Free. There is no cost to you for mediation.

Clarify the Role and Responsibilities of All Players in the System

An often-overlooked step in implementing a workplace system is the identification of the players who will interact with the system.[16] This step has three parts:

1. The design team creates a list of all roles involved in the workplace system.

2. The design team describes the responsibilities and collaborative behaviors expected of each player.

3. The team drafts job descriptions with behavioral requirements for each player.

To help define these behavioral requirements, ask what degree of personal ownership of their conflict you desire from individual employees and what levels of skills you expect from your stakeholders.

Each of the stakeholder groups will require customized education, which conveys substantive knowledge about the new workplace system, and training, which refers to skills-based learning. Each stakeholder group requires a blend of these two elements.

Among the numerous misconceptions about ADR training are these myths, observed by Costantino and Merchant:

- All stakeholders need identical ADR training and education.

- ADR training and education are best conducted by outside ADR experts and consultants.

- Only organizational stakeholders should be trained and educated.

- Once they have been trained and educated, stakeholders will use ADR.[17]

Train Supervisors to Support the System

The launch effort must focus directly on first-line supervisors. Many observers view supervisors as the primary obstacle to effective implementation of the ADR system. This perception arises for three reasons: supervisors view the workplace system as providing excessive power to their employees, the workplace system increases the supervisors' workload, and the workplace system requires skills in conflict resolution that supervisors do not currently have.

An interview by CPR's Peter Phillips with Richard Ross, senior associate general counsel with Anheuser-Busch Companies, highlights this example. When asked if there were skills that he wanted to make sure managers had in order to use the program, Ross responded:

> Problem resolution skills are extremely important because the great bulk of the complaints should be resolved at that first step, without need for either mediation or arbitration. So you're really putting managers into a new role, that of problem solver. . . . Having to address employee problems aggressively and creatively is a new experience for a lot of managers.[18]

Training supervisors to embrace the workplace system has two main goals: to convey substantive awareness of the system design and features and to build conflict-resolution skills. The primary skills that supervisors require are listening, channeling anger, and basic problem solving. If the organization has a training function, that often serves as the primary adviser and trainer at this point. Typically, the design team does not actually conduct the supervisory training.[19]

The training brochure from the Rural-Metro Corporation (an ambulance and fire protection business) describes the goals of its supervisors' training workshops. It states that managers who participate in their workshops will learn (1) how the new employment contract defines management actions when an employee elects to use the termination dispute resolution process; (2) key facts about the mediation process; (3) key facts about the arbitration process; and (4) the four responsibilities that govern the role of the supervisor during the mediation and arbitration process. Rural-Metro concludes each training workshop with a short simulation and an opportunity for general discussion.

PHASE SIX: INSTITUTIONALIZATION

In this final phase, the organization gives the system long life. It enables the system to become embedded in the organization by instilling incentives, maintaining credibility, reinforcing activity, analyzing results, and readjusting the system over time to ensure long-term success.

Build Incentives to Use the Workplace System

Employees' and supervisors' behaviors are significantly influenced by their perception of the risks and rewards associated with an action. Thus, progressive organizations need to ask two basic questions when implementing a workplace system: How can we minimize the risk or fear associated with using the system, and How can we encourage employees to use the system? These are not easy questions to answer because each system stakeholder group requires its own rewards and incentives. Organizations need to define what features will succeed in eliminating fears and what rewards will serve as incentives for each group.

The most obvious means to minimize the risk or fear of using the workplace system is to ensure that there is no retaliation by the immediate supervisor or other management personnel. Ensuring confidentiality is another means of neutralizing fear and encouraging use of the process. A leak or breach of information will be recognized and remembered for years. Systems must build in the ability to maintain confidences and prevent the disclosure of employee issues throughout the process. Although this is not as easy as preventing retaliation, confidentiality is a touchstone for effective system design

There are many ways to encourage use of a workplace system. One is to publicize success stories, either from statistics or actual stories that do not mention the employee's name. Another is for senior leadership to speak favorably of the system regularly and encourage its use by employees and managers. Another means is through the management performance appraisal system. Managers who are rewarded in their annual evaluations for successful use of the new system will be motivated to respond favorably to future claims made under it.

Following is Chevron Corporation's effort to reduce employees' fear of using their workplace system:

> *Should I worry about retaliation?* No. This is one of the first questions on people's minds. STEPS [Steps to Employee Problem Solution] has a strong policy that swings into action if anyone suspects retaliation for using the process. This includes any improper impact on pay, promotion, or assignments. Claims are to be immediately investigated and, if warranted, appropriate action taken. If you suspect retaliation, you should contact your HR Business Partner or an Ombuds.

> *Can I trust the process?* The answer is yes—and here's why. First, STEPS uses a variety of third-party facilitators who are involved because of their neutrality and impartiality. Second, STEPS is completely confidential. Third, the steps that make up the process are open for all to see. If an employee was denied access to all or part of the STEPS process, it would be immediately obvious. And finally, STEPS has the support of Chevron's senior leaders, who are committed to monitoring the effectiveness of the process.

Maintain Credibility Through Ongoing Education and Reinforcing Communications

After successful launch of a workplace system, there is an ongoing need for education and reinforcing communication. Ongoing education is for newly hired employees, new supervisors, and existing employees who may never have used the system or may have forgotten its value and features. Reinforcing communication serves to maintain awareness of the system and to present examples of representative success stories. Such communication should occur at least twice per year. Ownership for ongoing education is typically assumed by the organization's supporting structure, often the system coordinator or the ombudsperson. The budget for this work comes from the ongoing operating budget.

Conduct an Ongoing Assessment of Outcomes

Effective workplace systems require an annual assessment of their effectiveness. Earlier in the implementation process, the design team defined the usage data and performance metrics that would be collected and analyzed on a periodic basis. These criteria should measure client satisfaction and the efficiency and effectiveness of the system. Beyond the basic criteria, organizations should seek to answer the question, "Who wants to know what and why?" about how the system is working.[20]

The support person assigned to the workplace system (an ombudsman, for example) typically owns this data-gathering and evaluation effort. In some organizations, though, an external consultant is retained to perform the assessment, which includes analyzing the data and conducting interviews with stakeholders. Under either scenario, this step is crucial to ensure continued support by the organization. Without proper data and metrics, the workplace system is highly susceptible to being underresourced or totally eliminated during any downturn of the organization.

American Express is an example of a company that has developed careful measurements of the performance of its workplace system.

The ombudsman's office, for example, produces an annual report that contains a thorough assessment of the office's operation during the past year. In the 1998 annual report, the ombudsman reported that the office had received 3,276 inquiries from American Express employees, an increase of 15 percent over the number received during the previous year.

The report also noted that the ombudsman and her staff had conducted face-to-face visits with more than twenty thousand AmEx employees in thirty-eight countries. The office supplemented these face-to-face visits with a sophisticated array of employee communications, including newsletters, an electronic bulletin board, brochures, and posters. To ensure that all AmEx employees would have easy access to the ombudsman, the office had recently installed international, toll-free telephone lines and multilingual contact cards.

The ombudsman's annual report also provided statistics on the number and types of employees that had used the office's services as well as the major issues raised by these employees. Of the total number of inquiries received from employees in 1998, 49 percent were from "associates" (hourly or nonexempt employees), 36 percent were from managers, 5 percent were from financial advisors, and 2 percent were from contractors, vendors, or temporary workers. The major issues the office dealt with that year involved the company's counseling process, management decisions, compensation, manager-employee relations, medical benefits, and general quality of work life matters. The report noted that counseling issues had grown significantly over the course of the year.

Readjust the Workplace System over Time

The final step in implementing a workplace system is periodic modification of the design and features of the system. No workplace system is perfectly crafted the first time, and systems often need to be tweaked as the organization evolves.

Typically, the system coordinator accepts primary responsibility to initiate changes to the system. In some organizations, though, an advisory committee for the workplace system serves as the sounding board of the workforce as to the system's effectiveness. In either case, the system coordinator should not make unilateral changes. Instead, a more disciplined and participative approach should be used to ensure broad input and buy-in to the proposed changes. An external system design consultant is often retained to assist in modifying the workplace system.

CONCLUSION

Implementation of a workplace system is a highly complex process. The effort requires broad understanding of dispute resolution processes, organizational change initiatives, human resources, employment law, labor law, research techniques, stakeholder analysis, benchmarking practices, and project planning. There are many obstacles facing workplace systems, both along the design path and after the system is launched.

During the design process, some stakeholders will be resistant to the workplace system and will disagree as to the preferred model. After the system is launched, the initial system champion may leave the organization. Many organizations fail to ensure effective monitoring and evaluation. When budget cuts occur, the system is at risk.

We highly recommend that the design effort generally follow the steps in this chapter and that the effort not be started until the necessary capabilities and resources have been pulled together for a successful initiative. We believe that workplace systems are not a temporary fix to a presenting problem but rather a sustainable vehicle to proactive conflict management.

Chapter Eight

Evaluation of Conflict Management Systems

The evaluation of conflict management systems and subsystems can mean very different things to different people. To organizational policymakers, including those who participate in the creation of these systems, the entire point of evaluation is to measure whether the goals of the program have been met. This is done with an absolute standard in mind—for example, to lower litigation costs or to settle disputes at the lowest level possible. These standards are usually behind the creation of a new system.

These conflict management systems are private processes, however. In most cases, even if organizations have been willing to share, or even broadly publicize, their system and its components, they are unwilling to share the results of that system publicly. For this reason, research that has been conducted on conflict management systems has tended to be across, rather than within, organizations. Thus, we have less understanding and knowledge of internal systems than we would like.

To independent researchers, evaluation can mean something very different. A behavioral scientist looks at evaluation as the attempt to isolate and measure the impact, intended and unintended, of a policy change on the behavior of individuals within an organization and the organization itself. Thus, the behavioral scientist's goal is broader, indifferent to the stated goals of a systematic change, and more focused on the specifics of precise measurement and data collection. Although it is easy to understand the joint interests of the two evaluation processes, they often collide. Only rarely are the interests of both communities met by the results of a single evaluation. Academics are constantly urging organizations to submit themselves to external scrutiny and pleading for more research on conflict management systems. Bingham and Chachere have this to say about dispute resolution:

> There is much we do not know about why organizations adopt these programs or how third-party processes will function in a nonunion context. The structural characteristics of employment dispute resolution systems vary widely and warrant further research, particularly on how these design features affect participant outcomes. We also need to examine whether there is an empirical basis for the claims that employment dispute resolution programs will have some positive impact or organizational outcomes such as effectiveness of dispute resolution programs and organizational efficiency. Because these are confidential processes, it will not be easy to do this research. However, it is work that needs to be done.[1]

Practitioners just as consistently urge academics to tell them the answers to basic questions, and without the qualifying statements academics are so prone to make. Practitioners have fundamental information questions about the effectiveness and efficiency of conflict management systems, and they are often frustrated at the type of research that has been conducted on these questions.

Finally, evaluation can be an analysis of the impact of a public policy. Laws, regulations, and procedures can be changed with the intention of shifting the behavior of those affected by the policy. Whether those behaviors change in the intended direction, or at all, is the concern of the policymaker and of analysts of policy changes.

This chapter seeks to serve the organizational policymaker, the behavioral scientist, and public policy analysts. Throughout the chapter, we present information about specific cases that will illuminate the problem and prospects of evaluation.

SYSTEM EVALUATION BY ORGANIZATIONS

Why do organizations want to evaluate their systems? This seems like such a straightforward question with such an obvious answer that one wonders why it must be asked. Yet it is not so straightforward to organizations involved in conflict management change. Most often, the question of evaluation has such a low priority that it is not considered until very late in the system design process, perhaps even into implementation. By that time, evaluation is an afterthought that does not receive the attention it deserves. Some organizations have a fear of evaluating their system because the answers provided may not confirm preexisting biases about what should occur. A kind of low-level organizational fear also can influence the type of data collected: many organizations have questions they simply do not wish to ask because they are worried about the answer they will be given. Evaluation is also expensive, particularly when it comes to the creation and maintenance of data collection systems. For all these reasons, many organizations choose not to evaluate their own systems or stop at a very rudimentary level of analysis.

Evaluation can be a key component to the conflict management system, however. Organizations need to know whether the system works as intended. Most organizations would benefit substantially from knowing the benefits—monetary and otherwise—and the costs of the system. As has often been postulated, no change occurs without some unintended consequences. Being aware that the introduction of new elements in a conflict management system may produce unexpected behaviors can be a powerful part of evaluation. Finally, organizations should evaluate their systems in part to provide the basis for future improvement of the system through feedback about the parts of the system that are working as intended and those that are not.

Despite these powerful arguments, it is very uncommon for organizations to undertake a disciplined evaluation of their dispute resolution processes and conflict management systems. In all of our interviews and discussions with corporate and public organizational officials in charge of conflict management systems, we found few who considered evaluation a high priority in system design. Yet these organizations almost all craved benchmarking information on how other systems worked. What occurs in this vacuum of hard information is that benchmarking is done on system components, regardless of whether they have worked well. Certain shibboleths of the conflict management gospel are passed on from one organization to another without any evidence to support the underlying belief or assumption.

Key Elements of Evaluation Success

As noted in Chapter Seven, organizations with admirable evaluation schemes integrated evaluation into their system design work at an early stage of the process. Many of the fears of a comprehensive evaluation can be eliminated if an evaluation component is assumed to be a critical part of the overall system design. When this is the case, evaluation can often influence program design as design team members consider whether their expectations regarding system design are even measurable. This is particularly true when designers think about the reasons for change and the goals of the new system. If goals are poorly defined, it will be difficult to recognize success even if it occurs since it will be impossible to measure. When evaluation criteria and measures are defined around goals and objectives, evaluation can then be used as part of a continuous feedback loop. It is equally important for the designers to see evaluation not as a one-time event but rather as standard, routine, and continuous. Finally, evaluation works well when the designers think far enough ahead to be able to judge whether the evaluators will have the access they need to the information and data important to collect and evaluate.

Who Evaluates the Conflict Management System?

Another important feature of the design of an evaluation project is the question of who will be the data collector and who will do the analysis and evaluation. Objectivity and credibility are crucial for collecting the information from the participants in the system and their clients—whether they are lawmakers or corporate executives. Public policy analysis, unlike internal organizational analysis, tends to be performed by outsiders, with public scrutiny of the data and methodology an expected part of the evaluation process. Internal evaluations are nearly always performed by insiders, and thus public credibility is not the standard. Rather, credibility within the organization and with the employees is a more important criterion.

A Work Agenda for Evaluation

Internal organizational evaluation efforts can be summarized into a work agenda or checklist for evaluation. Companies with notable evaluation efforts did the following:

- Carefully defined the goals of conflict management
- Determined in advance the clients for the evaluation of the system
- Thought through the problem of measurement and data collection
- Developed a scheme to capture data
- Clearly assigned the evaluation task

Although very few organizations subject themselves to public scrutiny by releasing the data on their internal evaluations, many go through a thorough design process such as the one above.

An Example: Evaluation at Shell Oil

Shell Oil is one of the very few organizations that have evaluated their internal organization conflict management systems. In 1997, Shell began the RESOLVE system of conflict management, which had the following goals:

1. Supporting Transformation

2. Addressing Workplace Needs

3. Supporting Diversity

4. Protecting the Company

5. Equipping Us for the Future[2]

The principles underlying these global goals were clear: to view conflict as an opportunity for improvement and to resolve conflict at the lowest level possible so as to avoid delay and costly litigation. Shell used a wide range of neutral services, including an ombudsman office, mediation, and arbitration. After eighteen months, the RESOLVE office published a brochure that summarized the initial experiences with the program.

Shell is one of a very small number of organizations willing to reveal such statistics as the number of conflicts, type of conflicts, time to resolve conflicts, and the ultimate process of resolution. Clearly, this material is designed more for internal credibility than evaluation, but the tables and charts reveal a great deal about how the system is working. Shell values the surfacing of problems early, the speedy resolution of conflict, and solving a large proportion of problems within the RESOLVE system.

THE METRICS OF CONFLICT MANAGEMENT EVALUATION

No agreement has yet emerged on the best way to measure and evaluate conflict management systems. There is no consensus, for example, on the critical dependent variables to be measured or even what outcomes are desirable in a conflict management system. Because that consensus has not emerged, it is not surprising that there is no particular agreement on the independent variables either. This void leads to significant problems for all evaluators and researchers since the iterative process of evaluation, critique, refinement of measure, and method has not progressed beyond its early stages. In the end, the few evaluation studies that exist are mostly comparing apples to oranges.

Therefore, we will start with some basic model building on conflict management systems. We shall do that by working on the frame of reference for comparison, hypothesized outcomes (or dependent variables), and predictors of outcomes (independent variables). There has been a lot of speculation on hypothesized outcomes, somewhat less on the independent variables that affect those outcomes, and because of the difficulty inherent in experimental design and data collection, even less on the frame of reference. Thus, the state of evaluation in conflict management is probably typical of newly emergent problems of study. We are not yet at a very sophisticated analytical level. Rather, at this point in the development of models, the parties interested in system evaluation are stuck with simply identifying important variables and tracking the data

In attempting to evaluate the Administrative Dispute Resolution Act of 1990, Lisa Bingham and Charles Wise framed the following question: "How can one measure change across the federal government as a whole?"[3] They were attempting to assess whether a specific piece of legislation had been successful; not surprisingly, given the broad implications in the question they asked, they broke the question into impact and process evaluation. They defined impact evaluation as the examination of program outcomes and their impact on a targeted population.[4] Process evaluation seeks to measure whether a specific program is delivered as intended to the targeted recipients.[5] Although the federal government is a huge organization, the problem that Bingham and Wise describe is the same for any other organization attempting to assess the impact or effectiveness of its conflict management system.

The Frame of Reference: General Methodological Problems

The first question with any data collected on system evaluation is, "As compared to what?" Although it is relatively straightforward to collect information on disputes, time to resolution, and a myriad of other potential measures, without a frame of reference, the information is subject to any number of potential interpretations. In a pure design, we would like to set up an experiment in which one group is given a treatment (access to a new grievance procedure, for example) and a control group is not given that treatment. Then we would measure different outcome behaviors across the groups in an attempt to isolate the effect of the treatment.

Very few organizations would even consider such a scheme in order to satisfy the demands of rigorous program evaluation when preparing to launch a conflict management system. Organizational imperatives—getting the program under way, unfavorable reaction to denying the program to some while giving it to others, halo effects in both the experimental and control groups—would dominate the discussion and nearly always outweigh evaluation needs.

Given that classic experimental design is only a dream for the evaluation of conflict management systems, what substitutes are there? There are at least four practical options: before-and-after analysis, the rolling pilot, changes over time once the new system is put into place, and analysis across a number of organizations. Each has advantages and disadvantages in data collection and analysis.

Before-and-after analysis is based on the premise that other than the implanting of the new features of a conflict management system, we can largely control organizational variables so that the system is the only change. We could then measure changes in behavior and outcomes and attribute those changes to the effect of the new conflict management system.

This method has been used in at least one large-scale conflict management system change: the New York State Workers' Compensation System.[6] A new workers' compensation law passed in 1995 allowed construction employers and their unions to negotiate a dispute resolution system for workers' compensation cases. This system would replace the administrative judicial process for resolving conflicts over payment of indemnity and medical benefits. To measure the impact of that change in the law, Seeber, Schmidle, and Smith used a sample of workplace injuries for Local

3 of the International Brotherhood of Electrical Workers and the New York Electrical Contractors Association. They tracked workplace injuries the year prior to the negotiated change in the dispute resolution process and compared them to the injuries over the year following the change. The underlying assumption giving validity to the analysis is that there were no other significant differences between the before period and the after period. That is never perfectly true, but was approached in this case.

The practical problems for most organizations are, in fact, the inability to isolate a policy change and the lack of comparable data. The advantage in the workers' compensation example is that the nature of injuries did not change, and because of insurance companies' predilection to data collection, detailed information was available. Ordinarily, if a company designed a new complaint process to replace an existing one, it would be unlikely to stop there. It might very well change other things about the system: add an arbitration scheme or an ombudsperson office, change the scope of what is a legitimized complaint, and so on. Those multiple changes make a before-and-after comparison very difficult, if not impossible, to conduct due to the inability to isolate the effect of a specific change.

A second problem for most organizations with before-and-after evaluation is that even if a scheme for isolating the program impact is designed, the before data are often not available. Our interviews revealed very few organizations that had adequate data on current experiences to be able to compare even simple matters like complaint rates after a systematic change in conflict management schemes.

The second possibility for a frame of reference for comparison is provided by the *rolling pilot* implementation of a new program. Some organizations create natural experiments through the use of this technique. In such a situation, due to the complex nature or the size of an organization, a determination is made that it is best not to implement the new system throughout the organization at one time but rather piece by piece.

Two of us are involved in the establishment of the Mediation Alternative Pilot Program (MAPP) for the nineteen thousand employees of the New York State court system.[7] The court system is divided into geographical and jurisdictional districts across the state. A decision was made by the design team to implement the MAPP in a series of pilot programs, each one being informed by the experiences of those already under the new system. This is a potentially fruitful design feature that allows errors that are made to be corrected as the system is implemented throughout the state. Although this is not a perfect research design, it does allow approximation of an experimental group (the early districts in the pilot) and a control group (those not yet covered by the program).

Some organizations have also created a quasi-natural experiment not through the rolling pilot but through the deliberate decision to have two dispute resolution systems within their organizations. Our interviews at Kaiser Permanente revealed that its well-developed mediation and arbitration system for the resolution of patients' medical complaints was used only on the West Coast.[8] In other places where it did business as a health care provider organization and an insurer, it used more traditional methods of dispute resolution. Had Kaiser desired, and we are not aware that it has done anything like this, it might have gathered data and compared the effectiveness and efficiency of the two systems.

A third possibility for the frame of reference is a comparison between outcomes and behaviors in an initial time period in conflict system design and subsequent periods of time. If an organization has no before data and wishes to implement a system change all at once, it has the option of observing initial experiences under the new system and then comparing those experiences to later time periods. The advantages to this scheme are obvious in that dynamic change in a system can be measured. The critical disadvantage is that the new cannot be compared to the old. In addition, the organization is not able to do a comparative evaluation until at least two time periods under the new scheme have passed.

A final possibility lies with comparative evaluation across organizations. Although this has obvious appeal to academics, it has two drawbacks that make meaningful evaluation in this manner an unlikely event. First, organizations are unlikely to be willing to share information of this sensitive type. The evolving notion of the use of conflict management and maturing views on the value of conflict may have taken root in management culture. But most organizations now treat these kinds of data as an internal secret, to be discussed only behind closed doors or with very trusted advisers. Second, organizations are wise to create a customized conflict management system that suits the specific environmental needs of the organization. Features will differ organically across organizations, and that may preclude any meaningful comparison of any pair of organizations. The problem is multiplied when attempting to compare a number of organizations.

In sum, the establishment of a meaningful way to evaluate systems is difficult, and opportunities for classic experimental policy research are rare and likely to remain so. This will limit the growth of research in conflict management for some time to come because we are largely unable to do the kind of impact research to answer the general question posed by Bingham and Wise. What is often left is a large number of studies presenting results of various components of systems, without an appropriate context within which to place the measurements.

Expectations, Hypotheses, and Results

With very few experimental designs in place that allow empirically based conclusions to be drawn about conflict management systems, we need to think in a different way about how to summarize what we know about those systems and their component elements. There are many underlying expectations and assumptions about pieces of conflict resolution systems:

> "Disputants are more satisfied with a mediated solution because they had a part in creating the answer to their problem."

> "Arbitration is more private and simpler than litigation."

> "We can eliminate many of our disputes if we have an effective way of surfacing conflict in the organization as soon as possible."

All these statements, commonly made by both internal and external advocates of dispute and conflict management systems, reflect underlying beliefs about the likely effects of mediation, arbitration, and complaint processes. Internal advocates searching for the right answer in system design are often frustrated, however, by the lack of research and fundamental evidence about these elements of conflict management systems.

Here, we seek to make as much sense as possible out of the disparate streams of research that are available on conflict management systems and suggest an agenda for the future of research in this arena so that the next generation of system designers will not be operating in the dark.

Expectations About Conflict Management Systems. Much is revealed in the explanations of conflict management systems by those who create and promote them. For example, an excellent explanatory brochure distributed to all Chevron employees explained the STEPS program in ways that revealed the underlying assumptions that led to the creation of the system:[9]

> As an employee at Chevron, you have relationships with everyone you work with. For the most part, these relationships are probably good ones. However, when disputes occur, it's important to have a way to resolve conflict without causing undue harm. . . .
>
> The Steps to Employee Problem Solution (STEPS) process was created because Chevron wanted a fast and fair way to resolve disputes. STEPS is intended to be a neutral approach to resolving disputes before they can get worse. Disagreements typically worsen when they are exposed to a wider forum. An obvious example is when employees sue the company where they work. One of STEPS' benefits is to help resolve employee disputes early before they can progress to the time-consuming and adversarial lawsuit process.

Note the beliefs implicit in these statements. Chevron wants employees to mediate and arbitrate disputes because they believe that these are faster, simpler processes that will lead to fair outcomes. We can be sure that when Chevron benchmarked other systems (it mentions Brown and Root, TRW, and Bechtel in its brochure), enough evidence, or enough of other companies' beliefs, was passed on to convince it of the truth of these statements.

Another company that explicitly revealed its beliefs about various ADR processes and conflict management system results is Brown and Root. In a 1995 article, William Bedman, an associate general counsel at Brown and Root, stated, "There is every reason to believe that it (private employment dispute resolution) will deliver superior justice, superior speed and reduced cost."[10] These statements of the expectations of conflict management systems also reveal some underlying expectations of the program for the corporation, but as Bedman noted, "The hard data have yet to be gathered, and perhaps the hard questions have yet to be asked—about both litigation and private methods."

We could present several more public statements of organizations about their conflict management systems, but they would continue to reveal expectations about systems without the data necessary to measure their truth. Those expectations, however, are based largely on more theoretical hypotheses about the way in which these processes perform and about their impact on individuals, organizations, and dispute resolution systems.

The expectations about the behavior of individuals and systems reflect many of the implicit beliefs about ADR and its component pieces. There is a broad consistency between these beliefs and the hypotheses generated by academics and other system evaluators, both internal and external to organizations.

Our earlier research on the rise of the ADR movement revealed that most organizations state that they seek alternatives to dispute management for instrumental reasons: they wish to save time and money. That finding gives us one starting point for thinking about the dependent variables in conflict management systems, but it is only from the organization's perspective. While employees might want to see the organization save as much time and money as possible, it is more likely that they view the conflict management system through the lens of fairness or some other value or attitude, comparing it to internal standards of appropriate behavior. For this reason, other researchers have advocated a more complex set of outcomes as appropriate dependent variables. Under the rubric of system efficiency and system effectiveness, some researchers have started from the users' point of view to develop models of those outcomes.

We will examine each of these perspectives, map them into specific measures and hypotheses about those measures of conflict management system outcomes, and group possible outcome measures into three categories: direct efficiency effects, effectiveness effects, and indirect organizational effects.

Hypothesized Direct Efficiency Effects. *Direct efficiency effects* are outcomes of a conflict management system that, in comparison to the alternative, offer a hypothesized opportunity for improvement over existing outcomes. Most often we think of outcomes related to time and money, but there are other possibilities. Table 8.1 presents a summary of potential direct impacts of conflict management systems. All of these effects have been hypothesized by other researchers in one way or another, but they have never been brought together comprehensively as in this format. Nor have these hypothesized effects been studied in a comprehensive, complete manner. In fact, it may not be possible to gather the kinds of data we would need to test for all these effects.

Conflict management systems are expected to be more efficient than any other system of dispute resolution. As we have shown, managers and executives expect to save time and money from the use of ADR. These savings would be the direct efficiency effects of conflict management, but evidence on these points is thin. The most complete summary of research on components of dispute resolution systems was written by Lisa Bingham and Denise Chachere in 1999.[11] Many reports of high rates of mediation settlement exist, though, and we will present some of them in the evaluation case studies later in this chapter.

Table 8.1. Hypothesized Efficiency of Conflict Management Systems

Measure	Hypothesized Impact
Time from conflict to settlement	Less than litigation
Costs of system maintenance (transaction): Training, neutrals, administrators, information	Uncertain, but expected to be less than alternatives
Costs of outcomes or settlements	Equal
Costs of litigation or other existing process	Less
Settlement rates	High
Conflict or dispute rates (usage)	Perhaps higher than litigation
Opting out of system	Low, or nonexistent, depending on availability
Outcomes: favorable or unfavorable	Equal
Resolution at low level of system	High
Avoidance of litigation	High

Typical results are those presented in an analysis of over four hundred cases in business dispute resolution.[12] Brett, Barsness, and Goldberg reported that 60 percent of the cases analyzed settled at mediation, and another 18 percent settled subsequent to mediation but prior to the next step of the dispute resolution process, for an overall settlement rate of 78 percent. These settlement rates all occur within a specific context, however, and thus leave us with little satisfaction from comparison. Does a 60 percent settlement rate mean that 60 percent of the cases would have proceeded to litigation without the availability of mediation? Is mediation thus judged effective? It depends on one's absolute standard, but clearly mediation allows a substantial portion of cases to be settled that might otherwise go on to more costly and time-consuming processes of dispute resolution.

Unlike mediation, arbitration settlement rates are always 100 percent, and so the concept of a rate of settlement is meaningless.

Perhaps more interesting is to consider how the parties chose to use arbitration, given the broad deferral to arbitrators' decisions by the courts. That question concerns system design, however, a process that has not been modeled or tested.

It is usually presumed that the time from the initiation of a dispute to its resolution will be less under mediation and arbitration than under traditional dispute resolution through litigation. Given the clogs in the litigation system, this is an easy mark for most systems to meet. Measurements of relative improvements are few in the research on conflict management systems, though. One such estimate comes from the ADR Workers' Compensation study in which the ADR system overall was judged to quicken the dispute resolution process by approximately four months.[13] Reports on the time to settlement through the litigation process are available, but those measures are not fair comparisons to time to settlement in conflict management systems because many of those cases would not have reached litigation. In general, mediation and arbitration are expected to be quicker processes than any available alternative.

A second broad group of hypothesized efficiency effects is related to costs: the costs of conflict management compared to existing systems within organizations. Costs can be divided into two types: transaction and settlement. *Settlement costs* are the actual damages paid to those with disputes and are relatively easy to calculate in litigated settlements. In arbitrated or mediated settlements, those costs are often not made public and thus are difficult to calculate. We are aware of only one organization, Toro, that claimed to pay more in settlement costs under a conflict management system. That claim was made happily, however, because Toro had more than made up the increase in settlement costs through a significant reduction in transaction costs. Usually, however, organizations are not particularly concerned with an increase or decrease in settlement costs under a conflict management regime. Settlement costs are not expected to vary significantly.

Transaction costs—for example, the costs of creation of a group of system administrators, the training of participants that most organizations see as useful, the creation and training of a roster of neutrals, and communications about the new system—receive a significant amount of attention in the development and implementation of a conflict management system. Yet we did not find in our corporate research and interviews that the transaction costs of a traditional system were actually being measured in any meaningful way. Litigation expenses could be measured relatively easily, but most firms did not have that benchmark against which to measure any change. The indirect costs of a traditional system unresolved employee conflicts, uncertainty from delays in the system, lower employee morale—remain unmeasured in every organization we studied.

One of the problems in the implementation of a new conflict management system is that the system creation and maintenance costs are real while the benefits are often speculative and difficult to measure. (We revisit this problem in Chapter Nine.) The transaction costs are not insignificant and while most organizations hypothesize that they will eventually be outweighed by benefits, they often provide an important barrier to the adoption of a conflict management system.

The efficiency effects of a conflict management system, as we have shown, have not been measured in any comprehensive way, although there are many hypothesized effects of the adoption of such a system. Later in this chapter, we examine some of the more comprehensive system evaluations, but even in those cases, only some of the expected effects are actually measured. This area of dispute resolution demands much more rigorous research before these hypotheses can be tested.

Hypothesized Effectiveness Effects.   There has been a significant amount of research on satisfaction with particular features of conflict management systems and other aspects of the effectiveness of these systems.[14] Table 8.2 presents some hypothesized effectiveness effects of conflict management systems. These are grouped into three types of measures. The first group refers to the nature of the

Table 8.2.   Hypothesized Effectiveness of Conflict Management Systems

Measure	Hypothesized Impact
Access	Easy
Fairness	Compared to publicly available alternative
Due process standards	Compared to publicly available systems
Satisfaction with process, neutral, and outcome	High, but no absolute standards
Impartiality of neutrals	High
Adversarial nature of system	Lower than alternative

procedure: Is the system easy to access? Is it perceived to be fair and impartial by the participants? Is the system adversarial?

Although access to the system is difficult to judge, it is a cornerstone of an integrated conflict management system. Individuals must be able to take a conflict to a resolution process easily. Given the difficulties of accessing the courts and administrative agencies, nearly all conflict management systems are seen as comparatively easier to access. The comparative measurement to the courts is difficult, however. Joshua Pascoe measured the willingness to complain under two different conflict resolution systems, one union and one nonunion.[15] Other than that very narrow and controlled circumstance, there have been few, if any, attempts to try a measure of comparative access.

To say that fairness and impartiality are in the eyes of the beholder is a truism. There is no accepted standard for these terms. Most who have tried to draw conclusions about whether a system is fair look at the system through the eyes of the employees affected by it. This view creates one of the fundamental critiques of conflict management systems. From the perspective of those who believe that private due process is never as fair as public due process, it is presumed that these systems are unfair.

Most of the evaluation of systems in this vein comes from a due process standard perspective. The comparative evaluation of conflict management systems with judicial due process is really a search for the replication of public standards in private processes. Most systems do not fare well under this standard, with critics pointing to limitations on representation and to those few systems that require predispute waivers of access to public forums in statutory rights cases. Although some systems have been thrown out on due process grounds by the courts,[16] there has not been any attempt to truly measure the differences. Thus, in the end fairness *is* in the eye of the beholder, and any accepted standards for measurement of systems are far off in the future.

A second group of effectiveness effects are easily measurable and are the category on which most evaluations are focused. Satisfaction with a process combines elements of procedural justice with the simple opportunity to be heard or to have access. Many evaluations, including some that we detail later in this chapter, have conducted extensive surveys of individuals' satisfaction with the overall process, with the neutral and the techniques the neutral used, and the bottom-line question of whether the individuals would use the process again. Of course, as with the other effects, there are no comparative satisfaction studies for comparable cases, so the generally high measures of satisfaction reported with mediation do not mean as much as they might in the light of other data. As such satisfaction measures emerge in evaluation studies over time, some general standard of success will begin to be associated with satisfaction.

One of the great frustrations with traditional systems of dispute resolution is that they put the parties into an adversarial posture so early in the process. Process issues that should be unimportant to the eventual outcome, such as scheduling of sessions and discovery of relevant documents, can often turn into contests of delay and obstruction. Conflict management systems offer an alternative to that posturing by providing processes that focus at an early stage on settlement. Thus, the developers of systems often postulate that the adversarial nature of the system should be much less than the traditional methods of dispute resolution. Measuring adversarialism, however, is tricky business at best. Few studies have ever attempted to test this belief. Later in this chapter, we review the results of the REDRESS system at the U.S. Postal Service, which sought to measure, in an indirect way, the impact of a conflict management system on adversary behavior through a workplace climate assessment comparison between two periods of time.

Hypothesized Indirect Effects. Many claims have been made for the overall organizational impact of the proper introduction of conflict management systems in a variety of publications. Yet it is in this area that there is the most speculation and the least evidence on the questions at issue. Table 8.3 summarizes the claims that have been hypothesized by advocates of conflict management.

Table 8.3. Hypothesized Indirect Effects
of Conflict Management Systems

Measure	Effect
Employee morale	Could improve if system is seen as effective, could decline if system is viewed as favorable to organization
Managerial morale	Could improve or decline dependent on implementation
Avoiding unionism	Positive for organization
Flexibility	Greater flexibility for organization
Turnover, attrition	Could be lower if system transfers exit behavior into voice
Reputation	Long run could be higher
Changes in relationships of the parties	Expected to be better
Organizational communications	Expected to be better

Probably the most debated area is the impact of conflict management on employees as a group and on managers. Employees could be positively affected. A conflict management system might be introduced in a participative way, early experiences could be seen as effective, the system could be accepted as fair, and an increase in employee morale might result. If an organization violates any one of those premises, however, employees might see the system as an effort to channel conflict to a system working primarily in the organization's best interests. Managers, as a separate group, might very well welcome the opportunity to be held responsible for the cost and impact of conflict. Alternatively, the transition for managers could be difficult and unwelcome. As we noted in the opening paragraphs of this book, Schering-Plough rejected an ADR approach in part to protect managers from that shift in responsibility, valuing the old system as most beneficial to the corporation.

Is there any evidence on this topic? Recently, Batt, Colvin, and Keefe examined the impact of a wide-ranging set of human resource practices on quit rates, including nonunion grievance procedures, peer review, and a range of participative practices.[17] They concluded that once other human resource practices are controlled for, the availability of nonunion grievance processes and peer review systems has only an insignificant impact on quit rates. They make the important point that research on dispute resolution systems cannot focus solely on the availability of such systems, but must also account for their use. Voice unused would seemingly have no impact on individual behavior or organizational performance.

There is even less evidence on the other hypothesized effects of conflict management features on individual and organizational behavior. Some organizations adopt conflict management systems to forestall unionism.[18] It is not clear whether they have been successful, given the very low likelihood of success of union organization efforts in general recently.

For the other secondary impacts listed in Table 8.3, there is no credible evidence that advances these effects beyond speculation.

More evaluation of the impact of conflict management systems is clearly needed, but these subjects are very difficult to isolate and treat.

EVALUATION OF CONFLICT MANAGEMENT SYSTEMS: FIVE CASE EXAMPLES

Over the past few years, as public policy has changed in favor of experimentation with conflict management, a number of opportunities to analyze those public policy changes comprehensively have arisen. These resulting analyses shed some light on conflict management as it is implemented in organizations. We look at five such examples of evaluation.

Workers' Compensation and Conflict Management

Beginning in the mid-1990s, a number of states adapted some of the principles of conflict management to their workers' compensation systems. For many, the relatively high administrative costs of the system had been seen as an important determinant of premium increases. A significant portion of those costs is related to the resolution of disputes through lengthy administrative processes. Both California and New York allowed an experimental exemption for the construction industry in situations where the relevant union and contractor groups were able to develop and administer their own dispute resolution system. In both states, provision was made in the law for the evaluation of the results of the adoption of conflict management systems in workers' compensation dispute resolution. In both California and New York, several large employer-union groups have adopted the system, and with quite impressive results. Other states have experimented with ADR in workers' compensation on a smaller scale. Seeber, Schmidle, and Smith include a comprehensive review of these experiments and their results in their evaluation of the New York system.[19]

For California and New York, universities were charged with the data collection and policy evaluation, and in both cases, comprehensive analyses were performed.[20] The California analysts chose the construction project as their unit of analysis, which limited the conclusions that could be drawn about the program. The results were impressive there, however, despite those limitations. Mediation and arbitration of disputes led to quicker resolution, and overall costs associated with the workers' compensation system were significantly reduced.

The New York evaluation reports a more comprehensive set of results. An experiment was set up there that allowed for before-and-after comparisons of the two dispute resolution systems.

Prior to the implementation of the ADR system, workers' compensation dispute resolution in New York was typical of such systems. Once an on-the-job injury occurred, disputes could arise over the course of medical treatment, appropriate return to work, and the level and permanence of benefits due the injured worker. All these disputes led to the possibility of a hearing before an administrative law judge, a system replete with significant delays in scheduling and decision making. Moreover, conflicts were built into the system, as workers typically retained an attorney who had an incentive to continue the case as long as possible.

While a number of different union-management ADR partnerships were established in New York, the evaluation primarily focused on Local 3 of the International Brotherhood of Electrical Workers and the New York City Electrical Contractors. This was due to the size of the group—about twenty-five thousand covered workers—and the availability of historical data. The conflict management system the parties created in collective bargaining included several features designed to speed up the dispute resolution process and resolve problems at the lowest level possible before they became disputes. The system created an ombudsperson position, to which an injured worker could turn at any time with any question regarding the system's treatment of his or her injury. The analysis of the log of the ombudsperson's call records indicated that a large majority of the contacts simply were requests for information. Unanswered, these requests might have quickly escalated into disputes. The system also included the creation of a nurse advocate, a position designed to assist the injured worker with any medical questions and to facilitate quick and appropriate treatment for the injury.

A mediation and arbitration process was set up to resolve disputes that could not be facilitated by the ombudsperson or the nurse advocate. In the Local 3 agreement, a single individual was appointed to mediate, and arbitrate if necessary, all disputes that arose. The system produced fundamental efficiency results. In an analysis of over two thousand injuries that occurred under the ADR system, not a single dispute went to the final arbitration step, and very few went to mediation. Under the traditional system, it had been routine for many disputes to be enmeshed in the administrative law system for years before resolution. Therefore, it was not surprising that there was a significant reduction in the time elapsed from injury to case closure of all disputes and claims.

In New York, the adoption of an ADR system was rated highly by those who participated. The combination of the ombudsperson, the nurse advocacy function, and a permanent neutral all worked to surface any problems quickly and resolve disputes that did arise.

A significant by-product of the New York workers' compensation experiment has been a reduction of the legal profession's role. Fewer injured workers hired lawyers under the ADR system than under the traditional one. This change has been met with disapproval, to put it mildly, by the workers' compensation bar. The claim has been made that legitimate disputes were being rushed to settlement, ultimately to the detriment of injured workers. This is not confirmed, though, by the participants in the experiment, who were quite satisfied that they had received appropriate justice under the ADR system.

There was no significant reduction in benefits received when comparisons were made for comparable injuries under the traditional and ADR systems. In California, the program was evaluated on an aggregated basis (as opposed to evaluating the effects on individual injured workers as was done in New York) and substantial net savings were realized, but it was not clear that those savings came in the form of reduced benefits.[21] In New York, the savings accrued by the program could be more directly attributed to the reduction in administrative costs, as well as the reduction in medical costs for dual treatment.

In sum, the workers' compensation ADR experiments have been quite successful in introducing conflict management system principles into one workplace arena. Since workers' compensation systems are governed by rigid, institutionalized sets of laws and procedures that differ from state to state, an extension of these system changes will be difficult to achieve. Nonetheless, the results of these two experiments are impressive.

Evaluation of the Massachusetts Commission Against Discrimination Alternative Dispute Resolution Program

The Massachusetts Commission Against Discrimination (MCAD) is fairly typical of public agencies charged with enforcing discrimination law. In 1995, faced with a growing caseload and a declining budget, the commission began to consider alternatives to its enforcement mechanisms then in place.[22] Urged on by the recommendations of the Commission on the Future of Worker-Management Relations and by Arnold Zack, an arbitrator and one of a group who had created the Due Process Protocol, the commission developed a set of ADR policy guidelines. They subcontracted with an outside agency, the American Arbitration Association (AAA), to administer the ADR program. The AAA was assigned the task of recruiting, training, and maintaining a roster of neutrals for the program.

The process allowed for the mediation and arbitration of claims against employers as an alternative to the normal litigation process. After an adequate number of experiences with the mediation and arbitration alternative, Thomas Kochan and his colleagues at MIT were assigned the task of evaluating the MCAD ADR program. Their evaluation allowed a comparison along a number of dimensions of interest to evaluators that go well beyond the usual findings of mediation and arbitration as a more efficient process of dispute resolution than litigation. Kochan and his colleagues gathered information on over 150 ADR and traditional cases by interviewing participants, including representative attorneys, neutrals, and responsible agency officials. Although there were the usual methodological problems in studies of this type with a lack of a truly appropriate control group, the study draws some interesting conclusions and certainly contributes to our understanding of conflict management systems.

Unlike most of the other evaluation studies, the evaluation of the MCAD experiment identified several institutional features of interest to designers of conflict management systems. They noted significant problems with the start of the program associated with a leadership change in MCAD and the difficulty of getting MCAD staff trained and familiar with the mediation and arbitration option. There was also some initial reluctance on the part of the staff to encourage use of the ADR option. Although the subcontracting of the administration and neutral work to AAA was controversial (there were other bidders on the project, including an agency of the state of Massachusetts), it proved to be beneficial. The AAA was credited with sustaining the program through the initial period of difficulties at MCAD and with playing an active role in promoting the program to possible users.

One dimension the MCAD researchers were able to evaluate was the question of why individuals chose to participate in the mediation process. Approximately one-third of the cases that were offered the ADR program chose to try it. The attorneys who responded overwhelmingly cited the refusal of the other side to agree to mediation, in fact, as the primary reason the program was not used. Of secondary importance was the refusal of their own clients. This response is typical as parties usually blame the other party for the refusal to go forward.[23]

Cases that did enter mediation were settled at a reasonably high rate. Sixty-three percent of the ADR cases were settled at mediation, while only 21 percent of comparable cases that remained in the MCAD process were settled. There were other instrumental measures of the efficiency of ADR as well. Case processing was rapid: an average of seventy-seven days to completion in the mediation process. Respondents were also asked whether they thought they saved money by using mediation, and both claimants and respondents suggested that they did. Although the numbers are merely estimates, and thus of little use as exact figures, they were of a size that indicates substantial savings from the use of ADR.

Another aspect of this study was the evaluation of the mediation process itself. Satisfaction with the mediator and the outcome of the process was high among the respondents. The vast majority of respondents (77 percent) said they would use the process again, perhaps the best test of the overall success of the process for resolving this type of dispute. Like the U.S. Postal Service REDRESS evaluation, Kochan and his colleagues attempted to assess mediator strategies for settlement. Unlike the REDRESS program, though, the MCAD system had no particular preference for type of mediator strategy in dispute resolution. Kochan and his colleagues found that mediators used a mix of facilitative and evaluative strategies, and the most successful mediators were those who mixed those two approaches throughout the mediation.

The MCAD experience is similar to the other conflict management systems we review here in that it is agency driven across individuals and organizations. Although this experience in design is not directly applicable to internal organizational design and implementation questions, it does provide useful insight into the results of the mediation process.

Evaluation of the U.S. Department of Labor Pilot Program for Enforcement Cases

In October 2000, the U.S. Department of Labor issued a research grant to Cornell University, acting on behalf of the Alliance for Education in Dispute Resolution (AEDR), to develop a pilot program to determine the most effective means of mediating enforcement disputes arising within the jurisdiction of the department.[24] The AEDR was formally established in 1999 to address two related needs: (1) the need to ensure that mediators, arbitrators, and the users of this service had the knowledge required to guarantee fairness and equity in the use of ADR and (2) the need for professional associations, universities, and other organizations in the dispute resolution field to work together to achieve desirable objectives. By the time of the Department of Labor award, the Alliance had established training programs in employment mediation and was well prepared to put together a roster of mediators for the Department of Labor pilot program.

During the start-up phase of the pilot program after the award of the grant, the Alliance designed an administrative structure for the project, developed an evaluation scheme (including survey instruments for the participants and mediators), and selected and trained a roster of mediators to handle the cases referred from the solicitor's office. This start-up phase took approximately four months; cases began to be mediated in March 2001.

The U.S. Department of Labor is responsible for administering and enforcing over 180 statutes, including the Fair Labor Standards Act, the Occupational Safety and Health Act, and the Family and Medical Leave Act. In general, a complaint arising under a particular statute is first handled by the relevant agency or regulatory body within the department. If the complaint is not successfully resolved at the agency level, it is referred to the solicitor's office for enforcement. The solicitor has the choice as to whether to pursue the case through the court system or, at the time of the initiation of the pilot project, through a myriad of adjudication procedures. The potential advantages of mediation had long been debated within the department, and in spring 2000, discussions began about what would eventually become the pilot program.

Three objectives were established for the pilot program: (1) to make trained mediators available to the solicitor's office for use in enforcement cases, (2) to evaluate the effectiveness and efficiency of the mediation process for these cases, and (3) to make recommendations to the Department of Labor on the continuation of the mediation program.

A roster of thirty-six mediators was assembled for the pilot program with the Department of Labor. The mediators on the roster were chosen from three sources, allowing for a natural experiment in the effectiveness of different types of mediators. The three sources were the graduates of the Alliance's mediator training programs, experienced mediators from the staff of the Federal Mediation and Conciliation Service, and members of the National Academy of Arbitrators with experience in employment mediation.

The early results of the pilot program indicate that it is successful, although not without problems. Like the MCAD program, it has had difficulty achieving a high level of acceptance among the parties. By March 2002, after one year of operation, only seventeen cases had been referred to the AEDR by the solicitor's office. There was a high mediation success rate of 75 percent for these cases neither settled nor withdrawn prior to the mediation. It appears that the initial results indicate the effectiveness of this program, although the final analysis will not be completed until the end of the pilot, in late 2003.

Measurement and Evaluation of REDRESS at the U.S. Postal Service

The implementation of the REDRESS program at the U.S. Postal Service (USPS) in January 1998 was the culmination of over a decade of experimentation with various forms of ADR.[25] An opportunity for extensive data collection, both before and after the implementation of the REDRESS program, has allowed Lisa Bingham and her colleagues at Indiana University to conduct the most comprehensive evaluation of a conflict management system to date. Moreover, the USPS system meets the criteria advanced earlier for a true conflict management system.

The REDRESS system was initiated as a pilot program within the postal service in three Florida cities in 1994. It was designed around an attempt to mediate employment disputes at the local level. After an initial evaluation by Indiana University, the USPS decided to roll out the program throughout the system in 1998. Evaluation efforts are ongoing, but a preliminary set of results was presented and published in a variety of forums and journals beginning in 2000.

The primary goals of the REDRESS program were to resolve equal employment opportunity complaints and to improve workplace climate throughout the postal service. The design of the final system included a commitment to transformative mediation. So not only was the USPS the largest organization ever to attempt to implement a comprehensive conflict management system, it was the only organization to commit itself to a specific theory of dispute resolution.

Transformative mediation is a specific approach to mediation that focuses almost exclusively on the relationship between the parties and requires a discipline on the part of the mediator not to offer specific substantive suggestions as to how to resolve the dispute. The mediator's job is to support opportunities within the mediation process for the parties to achieve recognition and empowerment.[26] In the USPS evaluation, mediators were judged on their ability to apply the transformative approach effectively to mediation. Approximately three thousand mediators were used initially, about half of them being ultimately retained as mediators in the REDRESS program.

In the report issued by Lisa Bingham and her colleagues, the first issue considered is whether the USPS has been successful in introducing and implementing the transformative, as opposed to facilitative or evaluative, model of mediation. Mediators were observed and measured against Bush and Folger's ten hallmarks of transformative mediation. In addition, participants were surveyed on exit from the mediation process. The mediators were found to be familiar with the transformative mediation process and able to apply it effectively. The participants were generally satisfied with the mediation process and the mediators.

On the more conventional side of measurement and evaluation, the analysts reported that approximately 68 percent of the disputes were at least partially resolved during mediation. Although the context within which to place a settlement rate is not an established methodological question, this settlement rate seems quite good, especially when combined with the results reported on formal discrimination complaint filing by USPS employees. The use of mediation should lead to fewer formal complaint filings as many of the (perhaps easier) cases are settled prior to the formal complaint process. In fact, the study shows that a significant decrease in filings occurred in the USPS during the initial implementation and use of the REDRESS program.

The REDRESS program also sought to change the workplace climate in the organization. Through analysis of before-and-after interview data from the initial pilot cities, the evaluators concluded that although the interviewees preferred mediation over formal Equal Employment Opportunity Commission complaint filing and the union grievance procedure, there had been no significant difference achieved in changing the workplace climate. Although this could be attributed to the longer time span necessary to alter the nature of a workplace (the program had only been in effect for two years), it also suggests that some of the indirect effects of conflict management may be much more difficult to achieve and could be confounded by other contributing factors.

Overall, the REDRESS program is probably the leading example of a large organization's attempt to implement a conflict management system and then put significant resources to bear on evaluation questions. The results are promising, and the program will be watched closely as it matures.

An Evaluation of the Equal Employment Opportunity Commission Mediation Program

The Equal Employment Opportunity Commission (EEOC) is responsible for the administration and enforcement of Title VII of the Civil Rights Act of 1964. The agency fulfills its mission by investigating charges filed by individuals or the EEOC itself. Although the EEOC initially had no power to enforce the law, in 1972 the EEO Act was amended to allow it to file suits in federal court to enforce Title VII. Although the agency was granted enforcement powers, it has continued to rely on its historical tradition and mission of conciliation as the preferred means of settlement in cases arising under Title VII.

The EEOC has always had a large backlog of cases and a long delay in enforcement proceedings. Under several chairs, beginning with Eleanor Holmes Norton in 1977, schemes have been put in place to reduce the backlog.[27] In 1991, the EEOC began to experiment with mediation as a means of reducing its significant caseload. The initial success of this program led to the creation of a task force on the expansion of the use of mediation throughout the system.[28] By the beginning of 1998, each of the fifty field offices had a mediation program in place.

The EEOC program rates all of its potential cases that it might pursue to trial on a three-point scale. The program assigns those to mediation with some cause established and a possibility for settlement prior to trial. The charging party in those cases is made aware of the availability of voluntary mediation, and if the party chooses it, the regular process is halted while the mediation takes place. In 1999, a group of academics assigned the task of evaluating the program generated a sample of over thirty-two hundred completed surveys from mediation participants, with a relatively equal number of charging and responding parties.[29] The sample was representative of the EEOC's caseload during the period surveyed of cases initiated between March 1 and July 31, 2000.

Raw satisfaction with the mediation program was very high. Over 90 percent of both charging and responding parties said that they would be willing to participate in the mediation program again. The parties viewed the mechanics of the program as fair, reporting that they had adequate information about the process and the mediators prior to the mediation session. The fundamental elements of procedural justice were in place, with the parties responding that they had a full opportunity to present their case in mediation.

The mediators came from two sources: internal EEOC staff mediators and external contract mediators, including staff from the Federal Mediation and Conciliation Service. The evaluators did not report on the comparative effectiveness of the two groups of mediators, but in general satisfaction with the mediators was very high. The participants rated the mediators as helpful, neutral, and fair.

Not surprisingly, satisfaction with the outcomes was lower than satisfaction with the process. One of the few studies available that has examined questions related to perceptions of distributive justice, this study measured satisfaction with the outcomes of the mediation process. Satisfaction levels were related to the perception of whether the award was skewed in one direction or the other, with the party perceiving itself as the relative loser being less satisfied with the process.

CONCLUSION

Most of the evaluation research conducted in the assessment of conflict management systems has narrowly focused on measures of efficiency and effectiveness. Even in that vein, we know little more than levels of settlement, rates of settlement, and satisfaction with the processes. The studies that have been conducted, although well conceived and executed, have tended to focus on their specific evaluation and have not successively built knowledge based on the previous work. This is a young field, however, and perhaps it is too much to ask to expect more of the early, path-breaking studies.

We have looked at the evaluation of conflict resolution systems from a number of different perspectives. At this point in the development of research in this field, research is spotty, and lines of inquiry are not particularly well developed. The adoption of conflict management systems by organizations has proceeded largely in the absence of hard evidence suggesting that the decision to do so makes sense. Only the future will tell whether the rather high expectations for the performance of these systems will be met.

Part Three

The Future of Conflict Management Systems

Chapter Nine

Barriers to the Growth of Conflict Management Systems

In our earlier discussion of the important reasons that major U.S. corporations do not use ADR (in Chapter Three), we noted that the difficulty of negotiating ADR agreements with reluctant adversaries appears to be the principal impediment. Although we believe in the merits of ADR and share many of the convictions of ADR's most ardent champions, the research we have conducted suggests that there is nothing inevitable about the ultimate triumph of ADR. In some of the organizations we have studied, in fact, the use of ADR may have already peaked, and a return to more traditional approaches to conflict management may have begun.

The research we have conducted underscores our belief that the future of ADR in U.S. corporations depends on the extent to which ADR policies and practices become institutionalized—that is, whether they become a more or less permanent part of the culture of the organization. The future is uncertain, of course, but it is entirely possible that the worst fears of ADR's champions—and the fondest hopes of its opponents—may come to pass: instead of advancing steadily into the future, ADR may find itself in retreat. Because we personally believe the advantages of ADR significantly outweigh its disadvantages, we would regret such a development. As social scientists, however, we need to report the truth as we find it. We hope our research will serve to strengthen the resolve of ADR's proponents rather than give comfort to its opponents.

In this chapter we expand on the discussion in Chapter Three to a consideration of the barriers deterring organizations from establishing workplace conflict management systems. It may be difficult to institutionalize either ADR policies or conflict management systems, but our research and our experience suggest that systems, if properly designed and implemented, have greater staying power than do mere policies and procedures. We discuss in detail several barriers we have observed that prevent the spread of conflict management systems. We believe that unless these barriers are lowered or removed experimentation will not become institutionalized.

THE LOGIC OF CONFLICT MANAGEMENT

There is a fundamental logic to the adoption of conflict management systems that seems to be accepted by organizations moving in that direction. That same logical chain is treated with skepticism by many organizations as they debate the merits of conflict management systems. The accepting organizations believe that some workplace conflict is inevitable as those with different priorities clash in a natural way within organizations. These organizations recognize also that no matter how extensive systematic checks and balances might be within organizations, there are individuals who discriminate, treat employees poorly, and in general are a source of conflict.

Other organizations, for reasons that we have not detected and cannot yet explain, seem wedded to the notion that when conflicts arise, they are an aberration. Working through extensive training and other efforts meant to eliminate conflict and errors, these organizations seem to believe in the triumph of hope over experience. That is, they act as if the real investments should be made to rid the organization of conflict rather than to treat its results. There is no real reconciliation of these two points of view. Organizations seem to differ in their cultural outlook and view of conflict.

A second point in the chain of the logic of conflict management is that employees have rights, both legal and those granted by the organization or as a result of collective bargaining. All organizations seem to recognize these rights as potential and legitimate sources of conflict; they do not seem to differ on this point. However, conflict is treated as a source of information in some organizations; although these organizations do not welcome disputes over rights, they treat them as informative and use them to repair the organization.

The final point in the logic of conflict management is that conflict costs money. Significant resources can be devoted to conflict and the eventual disputes that arise from it. There is no dispute among organizations about this, merely differences in the action that occurs as a result of it. Some organizations see this logic—that conflicts are inevitable, employees have rights that are at the root of those conflicts, and those conflicts cost money—and believe that conflict management is the best way to reconcile that chain of events to an organization's advantage.

Other organizations see those three points as not necessarily interlocked and believe that each of them can be treated separately and distinctly. Among these organizations, some that we have studied attempt to minimize or eliminate the sources of conflict. Others are reluctant to grant employees rights or try to minimize those they do have. And others try to minimize the costs of conflict by using traditional methods of litigation cost management. Thus, there is clearly a barrier to the extension of conflict management systems that results solely from the organizational view of conflict and its impact.

STAKEHOLDER MOTIVATIONS AND OBJECTIVES

Numerous groups have vital stakes in the design and implementation of fair and effective dispute resolution systems. The motives and objectives of these stakeholder groups frequently serve as barriers to the adoption of ADR techniques and conflict management systems. In addition to employers and employees, the stakeholders include government agencies and unions, civil rights organizations, members of the bar, arbitrators and mediators and the organizations that represent them, and others. And society itself has a critical interest in workplace dispute resolution systems because of the close and obvious link between these systems and its interest in achieving equity and efficiency in the operation of its workplace institutions. There is general, if often tentative, support across most stakeholder groups for the use of dispute resolution systems in employment relations. The motives underlying the stakeholder groups' support, however, differ across these various groups and are not necessarily compatible.

The challenge in establishing fair and effective dispute resolution systems is to take account of the sometimes compatible but often conflicting objectives of the various stakeholders. There are many pitfalls for organizations that are not able to overcome all of the potential barriers from stakeholder groups with significant interests in conflict management systems. Systems can be put at risk by ignoring stakeholder interests and can be strengthened by taking those interests into consideration at an early stage.

In this section, we examine the motives and objectives of four key stakeholder groups, two internal and two external to the organization: employees, unions, public agencies, and organizations representing neutrals.

Employees

Of all the stakeholder groups, employees are the most difficult to read because, unlike unions or governmental agencies, they have no formalized voice through which to express their displeasure or support with the course of dispute management within an organization. Thus, this section is probably the most speculative of this chapter.

We have repeatedly emphasized in this book the value and desirability of including employee voice in the design process of conflict management system development. Organizations that have proceeded in the design of their systems in this fashion often report significant employee buy-in and acceptance of the resulting process. Organizations that do not include employee groups in their design process are never quite sure what their employees truly believe until the system is available for use.

We have had some organizations express curiosity, and fear on some level, about the launch of their new systems. They are not quite sure whether there will be a flood of employee complaints, confirming their worst fears about the availability of a new opportunity for complaint, or whether, even worse, no one will step forward to use the system. Organizations that have not included employees in their design process are unsure as to how to interpret either of these behaviors.

Employees may have good reason to mistrust the motivations of organizations that create conflict management systems. While we have focused much of this book on those organizations that have introduced conflict management with employees in mind, we are left with the bottom-line motivation of the Fortune 1000. They report the adoption of ADR techniques to save time and money, not to make things better for employees. Add to that what some see as the specter of predispute arbitration agreements, and we can be left with a recipe for employee mistrust of the system. There are no good survey data, either within or across organizations, on this question for employees other than the surveys reported in Chapter Eight on the evaluation of conflict management systems.

The main point here is that employees can be a significant barrier to the effective implementation of a conflict management system. Organizations that fail to consult them in the design and implementation phases of system construction may not have a system that employees perceive as fair and effective. The effect of this will not work to the organization's advantage.

Unions

Unions have viewed dispute resolution systems with some skepticism. Many fear that employers often institute workplace dispute resolution systems as a means of avoiding unionization. Because most employers will not freely admit to antiunion motives, hard evidence regarding this concern is not available. There is, however, sufficient anecdotal evidence to suggest that labor's fears are justified in some cases.

Nevertheless, many unions support the design and implementation of fair and equitable dispute resolution systems. They believe such systems are capable of protecting the best interests of both their organizations and the employees they represent and can be entirely compatible with a collective bargaining agreement. Many unions recognize that certain types of employee complaints cannot readily be handled through traditional collective bargaining channels. Employee concerns ranging from the quality of their relations with supervisors and fellow employees to the adequacy of their computers and office equipment are usually matters that are not easily handled through the grievance procedure, for example. Some unions have discovered that employee complaints that fall outside the purview of the mandatory topics of bargaining may be addressed effectively through a dispute resolution system designed jointly by the parties. So some unions have embraced ADR with enthusiasm, not only valuing its potential benefits for their members but also recognizing that ADR systems can extend the authority and influence of a union into areas normally considered to be management prerogatives.

More significant, perhaps, is the manner in which unions and employers handle employee allegations of statutory violations. In some union-management relationships, many, if not all, statutory claims are channeled through the grievance and arbitration procedures contained in the collective bargaining agreement. But an increasing number of unions and employers have established dispute resolution procedures for certain types of statutory claims that stand outside the collective bargaining contract. For example, some unions and employers have established special procedures to handle sexual harassment complaints. Also, employee assistance programs, established to deal with employees suffering from alcoholism, drug abuse, and related problems, sometimes contain their own dispute resolution procedures, another form of ADR that can coexist with conventional grievance procedures.

Public Agencies

As Bingham and Chachere have noted, "Adoption of ADR in the public sector is somewhat different from the private sector. In the federal sector, Congress enacted the Administrative Dispute Resolution Act (ADRA) in 1990 to spur agencies to consider using ADR. In a 1994 study [by the General Accounting Office], 31% of federal agencies had some form of ADR in place for employee complaints. By 1996 the federal agency rate had increased to 49%."[1] In the mid-1990s, a task force appointed by the secretary of the U.S. Department of Labor examined employment relations in state and local government and concluded that in some respects, the public sector led the private sector in the adoption of ADR systems: "Overall, it appear[s] that the public workplace might be more receptive to [ADR] systems, particularly to setting them up in a manner that protect[s] the fact and appearance of neutrality and independence, and providing employees' access to the court if they felt their case was meritorious or did not choose to use the ADR system."[2]

A recent survey has shown "that the vast majority of cabinet and non-cabinet-level agencies were experimenting with the use of mediation in personnel and employment disputes." Very few federal agencies, however, have made use of arbitration.[3] Yet apparently the rate of adoption of ADR procedures in some public jurisdictions has been slower than the rate of adoption in major U.S. corporations. Despite the requirements of the ADRA, some federal agencies have lagged behind major private sector employers in part because federal workers have had for many years "multiple avenues for redress" of their complaints and grievances.[4] Many types of grievances in the federal sector are adjudicated by the Merit Systems Protection Board, established by the Civil Service Reform Act of 1978, and some federal sector managers have been reluctant to establish ADR systems that would constitute yet another avenue for redress for the employees of their agencies.

Surveys suggest that the adoption of ADR procedures and systems by public sector agencies and their unions in the United

States apparently quickened in the 1990s, spurred on by various statutes and regulations and frequently supported by elected officials generally motivated by the same set of factors operating in the private sector.

Neutrals and Their Organizations

Obviously the professional organizations that represent arbitrators, mediators, and other workplace neutrals have a vital stake in the evolution of employment dispute resolution systems. In the United States, these organizations include the National Academy of Arbitrators, the Association for Conflict Resolution, the American Arbitration Association, and the Dispute Resolution Section of the American Bar Association.

The controversies surrounding the rise of employment arbitration have generated intense debates within the National Academy of Arbitrators, which has responded in a preliminary fashion to the changing realities of employment relations through its endorsement of the Due Process Protocol for Mediation and Arbitration of Statutory Disputes Arising out of the Employment Relationship. As noted earlier, the Due Process Protocol was developed by a task force consisting of representatives from the academy, the Labor and Employment Law Section of the American Bar Association, the American Arbitration Association, the Society of Professionals in Dispute Resolution, the U.S. Federal Mediation and Conciliation Service, the National Employment Lawyers Association, and the American Civil Liberties Union. The task force debated the question of the mandatory predispute arbitration agreement as a condition of employment but did not "achieve consensus on this difficult issue" other than to agree that such agreements should only be knowingly made.

The task force did agree on a set of "standards of exemplary due process," however, including the right of employees in arbitration and mediation cases to be represented by a spokesperson of their own choosing, employer reimbursement of at least a portion of employees' attorney fees, especially for lower-paid employees, and adequate employee access to "all information reasonably relevant to mediation and/or arbitration of their claims." The Due Process Protocol also calls for the use of qualified and impartial arbitrators and mediators drawn from rosters that are diversified on the basis of gender, ethnicity, background, and experience. To guarantee an adequate supply of qualified neutrals, the protocol calls for "the development of a training program to educate existing and potential labor and employment mediators and arbitrators."[5]

Concerned that unfair procedures in employment arbitration and the involuntary predispute exclusion of employees from access to the courts and regulatory agencies were tainting the image of all workplace arbitration, the academy went on record at its Fiftieth Annual Meeting in Chicago, in May 1997, as being opposed to the mandatory arbitration of the statutory rights of employees as a condition of employment where such schemes preclude recourse to the courts and statutory tribunals. Recognizing at the same meeting that such arbitrations are nevertheless lawful, as confirmed by *Gilmer v. Interstate/Johnson Lane Corp.*, the academy promulgated guidelines to assist its members in conducting employment arbitrations that involve the adjudication of statutory rights. The guidelines strive to ensure fairness and due process, giving the fullest scope to the procedural protections, evidentiary burdens, and remedies available under the statutes themselves. To further its interest in protecting the integrity of the arbitration process, the academy has also intervened as amicus curiae in a number of cases before the courts involving the application and refinement of *Gilmer*.[6]

LEADERSHIP AND THE UNCERTAINTIES ABOUT THE EFFECTS OF CONFLICT MANAGEMENT

A different barrier to the spread of conflict management systems is a result of the paucity of analysis of existing systems. Leaders of organizations often find themselves confronting a dilemma caused by a lack of information. Organizations often have champions of conflict management systems, who believe in the logic of conflict management, have often benchmarked other systems in shaping their own, and have pushed their organization in the direction they believe best. How effective those champions are in spreading their beliefs to other key figures in the organization often determines whether the system will survive their departure. The lack of analysis of the performance of systems in general gives champions trouble making their case to others in their organizations and to the organization's leadership. Thus, leaders either accept the views of the champion or, more likely, ask for the results of the systems.

This is where the lack of evaluation tends to break down the institutionalization and spread of conflict management systems. Conflict management systems, often implemented to save money, have real costs associated with their adoption. Training, monitoring, resolution, and system maintenance are all real, observable costs of conflict management systems. Benefits, however, tend toward the speculative and immeasurable. Leaders of organizations, even if they believe in conflict management, are often faced with going forward in the absence of any hard evidence about the benefits of the system.

In addition, there is some uncertainty over the legal landscape surrounding arbitration of employment disputes. Although the fundamental issue seems to have been resolved in the Supreme Court, the details of what the courts will find as appropriate due process leave many systems that include arbitration in some doubt. Even the systems that do not include arbitration, but attempt to resolve statutory claims through mediation, leave organizational leadership with some uncertainty. What proportion of statutory claims can be expected to be resolved short of leaving the system for the courts? High mediation success rates are common, but even in the most successful circumstances, mediation will not resolve all statutory claims. Thus, even with a well-functioning conflict management system, the organization may still face the very courts and administrative agency processes it sought to avoid. And some of the more difficult cases may be the ones that exit the system.

Given all this uncertainty surrounding conflict management systems, it takes an organization with strong and committed leadership, viewing conflict management system success over the long run, to sustain its commitment to conflict management. Not surprisingly, given the short-term outlook of many organizations and the short-term tenure of many champions and other leaders of those same organizations, these uncertainties provide an important barrier to the creation and spread of conflict management systems.

DOES EXPERIMENTATION BECOME INSTITUTIONALIZED?

We have described a number of examples of ADR policies and systems in various stages of development and formality. We have difficulty concluding, however, that many of the corporations we have studied have reached the stage of institutionalizing their ADR systems, even those we include in the prevent category. By institutionalization, we mean a system or function that has become a more or less permanent part of the fabric of the organization in the same sense as functions such as marketing, finance, human resources, and the counsel's office itself. ADR policies and practices are relatively recent, developed largely in response to certain shifts in the environment of the corporation. The emergence of corporate conflict management systems is an even more recent phenomenon.

When we began our investigation, we expected to find the diffusion of ADR experiments across firms, particularly firms within the same industry. We also expected to find that a corporation's adoption of ADR techniques for one type of dispute would lead to the adoption of those techniques for other types of disputes. For example, if a corporation had successfully used ADR in consumer disputes, we expected it to use ADR in employment and environmental disputes. In other words, we hypothesized the existence of a corporatewide conflict management strategy within the organization.

Others have studied the phenomenon of diffusion of human resource practices across and within organizations.[7] That research seems to suggest that there are many paths to change in workplace practices and that it will take some time for new models to become institutionalized, even after the new practices themselves are widely accepted. We are in an early phase of observation about conflict management systems. Each of the systems we have studied seems to present unique solutions to unique organizational issues. There is enough similarity in these systems, however, that we might conclude that after a longer period of time, the features that diverge from one another will disappear and there will be a standard model of conflict management. There is no guarantee that will occur, though, and the diffusion of conflict management processes may not proceed in any discernable pattern. It is certainly too early in the development of these systems to be able to reach conclusions about them.

In fact, we did not observe a high degree of diffusion in our research—certainly not to the extent we expected. Many of the corporations we studied engage in a considerable amount of bench-marking, keeping close tabs on the conflict management practices and strategies of other companies, particularly in the same indus-try. But benchmarking does not necessarily lead to diffusion; indeed, it can deter diffusion if the corporation doing the bench-marking concludes that another corporation's experience with a particular practice has been less than satisfactory.

Another hypothesis we had when we began our research con-cerned the relationship between a company's use of ADR and workplace systems and its experience in collective bargaining. We assumed, perhaps naively, that companies that had used mediation and arbitration under collective bargaining would have a favorable view of those processes and be more inclined to adopt those processes as part of their ADR programs. In other words, we hypothesized there would be a positive spillover from collective bargaining to other aspects of a firm's employment relations. Indeed, in our 1997 survey, we discovered a fairly strong positive relationship between the degree to which a corporation was union-ized and its reliance on ADR techniques. The most unionized cor-porations also tended to be the most pro-ADR companies.

In our field research, however, we came to realize that unionization and the use of ADR do not always go hand in hand. In some companies, experience with mediation and arbitration under collective bargaining has deterred the more general use of ADR. One of the respondents in our Fortune 1000 survey told us, "My company has had so many bad experiences in grievance arbitration cases that I wouldn't want to use arbitration with our non-union employees."[8]

At times a corporation's adoption of ADR policies seems idiosyncratic, dependent on the values and inclinations of the CEO, the evangelizing of an effective champion, or some other factor unique to the corporation. The variance in conflict or litigation management within a corporation can be quite astonishing. The employment counsel might be an ardent ADR champion, but the firm's chief litigator might be anti-ADR. Of course, variance in conflict management within a corporation can be a perfectly rational response to differences in the corporation's objectives and values in different types of disputes.

There are many possible explanations for this lack of institutionalization of ADR, and we explore a few of the hypotheses we believe have the most credibility. Consider, first, the environmental factors that appear to have brought about the rise of ADR. Over the past twenty years, changes in these factors all served to buttress the business case for ADR, but all of these factors could potentially move in the opposite direction, thus undercutting the case for ADR. For example, global competition intensified dramatically over the past two or three decades, but it is not certain that global competition will have the same influence on corporate strategy in the future that it had in the past. Given the increasingly chronic weakness of the Japanese and other Asian economies, global competition may not be the same spur to corporate action that it once was. Also, government regulation, particularly of employment relations, grew dramatically in the 1960s and 1970s, helping to fuel the alleged litigation explosion. Clearly the Bush administration is not disposed to favor the further regulation of U.S. business. If market competition and government regulation have reached a plateau, two important factors that brought about the rise of ADR will no longer be significant.

We noted in Chapter Two that some scholars questioned the validity of the litigation explosion. By most measures, the upward trend in litigation probably came to an end in the early 1990s, and caseloads in most courts have leveled off. Ironically, the success of ADR may be partly responsible for that, and although tort reform has not been enacted at the federal level, it has advanced steadily at the state level. (Efforts in Congress in 2001 to pass a patients' bill of rights giving patients the right to sue their health maintenance organizations might have triggered a new wave of litigation.) The courts themselves, at both the federal and state levels, have made strenuous efforts to introduce internal reforms, and most now have established ADR programs. If there is any prospect of a litigation implosion and if the courts succeed in improving their management of litigation, the impetus for corporations to institutionalize ADR will be substantially diminished.

As unlikely as it may seem, some of the employment trends that have favored the development of ADR could be reversed as well. For example, the reemergence of the union movement as a significant institution in the private sector would almost certainly decrease corporate interest in ADR programs. Also, it seems clear that we are at or near the end of the expansion of individual employment rights through state and federal legislation. Any or all of these changes would make ADR marginally less attractive to many corporations.

There are other factors within the corporation that deter the institutionalization of ADR programs and systems. Consider, for example, the phenomenon of the precipitating event: some of our interviewees noted that the further into the past a precipitating event receded, the less compelling that event was as a factor motivating the corporation's development of an ADR program. To the extent that the creation of an ADR program is the corporation's short-term response to a crisis, the foundation for institutionalizing such a program remains tenuous. Moreover, as we noted earlier, we have found very little evidence of the diffusion of ADR policies and practices across dispute areas within firms. Nearly all of the firms we studied confine the use of ADR to certain types of disputes. Conflict management systems of the type we have described in this book are most frequently used in employment relations. They are almost never used for—and indeed would have little application to—other types of disputes. (A conflict management system might arguably be useful in customer, client, and vendor relationships, but it is difficult to imagine the use of a system as we have defined it in financial disputes.) When we asked our respondents whether their corporation planned to apply an ADR strategy they were using in one dispute area to a different dispute area, most said they did not consider it a possibility. Indeed, we cannot cite a single example of a corporation that employs a truly integrated and consistent strategy toward all disputes it potentially faces. On the basis of our case studies, we conclude that the vast majority of corporations favor dispute management over conflict management.

Most U.S. corporations that have adopted ADR in one form or another have done so because they hoped it would save time and money. In our survey of the Fortune 1000, as we noted in Chapter Three, about 80 percent of the respondents told us that saving time or saving money was the primary reason the corporation had used ADR. There is in fact very little hard evidence that corporations actually do save time and money by using ADR, however. Furthermore, it is not clear to us that many corporations are even gathering the information necessary to make a cost-benefit analysis. We pressed our respondents to tell us what they were doing in this regard, and most gave us vague responses or admitted they were not doing much. Some corporations apparently do have internal tracking systems (Alcoa and the FMC Corporation come to mind), but we were consistently surprised at the lack of rigorous data collection and analysis of ADR within corporations.

The lack of analysis is in part a consequence of the fact that there is no accepted paradigm in the dispute resolution field for conducting the analysis. The task of developing appropriate metrics in dispute resolution has not yet been undertaken, and until it is, the success (or failure) of ADR will be problematic.

We noted the important role that champions have played in developing ADR systems within corporations. In the course of our research, we have met many champions, and we admire almost all of them. It often takes courage to be a champion within an organization. But the critical role played by a champion works against the institutionalization of an ADR program. Time and again, we encountered champions who had become frustrated and discouraged, and some had simply given up. Any movement that relies heavily on the heroic efforts of individual champions is a fragile movement indeed.

Nevertheless, ADR certainly has become institutionalized in some settings. For example, it seems to be a continuing and integral part of a number of firms in the construction industry and in the securities industry. Tentatively, we conclude that institutionalization is most likely to occur in the following situations:

- The corporation faces, on a regular and continuing basis, a large number of the same type of dispute.
- The disputes do not typically involve high stakes in terms of money or principle.
- The disputes involve the interpretation and application of contracts rather than statutes.
- It becomes indisputably clear to the corporation (even if it does not conduct a concrete cost-benefit analysis) that the time and money saved from using ADR rather than litigation is highly significant.

We do not maintain that these conditions are the only ones that can lead to institutionalization, only that institutionalization is more likely when these conditions are present.

Our research has led us to at least one conclusion we did not anticipate. Contrary to much of the popular literature and perceptions regarding ADR and somewhat surprising to us, we do not believe that the ADR movement has achieved the critical mass necessary to institutionalize it within most large businesses or other organizations. Although the use of ADR procedures by U.S. corporations is very widespread, support for ADR policies in many corporations is confined (often to one or two champions) and frequently has not penetrated the upper reaches of management. Unless ADR becomes more embedded in corporate culture, the ADR movement is likely to stall or even retreat in the coming years. Specifically, our research has revealed four major points.

First, in most organizations, ADR is a reactive response rather than a strategic choice. Our corporate survey led us to believe that a growing number of managers supported ADR policies and were creating systems as part of a larger strategy of conflict management. In the case studies we conducted, however, we found that the use of ADR was nearly always an ad hoc response to a specific, repetitive set of disputes faced by a business.

Second, the rise of ADR in business in the United States was the consequence of changes in a set of environmental factors (such as the perceived litigation explosion), and a reversal of direction of these factors could very well lead to a decline in the use of ADR. Although ADR has been institutionalized in a handful of corporations, it has not become part of the corporation's standing policies in the vast majority. Without further institutionalization, ADR may prove to be a transitory phase rather than a permanent shift in corporate conflict management. Our survey results and our on-site interviews revealed that a number of societal forces had developed over the past twenty years or so that have strongly encouraged businesses to consider ADR as a dispute management tool. More recently, many of those forces have lost their potency and may even be moving in an opposite direction. ADR has not taken such a strong hold in U.S. corporations that it cannot easily be abandoned if the environmental reasons for using it disappear.

Third, it is important to distinguish conceptually between dispute management and conflict management. Our research demonstrates that dispute management overwhelms conflict management as the dominant mode of corporate behavior. When we began our field research, we expected to find corporations moving beyond the use of ADR to manage disputes toward the establishment of conflict management systems, which in theory have the purpose of preventing or eliminating conflicts before they rise to the level of explicit disputes. In fact, with the exception of the handful of corporations noted earlier, we have found almost no such behavior on the part of U.S. business.

Fourth, our corporate survey revealed that companies used ADR for instrumental purposes. That is, typically corporate managers and lawyers valued ADR because they believed its use served larger corporate objectives. Almost all of our interviewees were attracted to ADR because of its potential to save time and money through more efficient dispute resolution. Almost none of them supported the use of ADR because they thought it was a fairer and more just means of resolving disputes. On balance, our corporate respondents believe conventional litigation provides better procedural safeguards than ADR does, but they were willing to forgo these safeguards if there was a reasonable chance of saving time and money.

We do not have a crystal ball that allows us to predict with certainty the direction ADR will take in the future. We merely want to note that our analytical model suggests that ADR in the corporate community may grow in significance or may decline, depending on the direction taken by the environmental and organizational factors we believe determine the corporation's choice of a conflict management strategy. Our friends in the ADR movement may find our analysis dismaying. We hope that rather than being dismayed, they will resolve to make an even more strenuous effort to achieve their objectives. In the end, we conclude that we are some distance from institutionalization of conflict management systems.

CONCLUSION

There are extensive barriers to the future growth of conflict management systems. When the four problems we described in this chapter are taken together, it seems clear to us that we are at somewhat of a crossroads in the development of conflict management in organizations. The logic of conflict management will not be accepted or spread further without some evidence as to its fundamental truth. Leaders of organizations clearly need to be convinced, and the uncertainties surrounding conflict management systems minimized or removed, before those leaders are likely to push development further. Stakeholders need to be reassured and convinced that the benefits of conflict management do not accrue completely to the organization but rather that conflict management may be of benefit to everyone. And finally, institutionalization of systems within organizations needs to occur before the early experimental efforts can be reversed by changes in leadership or the lack of short-term evidence as to the efficacy of conflict management systems.

Chapter Ten

The Future of Workplace
Dispute Resolution

In the first chapter of this book, we presented a plan for discussing our research on why conflict management has become an important subject for organizations and how these organizations have approached the implementation of conflict management systems. In this final chapter, we will address the question of where the field is going. We will explore what we think are the long-term trends affecting workplace dispute resolution, make some predictions for future organizational use of these systems, and comment on the effect of the external environment on conflict management.

We believe that the long scope of economic and organizational history in the United States suggests that there will be continued privatization of dispute resolution in our society, including the privatization of employment dispute resolution. Although every set of employee–employer disputes that has arisen has been met first with regulation, the parties ultimately have sought to resolve disputes themselves, in private, and policymakers have encouraged them to do so.

When unions first gained strength in the latter quarter of the nineteenth century, for example, employers commonly turned to the courts for injunctions and penalties rather than to negotiate. This strategy was often successful, but it usually served only to forestall negotiations. The policies of the United States supported those negotiations, first through the Railway Labor Act in 1926, then through the National Labor Relations Act in 1935, and eventually through various other state laws in the 1960s and 1970s. This policy was reinforced by the deferral of the courts to arbitration and the support for private negotiations of the mediation services set up by the federal government and various states. Thus, the first privatization of employment disputes was collective bargaining.

The second privatization arena was that of individual employment rights, and it is now less than forty years since the federal government's initial foray into that area. It is unlikely that when the U.S. Congress passed the Equal Pay Act in 1963 anyone thought that it would be the first of a flood of individual employment rights created by the federal government. Not long after that, however, efforts began to try to move toward private systems for the resolution of those disputes and the disputes arising from all of the laws that followed. The deregulation of whole segments of the economy has also furthered the trend toward the use of ADR to resolve disputes formerly heard in federal courts. Even the judiciary has supported this trend with court-annexed ADR programs for a wide variety of disputes.

The conclusion we draw from the longstanding trend toward private dispute resolution, combined with the more recent move in that direction, is that the conflict management systems we have detailed in this book are probably just the next wave of privatization. The area up for debate is not the direction of the trend but rather the pace at which it will proceed. It seems clear to us that while there might be minor setbacks and there are barriers to further growth (as we suggested in Chapter Nine), these systems will continue to be newly implemented in organizations and will be more widely accepted in the coming years.

In the remainder of this chapter, we discuss what that continued growth means. We present some predictions about how we think these systems will develop within organizations and then examine the impact of the external environment on the growth of conflict management. Although we see a somewhat more negative outlook for the rapid growth of conflict management, we believe the environmental difficulties will provide only a small barrier, or at worst a short step backward, in the longstanding historical movement toward private dispute resolution.

ANTICIPATED CHANGES TO THE ACCEPTANCE AND ROLE OF WORKPLACE SYSTEMS

We anticipate changes in the size and range of organizations that create workplace systems, the institutionalization of these systems, and the integration of the systems with other corporate values and processes. We believe that the borders of the United States will be a border to dispute resolution systems as well. We think that global organizations will continue to customize dispute resolution regionally or even country by country if necessary.

Broadening Acceptance

We believe that there will be increased acceptance of workplace systems in a broader range of organizations. For the next few years, this trend will occur mainly with larger employers because they are the organizations that commonly have the precipitating event that triggers the concept. These triggering events, described in Chapter Seven, include an internal crisis, a clear threat (such as union organizing), or burdensome litigation. The resources needed to build and manage workplace systems are also found mainly in larger organizations. As we discussed in Chapter Four, our field research placed organizations in three categories of conflict strategy: contend, settle, and prevent. Over the next ten years, we believe that employers in the settle category will move into the prevent category and begin to become proactive in managing conflict.

We also believe that workplace systems will be accepted increasingly in midsized organizations, a trend motivated by an increasing recognition that a workplace system is simply good for business. Midsized employers will recognize that organizational conflict can be a source of creativity and productivity and that workplace systems effectively channel such conflict to constructive ends. Midsized employers have the same core interests in resolving conflict as do large employers. For these reasons, we expect workplace systems to migrate into midsized employers.

We do not expect formal workplace systems to be accepted into smaller organizations, mainly because of cost: systems require more ongoing resources than smaller firms feel they can afford. Most organizations do not hire a dedicated human resource professional until they reach at least two hundred employees. An employer without a human resource function will not focus on workplace systems.

There is, however, the potential for one exception: organizations working with professional employer organizations (PEOs), private organizations that provide human resource administrative support to small employers. In some cases, the PEO employs the administrative staff. For example, PEOs will contract with a doctor's practice to employ and supervise the clerical or nursing staff. The PEOs are owned and managed by highly progressive human resource experts who understand the potential of a workplace system. In these situations, we expect to see elements of conflict resolution features used in smaller organizations.

Will Workplace Systems Go Global?

Our field research indicated that no employers have adopted workplace systems for their international operations. Some have considered it and chosen not to do so. There are many reasons for this. First, the precipitating events that typically trigger the creation of workplace systems, such as litigation, are often unique to the United States. Second, the laws of some other countries already provide many of the options inherent in a workplace system. Most European countries, for example, provide both statutory avenues of appeal in cases of discharge and mandatory workers' councils. Third, there is a perception that global dispute resolution is different from, and in some cases behind, dispute resolution in the United States. Specifically, the pro-employee laws of many other countries focus on a rights-based orientation. There is a perception that foreign employees would not accept a model that encourages self-initiative and offers significant freedom of choice as to rights-versus interest-based solutions. Because of these legal and cultural differences, we do not foresee workplace systems being broadly implemented in international operations.

Workplace Systems Will Become Institutionalized

The general commitment to ADR in organizations has historically been fragmented at best. As we have described in prior chapters, our research established that conflict resolution strategies are valued in some functions but not others. Mediation may be used in employment litigation but not in product liability. Arbitration may be used in consumer disputes but not in environmental disputes. Even in the same law department, some attorneys embrace ADR and some resist it. Overall, ADR has been very slow to become institutionalized in organizations.

We believe that conflict management systems will become institutionalized in the future, however, by employers that recognize their value and remain committed to their credibility. By this, we mean that the system will become a universal part of the workplace culture, that its success will be firmly accepted by all parts of the workforce, and that commitment to the system will not waiver through the passing of leadership and tougher financial times.

This will occur for many reasons. First, although a lot of existing workplace systems were built through the efforts of an internal champion, occasionally, corporate commitment to its workplace system has faltered when the champion has moved on to other opportunities. Internal champions, although not always experts on ADR, do understand the concept and work to achieve support among the senior leadership team. Our reseach suggests that the survival of workplace systems need not be affected by the departure of a champion.

Second, the newness and suspicion of workplace systems will disappear. Employees will eventually view proactive conflict resolution as the norm. Finally, we believe that workplace systems will become institutionalized because their values, philosophy, and features will become ingrained in the fabric of the organization. Success stories will build up around the workplace system. Substantive differences between the workplace system and other human resource strategies or initiatives will be ironed out, and workplace systems, including their values and features, will be seen universally as "the way we have always done it around here." That is the real definition of institutionalization.

Integration of Systems with Other Corporate Values

Larger organizations are increasingly defining their values—those principles intended to guide both employee conduct and business strategy—as a source of competitive advantage. Examples of corporate values include integrity of conduct, customer commitment, innovation, environmental compliance, process and product quality, and respect for employees. Organizations believe that employee behavior can be broadly influenced by defining, encouraging, and rewarding employees to act consistent with corporate values.

We believe that in the future, there will be continued integration of these corporate values with the core values inherent in workplace systems. In Chapter Five, we defined many of the core values of a workplace system: voluntariness, protection of privacy, impartiality of neutrals, and prohibition of retaliation, among others. Our field research concluded that employers that have effectively implemented workplace systems have, for the most part, introduced new values and options into the workplace and integrated these two sets of values. We believe that in the end, there will be no differences in values.

Alignment of Systems with Other Workplace Processes and Initiatives

Workplace conflict management systems are not stand-alone features in an organization. They must be carefully aligned with other workplace processes, programs, and initiatives. If the design of the workplace system is inconsistent or at odds with these other organizational processes, the system will be less effective. If the core values of the workplace system are at odds with other dominant processes, the system will fail. These other workplace processes (they may also be systems) include workforce staffing, employee orientation, employee communications, compensation, the promotion system, workforce training, and discipline and discharge. Examples of common organizationwide initiatives include quality programs, systemic learning initiatives, and implementation of team concepts. We will examine the alignment of each of these other workplace processes with the conflict management system.

Alignment with Human Resource Processes. To be successful, conflict management systems must be carefully aligned with the core human resource strategies and processes. Procedural differences between these two systems are acceptable, but value differences are not. Proper alignment of the two systems facilitates employee understanding and acceptance of the conflict management system. Such alignment requires supervisors to be trained and rewarded in using conflict resolution skills through the training and compensation processes. It requires that the prohibition against retaliation by users of the workplace system be enforced through the discipline process and that the discipline strategy provide for access and use of options within the workplace system. It requires that—for those employers selecting mandatory arbitration—a clear and knowledgeable waiver of employee statutory rights be obtained through effective employee communications in the orientation process. It also requires success stories arising from the workplace system to be conveyed during employee orientation. All of these alignment features will be required before one could conclude that dispute resolution systems are fully integrated with more general human resource policies. This is a difficult task, and not all organizations will find this integration to be a smooth transition. We believe, however, that despite the difficulties present, successful workplace systems will increasingly become aligned with internal human resource processes.

Alignment with Quality Initiatives. Most large organizations today have adopted the general principles of the quality movement, also known as process improvement, continuous improvement, or Six Sigma. The general principles of the process are understanding customer satisfaction, mapping the process, creating process goals, monitoring performance toward those goals to achieve zero defects (statistical control), and continuously refining the process. Although the quality movement once focused mainly on the manufacturing process, more recently it has been broadened to include staff functions and employee satisfaction. Human resource and law departments have been transformed through this quality process.

Growing numbers of organizations have embraced conflict management systems as part of their quality initiative for employees. They view the management of workplace conflict as a business strategy that can be analyzed, mapped, and quantified. These employers use the quality process to develop their workplace system, including employee focus groups, monitoring of progress, and statistical control. These organizations report significant satisfaction through the use of this quality methodology.

Alignment as a Learning Organization. In the past decade, numerous large employers have tried to become learning organizations, a term often credited to Peter Senge and others in their pathbreaking book, *The Fifth Discipline*.[1] A corporatewide initiative to build organizational capability, this process calls for systems thinking, mental models, shared vision, and team learning. The organizations using this initiative view knowledge and systems thinking as broad organizational capabilities that can be transformed into a source of competitive advantage.

Increasingly, progressive employers have embraced thinking about workplace conflict as a social system worthy of analysis. They encourage individual employees to enter the workplace system at will but not to stop there. These systems thinkers examine the sources and nature of conflict for their root causes. Whatever knowledge they glean during the examination process is broadly exchanged across the organization for reflection and adjustment. In this way, learning is continuous across numerous locations using the workplace system, and the system's effectiveness is accelerated over time. If one site identifies a flaw in the design, for example, this information is quickly inventoried and distributed to all sites for their fix. If five remote sites have similar claims arising from the retirement plan, these cumulative data are noted and addressed by the system coordinator. These systems thinkers report significant satisfaction with this strategic initiative, and we believe that workplace systems will increasingly become a learning tool.

Alignment with Team Concepts. A significant movement embracing team concepts has evolved since the 1980s in large and small organizations. This movement encompasses principles of innovative changes in work structure, the absence of clear supervision and leaders, and radical expectations for self-initiative. These team principles can take the shape of temporary cross-functional work groups, permanent cross-department teams, work groups without clear leaders, and greatly reduced time frames for decision making. In the Xerox Corporation, for example, many employees work full time on teams outside the traditional hierarchy. The goal of this initiative at Xerox is increased productivity, enhanced innovation, higher quality, and faster turn-around times.

Employees selected for these work teams (at Xerox) receive extensive training in processing information, clarifying options, making decisions quickly, and resolving disputes. Conflict and disputes in work teams are inevitable. They occur at several levels. Some are interpersonal among team members. Some are with other teams. Some are over the interpretation of data or the allocation of resources. To resolve these conflicts, an increasing number of these organizations have embraced conflict management systems. These employers have reported that workplace systems have effectively supported the social process values and skills required for these work teams to be successful.

Flatter and More Agile Organizations

Since the 1980s, organizations have become flatter and more agile in structure and process. Layers of managers have been removed, leading to greater spans of control among those remaining. Functions are now expected to be more adaptive and more accepting of new strategic direction as market conditions change in their industry. Such a situation inevitably leads to conflict and disputes over strategy, resources, data, assignments, and job performance. In the past, managers had the time to resolve functional conflicts, and the slow pace of change allowed conflict to be resolved through existing processes. This is no longer the case.

In logic similar to work teams, organizations have embraced workplace conflict management systems to provide a cultural foundation and clear options, training, and specific tools to channel and resolve conflicts arising from this new organizational reality. Employers who have implemented workplace systems as an enabling vehicle in flatter and more agile organizations have reported success in their results. Thus, we believe that workplace systems will increasingly be accepted by flatter and more agile organizations.

Marketing a System as a Competitive Benefit

Competitive benefit is generally defined as an organizational capability that is publicly recognized and encourages candidates to select one employer over another. In essence, it creates the image of an employer of choice. The marketing legacy of Procter & Gamble Corporation is a competitive advantage in college recruiting, for example. The world-famous Crotonville Learning Institute is a competitive benefit of General Electric Corporation in the retention of career-minded executives. The technology prowess of Microsoft has made it a national employer of choice for technology-oriented people. Other companies gain competitive benefit through their salary structure, medical benefits plan, retirement benefits, growth history, and even location.

Our field research included interviews with numerous corporate executives, including presidents, chief financial officers, vice presidents of human resources, and general counsels. During these interviews, we raised the question as to whether workplace systems already are or will be viewed as a competitive benefit in the marketplace. We received a variety of responses. As one would expect, all users of workplace systems emphasized that the system must be effective to become a competitive benefit. This means that the system must be credible, must be used by employees, and must have an established track record of corporate commitment.

The majority of executives interviewed did not yet view the existence of a credible workplace system as a competitive benefit for candidates and employees. They believed that most systems are too new to gain this status. They also believed that most employees do not fully understand conflict resolution and the advantages resulting from a systemic channeling of conflict. In a few interviews, executives commented that the image of their workplace system is linked to whatever event precipitated building it—sometimes embarrassing litigation or a union organizing campaign. Most executives voiced a hope, however, that an employer with a workplace system will eventually be recognized in the talent market and will be viewed as an employer of choice. They believe that the existence of workplace systems will become linked to a friendlier culture, higher morale, higher-quality decision making, and a more professional work environment. In a few organizations, candidates are informed about the workplace system as a recruiting tool. We believe that in the next decade, workplace systems will be marketed as a competitive benefit for retention and recruiting purposes.

New Frontiers of Workplace Dispute Resolution

Historically, negotiations over business disputes have occurred face-to-face. There was a paradigm that people required physical and visual presence to create movement and settle a dispute. Both law schools and business schools taught it that way, and everyone believed it. In the past twenty years, though, this model has been modified: negotiations started to occur over the telephone. Although some adjustments were required, parties recognized the savings in time and convenience. As a result, telephonic negotiations are now a commonly accepted option during the dispute resolution process. Many disputes have been resolved over the telephone outside the physical presence of the parties.

We believe that the next frontier in conflict resolution will be based on the Internet. In fact, this frontier is already being explored. Aware of the Internet's potential, parties are trying it out. An explosion of on-line dispute resolution services, such as Cybersettle.com, NAM/Clicksettle.com, Squaretrade, and eResolution, has occurred in the past five years. These are the new wave of ADR providers, perhaps destined to challenge and supplement the services of established providers such as the American Arbitration Association (AAA) and JAMS. These on-line providers use software technology to connect disputants, schedule negotiations, frame issues, propose options for settlement, encourage movement, and draft agreements. They are gaining experience, refining their technology, and increasingly understanding and responding to customer requirements. Even state and federal courts have begun to implement on-line technology for the communication of critical documents.

The rationale behind the use of on-line providers for workplace disputes in larger organizations is compelling in many ways. First, it provides access in a distributed environment. Parties in different locations can log on and problem-solve immediate issues. Second, it is efficient. Travel costs can be greatly reduced and managerial time focused in a just-in-time basis. Transactional costs are reduced in scope. Third, the on-line system is flexible. There can be different software applications for different types of disputes. A consumer dispute can have a different on-line process from an employment dispute, and a claim alleging age discrimination can have a different process from a claim alleging a discriminatory denial of promotion. The parties will, in fact, expect a customized process.

Fourth, technology can provide the opportunity for fast resolution. In a world where time is money, it can be a major advantage to have conflict immediately addressed and resolved in days rather than years.

This on-line dispute technology is already delivering results in limited cases. One prominent labor arbitrator we know has adopted on-line technology in his practice. Whenever possible, he conducts prehearing conferences and "live" hearings from his home over the Internet, using video-streaming equipment and other technologies. In the past, this arbitrator reports, he would have resisted the technology because of a perception that he would lose the ability to assess the credibility of witnesses. Over time, though, he has not found this to be the case. He claims that most cases do not turn on visual impressions of witness credibility and that, when required, there are other techniques to evaluate the credibility of testimony.

Of course, the precise direction of on-line dispute resolution cannot yet be predicted. There are numerous barriers to its full acceptance. One is security: ensuring the privacy and confidentiality of settlement discussions and agreements. Another is jurisdiction: How do real-world jurisdictional disputes translate into cyberspace? Another is creating legally binding Web agreements. Another is defining and respecting the procedural rules of the on-line process. Despite these current barriers, we believe that on-line dispute resolution represents the new frontier for workplace conflict resolution. Disputes do not necessarily have to be settled face-to-face. We see on-line dispute resolution as a tremendous opportunity with broad appeal to a variety of large and small organizations.

ON THE OTHER HAND

Although we have presented a strong case for the probability of the continuing development of conflict management systems, potentially significant problems could slow the pace of that growth. For organizations that have hesitated to this point, important issues remain that might give leaders pause as they consider whether to develop and implement a conflict management system.

Here, we present what we believe to be the key challenges to the pace at which the privatization of conflict and dispute resolution will proceed. All of the problems we examine are related to the external environment faced by organizations seeking to develop conflict management systems (there seems only to be a limited potential for influence of internal design features). The threat of the courts, problems with neutrals, and the evolving role of neutral providers may give pause to organizations currently debating the strategic question of whether to create their own system.

Legal Problems Could Slow Conflict Management Growth

The U.S. Supreme Court is now clearly and firmly in favor of employment ADR. The line of cases that began with *Gilmer*, extended to *Circuit City*, and was seemingly finalized in *Waffle House* has created a series of precedents that seem unlikely to be challenged in the near future. In *Waffle House*, the Supreme Court carved out an agency exemption for a predispute waiver by retaining agency rights, where they exist, to not be a party to an arbitration system the agency did not voluntarily accept. Thus, the fundamental legal issue is not whether these schemes are legal, as it was throughout the 1990s, but whether there has been enough chipping around the edges to make arbitration difficult to enforce and less final and binding than users would hope for.

Other than that exception, the important legal actions to come seem to be the continuing efforts by the courts to define a set of standards for due process in dispute resolution systems. A large and growing number of recent cases, primarily decided at the state court level, have focused on carving out due process standards for those conflict management systems that contain arbitration waivers.

Representation of Plaintiffs. One of the more contentious legal issues concerns the representation of plaintiffs in arbitration. Many conflict management systems contain the noble idea that conflicts should be resolved at the lowest possible level of the organization, with only the parties themselves present at the discussions. As an ideal for a lot of common workplace problems, this is very laudable. But in practice, the employer is far more likely to have greater access to information and greater expertise in the subject matter under discussion, and thus to have a powerful advantage over the employee. The courts, appropriately, have expressed significant concern when the possibility exists that during the arbitration process these discussions could veer into areas where legal issues are at stake. It is those cases in which the resource and information advantage may be the most important and independent representation of the employee the most critical.

Other systems limit representation through the amount of money or time provided to the employee for counsel. While not as troubling to the courts as having no representation at all, these systems still present important issues. Although the lack of a right to representation is troubling in these systems, it primarily affects only systems with arbitration instead of the courts at the end of the dispute resolution process. Where the conflict management system contains a mediation step short of action in the courts or through agency enforcement, the courts have expressed less concern about the lack of representation. Nonetheless, lack of representation, even in a mediation process, can still be a significant hurdle for an employee to jump.

If the courts were to make an important ruling on the right of representation in conflict management systems, it could discourage some companies from jumping on the conflict management bandwagon. The primary motivations of saving time and money might not appear so clearly attainable under a system requiring employees to be represented. Another subject of concern here is the extension of Weingarten (under the National Labor Relations Board rules) rights to nonunion employees. Weingarten rights are derived from NLRB case law, in which it has been held that employees facing the potential for disciplinary action have a right

to an accompanying representative in any meeting. A parallel ruling extending those rights to every workplace would be a potential
burden on many conflict management systems. We know of no system that encourages this legal right in disciplinary discussions.

Predispute Waivers. Another significant arena for state-level litigation involves the predispute waivers themselves. A number of
courts have held that some waivers are unconscionable contracts.
Although a well-considered conflict management system will have
nothing to fear from this area of litigation, some employers have
been judged to overreach in the waivers they require employees to
sign at the time of employment. Although we believe that high-
level executives and some other employees have the means and the
education to make themselves knowledgeable about the employment contracts they are signing, the fact is that most employees
sign these waivers without an adequate information base. We have
seen many waivers that are very clear and many programs (even
including video presentations) that attempt to inform potential
employees extensively about what they are signing. It seems to us
that a conflict management system designed with the principles
suggested earlier in this book will have no difficulty meeting state-
level court tests regarding clarity and knowledgeability.

Potential for Taking Advantage. A final legal barrier could occur
in either Congress or state legislatures. It is not too farfetched to
imagine some companies pressing their advantage in the creation
of conflict management systems to the extreme disadvantage of
their employees. A single well-publicized scandal involving the
wholesale sacrifice of employee rights under conflict management
could lead legislative bodies to attempt to regulate or even prohibit
these schemes. Clearly, the U.S. Congress could reverse the entire
Supreme Court line of pro-ADR cases should it choose to do so.
Although we consider that extremely unlikely, we recognize that
some state legislatures, most notably California's, have shown a
tendency to scrutinize the entire field of conflict management

closely. Obviously, no state could overturn the Supreme Court's ADR cases, but there is much that state courts and legislatures can do to change the impact of those rulings effectively.

Problems with Neutrals. Most conflict management systems rely on neutrals who are external to the organization. Yet not all observers accept the fact that arbitrators are somehow inherently neutral when they are providing services in a dispute. Some court cases have commented on the bias inherent in a system in which the neutrals are paid by the organization but are expected to be entirely neutral on each case in which they are involved. This can be particularly true when an organization uses a single neutral or a very small pool. Such an arrangement may be efficient, but it can lead to employees' suspicion that the system is somehow fixed against their interests.

The leading professional organizations in the field of dispute resolution have tackled this problem, recognizing that it calls into question the integrity of their members and their profession. The National Academy of Arbitrators confronted the ethical dilemmas directly in a 1999 survey by asking its members their views on a wide range of ethical issues presented by arbitrator participation in conflict management systems. The Association for Conflict Resolution, more a group of mediators than arbitrators, has also addressed the issues in its policies on conflict of interest.

The bottom line is that employees and policymakers, as well as the promulgators of workplace conflict management systems, have to have a high level of confidence in the neutral profession. Otherwise, no matter the pace of growth, the movement will be stunted by this problem.

One means of addressing the neutral question is through credentialing. At this point, there is no standard for minimum qualifications or training for arbitrators and mediators. We believe that these standards will be developed over time, although it is impossible to say when. The inevitability of credentialing may not seem so obvious to all the groups trying to prevent it, but it seems to us that the field would be well served by at least some minimum statement of qualifications.

Credentialing could address or even resolve the question of whether all disputes that involve even the smallest legal matter require neutrals who are lawyers. It also could resolve whether all lawyers or former members of the judiciary are automatically qualified to conduct mediations of employment disputes with a legal issue at the core. Credentialing could be implemented through minimum hours of training, written tests, skill-based tests, client evaluations, or apprenticeship, and it could legitimize providers of training for neutrals, a field in which reputation currently counts for more than the quality or content of the training itself.

Credentialing of neutrals has not proceeded easily to this point. In 2000, the Federal Mediation and Conciliation Service proposed a set of guidelines for the training and experience required to meet its standards for a four-grade system of classification of mediators. To put it mildly, these standards were not accepted by the other providers of neutral services or by the neutrals themselves. The Maryland Mediation and Conflict Resolution Office of the Maryland court system is engaged, at this writing, in a grassroots effort to determine appropriate minimum standards for mediators in the state. The Association for Conflict Resolution has had a task force address the issue, but without being able to form a consensus, much less put it before the membership. Although many organizations have contemplated a solution to this problem, we believe it unlikely that one will emerge. In the absence of agreed-on standards for the qualifications of mediators and arbitrators, the open market will determine how neutrals obtain work.

Providers of Neutrals Will Evolve. As the number of conflict management systems expands, so will the demand for qualified neutrals and for the sources of neutral services. Since it is inefficient for individual mediators and arbitrators simply to advertise their services as employment neutrals, organizations, particularly large ones, will require outside groups to recruit, select, and certify neutrals for them. We believe it is unlikely that such traditional providers as AAA and the Federal Mediation and Conciliation Service (FMCS) will be able to handle the increase in demand. The AAA and the FMCS have well-deserved reputations as consistent providers of neutral services across the entire country. It is not clear to us, however, whether either organization will be able to create the customized services required by every organization. In addition, it seems clear to us that others will jump into this marketplace, on both a profit and a nonprofit basis. For example, our university (Cornell) is part of the Alliance for Education in Dispute Resolution, a nonprofit provider of mediation and arbitration training. The Alliance regularly fields inquiries from organizations and law firms regarding the availability of rosters of Alliance-trained neutrals for use in class actions and conflict management systems. We do not believe that this is a unique experience; we think that many organizations are searching for alternatives to the national providers of neutral services.

The Unlawful Practice of Law.   Mediation as the unlawful practice of law is a legitimate issue and one of major concern to the profession. The Dispute Resolution Section of the American Bar Association has repeatedly claimed that mediation is not the practice of law. That opinion has not convinced everyone, however, as the bar associations of the states of North Carolina and Virginia currently claim that it is, under certain conditions. Should that view eventually hold, the profession of mediation could be largely closed to nonlawyers and the supply of qualified mediators further restricted. The ACR has had a task force on mediation as the practice of law for two years and has not been able to reach a consensus on the question.

It is clear that the nature of the neutrals working in employment dispute resolution is an issue that needs some resolution if conflict management systems are going to continue to grow. Employees and policymakers have a right to expect qualified, truly neutral mediators and arbitrators to be working in these systems before they will grant their full endorsement. We believe this is a critical area to watch over the coming years.

ADR Providers Will Be More Closely Scrutinized

The role of the ADR provider is evolving rapidly in the early part of the twenty-first century. The traditional full-service model of the AAA is being threatened by both users of the services and regulators. The AAA traditionally was brought into labor-management agreements, and other institutional arrangements, as a complete administrator of dispute resolution programs. It routinized case filing, offered a complete set of rules for the conduct of mediation and arbitration, provided a roster of neutrals and a means of choosing one from among the proffered list, and even provided a neutral site for the conduct of hearings. For neutrals, it provided a means of obtaining work, and the quality and reputation of the organization served in a *de facto* fashion certification of the qualifications of the neutral.

Many organizations have chosen another model in their development of their conflict management systems. These newcomers to dispute resolution have sometimes created a system that demands a flexibility and a cost structure that does not fit within the traditional provider model. Whether the traditional providers will respond with more customized offerings remains to be seen. Thus, it is our belief that sources of neutrals and neutral services will continue to expand in response to this need for flexibility.

Providers have also been criticized for the very feature that makes them attractive to so many of their customers. Users have questioned the quality, consistency, and contemporary knowledge of their panels. The providers' response has been to weed out their panels. AAA recently moved to a professional roster of full-time neutrals and removed approximately 70 percent of its occasional neutrals. It also recently began requiring annual educational updates for members of its rosters. These moves are clearly in response to the market and the demand for high-quality rosters.

Many regulatory trends begin in California. If that is true in conflict management, neutral providers may be in for a rough period of scrutiny. In the spring of 2002, the California legislature held hearings on neutral providers and ultimately passed the first significant regulation of the organizations that provide these services. The California legislature was particularly focused on conflicts of interest. Some neutral organizations had a long-standing practice of investing funds in corporate customers that contracted with them for mediators and arbitrators. The California law now very specifically defines and prohibits conflicts of interest for neutral providers. The law also requires extensive disclosure of any prior neutral history with the parties in order to avoid even the appearance of a repeat-player effect, in which employers are favored over employees. In response, some providers hired lobbyists and threatened not to do business in the state or to pull completely out of California.

CONFLICT MANAGEMENT AND THE TIPPING POINT

In his book *The Tipping Point*, Malcolm Gladwell advances a thesis to explain the spread of social and behavioral epidemics.[2] His fundamental premise is that some social and group behaviors move from trends to epidemics when they reach a "tipping point," that is, the point in time at which the growth of a phenomenon suddenly and inexplicably becomes epidemic—everyone is doing it. Gladwell uses his idea to explain phenomena as diverse as the decline in crime rates in New York City and the explosive growth in sales of Hush Puppy shoes in the mid-1990s.

We believe that Gladwell's idea is useful as a frame through which to view the future of dispute management. The fundamental question we wish to address is whether we are at a point where the trends we have discussed in this book are likely to become an epidemic. Will we look back in a few years and see the tipping point at which conflict management systems became as essential to organizational life as any of a dozen other features of human resources?

With all apologies to Gladwell for oversimplifying his ideas, let us summarize his thesis. He postulates that there are three rules that all epidemics follow on their way to the tipping point: the Law of the Few, the Stickiness Factor, and the Power of Context. The Law of the Few says that a small number or group of people—Gladwell calls them Connectors, Mavens, and Salesmen—make all the difference in spreading an idea or a behavior. *Connectors* are essential to reaching the tipping point because they know many others, easily communicate ideas, and are simultaneously parts of many different circles. *Mavens* have information that the rest of us are not yet aware of; they always know where to get the best deal on a product and how to manipulate situations to their advantage, and they are often aware of trends before the rest of us. *Salesmen* are exactly what the title suggests: persuaders of others. They take ideas, products, or whatever else and convince the rest of us of their value.

The Stickiness Factor suggests that, in Gladwell's words, "There is a simple way to package information that, under the right circumstances, can make it irresistible."[3] In other words, it matters not only how an idea is packaged and sold, but when as well. The greatest solution might come along at the wrong time, or be presented in the wrong way or by the wrong person, and it will fail. The idea being presented has to "stick" to us in some way. Thus, when the right method lines up with the right salesmen and the right timing, individuals will be almost powerless to resist the stickiness of the message.

The final piece of Gladwell's thesis is the Power of Context. He tells us that we are very sensitive to the context in which we receive information. Our environment and other forces shape how we receive an idea. We all have heard the phrase "an idea whose time has come." In some ways, Gladwell is explaining that phrase to us by sensitizing the reader to the absolute power of an idea in a certain context and the same idea's unimportance in another context.

Gladwell's thesis can be overly simplified to tipping points in social epidemics being reached when the right people arrive with the right message at the right time. When we read the *Tipping Point*, we immediately saw parallels to our study of conflict management. One needs look back only ten or fifteen years and see that most of the material we have written about in this book had not yet occurred. How did this rapid development of conflict management occur, and will it continue past a tipping point to standardization?

We first thought back and realized that there are clearly people and organizations that are mavens, connectors, and salesmen in conflict management circles. Although we have not conducted a detailed study, nearly all organizations that have considered questions of conflict management cite a very small number of benchmarks. Halliburton, for example, is nearly always included. Individuals nearly all cite the pathbreaking book of Costantino and Merchant.[4] Moreover, they have all attended presentations at conferences by this same small number of individuals and organizations. These conferences are hosted by a very small number of professional and private organizations, such as ACR and its forerunners or CPR, and led by individuals who believe in the power of conflict management. Thus, Gladwell's Law of the Few seems to be true in the field of conflict management.

Whether the Stickiness Factor is present is not quite as apparent. It is clear that the message about conflict management is not always received as intended. Whether the messengers are not trusted completely, or the evidence in support of the message is not as persuasive as is hoped, we certainly found individuals and organizations that did not accept the logic of conflict management systems. Conflict management clearly does not stick to everyone.

The context in which this trend is occurring may in fact still be changing quite rapidly. Two beliefs that we have not fully explored in this book are currently being challenged, for example. First, it has been assumed by most that public justice and dispute resolution are always better than privately administered justice.

Many of those who have attacked conflict management systems have done so solely on this premise—ceteris paribus, private systems have to be inferior to public systems. The well-documented problems with the courts and administrative agencies charged with enforcing the employment laws in the United States have caused many to reevaluate their support of this premise, however, and without significant change in the public system, more may come around to that point of view.

It is also assumed by many that collective bargaining through independent trade unions provides the only true voice in the workplace. Even without challenging the truth of that belief, its underpinnings may be coming apart. As private sector unionism continues to decline toward near insignificance, the real choice is not between collective bargaining and nonunion employment, but rather between nonunion employment and publicly available systems of dispute resolution. When added to the other evidence that we provided throughout this book, the context for the argument about conflict management may have shifted in a direction where a tipping point could occur.

The tipping point for portions of the conflict management movement has certainly been reached. When President Truman convened the 1945 labor-management conference, it is not clear that arbitration was on the threshold of universal acceptance and application in the world of collective bargaining. Yet that is exactly what happened. At the Pound Conference on the Causes of Popular Dissatisfaction with the Administration of Justice in 1975, few believed that mediation would achieve the wide-ranging applications it has in the past quarter of a century. Only in the past decade has ADR itself, as a concept embodying a number of techniques, been hailed by almost all as a useful approach to dispute resolution.

Will we reach the tipping point for conflict management? It is uncertain, for there are persuasive arguments on both sides. Perhaps conflict management is one more passing fad of organizations ever eager to press their advantage over their own employees in the resolution of disputes. There is enough uncertainty in the environment to give pause to many organizations that might otherwise follow the pathbreakers. Arbitration itself has problems. Increasing legalism in the process and the potential lack of final and binding awards in the wake of *Waffle House* may make its advantages much less attractive to those who would use it. There is significant institutionalized opposition to the growth of conflict management in the legal profession and the judiciary. The rigidity of this opposition cannot be underestimated.

On the other hand, the long-term trend toward the privatization of dispute resolution is a social and cultural reality. Given that trend, conflict management by organizations will merely systematize the privatization under a new regime. Certainly, contemporary trends seem almost overwhelmingly to favor the continued creation of conflict management systems. In Chapter Two, we discussed the dismantling of the old social contract in employment and the construction of a new one. We believe that the new social contract, once created, is likely to be durable for a generation at least. To the extent that conflict management and private dispute resolution are part of that new social contract, these ideas will become institutionalized in a very powerful way. Reversal in that context is unlikely to occur easily. Finally, the context for conflict management continues to change, in a direction that favors the continued creation of more and more conflict management systems.

One of the features of Gladwell's thesis is that we are able to recognize the tipping point only in retrospective examination; we are not yet able to forecast the existence of a tipping point or to identify in advance the exact point at which we will reach it. In part, that is what makes this dynamic field of study and practice so interesting. We will watch the developments over the next few years with an interest as intense as those who debate the advantages and disadvantages of conflict management for their own organizations.

A List of Corporations and Other Organizations Studied by the Authors and Referred to in This Book

Alcoa

American Arbitration Association

American Express

Anheuser-Busch

AOL Time Warner

Beau Rivage

Bechtel

Bellagio

Boeing Company

Brown and Root

Caesars World

Chevron

City of Phoenix, Arizona

Coca-Cola Enterprises

Eastman Kodak

Emerson Electric Company

Exelon Corporation

FMC Corporation

Golden Nugget

Halliburton

Hewlett Packard

Honeywell Corporation

Inland Container Corporation

Kaiser Permanente

Kaufman and Broad

MGM Grand

Mercy Healthcare Arizona

Mirage Resorts, Inc.

PECO Energy

Phelps-Dodge Corporation

Prudential

Rural-Metro Corporation

Schering-Plough

Sears, Roebuck and Company

Shell Oil Company

The Great Indoors

TRW

Unified Court System of
New York State

U.S. Department of
the Interior

Universal Studios

USX Corporation

Warner Brothers

Wells Fargo

Appendix B

Glossary of Terms

Arbitration. A method of resolving a dispute in which the disputants present their case to an impartial third party, who then makes a decision for them that resolves the conflict. This decision is usually binding. There are many forms of arbitration. *See also* Compulsory arbitration; Final offer arbitration; Nonbinding arbitration; Voluntary arbitration.

Adjudication. Any of the forms of dispute resolution in which the parties to the dispute present proofs and arguments to a neutral third party, who has the power to deliver a binding decision. Although it can include arbitration, adjudication usually is used in reference to publicly available dispute resolution forums, such as the courts or administrative agencies.

Alternative dispute resolution. A broad range of processes designed to resolve disputes outside publicly available courts or agencies; includes mediation and arbitration, as well as many other less used processes.

Comediation. A form of mediation in which there are two mediators who conduct the process jointly. Used in settings where two mediators with different expertise could be useful.

Compulsory arbitration. Arbitration of disputes the parties are obligated to submit to arbitration by prior agreement or pursuant to the provisions of a statute. Sometimes referred to as *predispute arbitration* or *mandatory arbitration*. In contemporary usage, *compulsory arbitration* may refer to arbitration pursuant to the provisions of a statute, and mandatory arbitration may refer to arbitration required by prior agreement by the parties. *See also* Arbitration.

Conciliation. An informal process in which a passive third party is used to create a channel for communication between the disputants, which will allow them to reestablish direct communication and identify common interests.

Discovery. In litigation and other legal proceedings, the acquisition, disclosure, and exchange of knowledge, facts, and observations with the opposing party or parties in the proceedings.

Early neutral evaluation. A process in which a neutral evaluator holds a confidential session with each of the disputants and listens to their cases. The neutral evaluates strengths and weaknesses of the parties' positions and issues a nonbinding assessment of the merits of the case.

Facilitation. A collaborative process that uses a neutral to design and oversee a group process. Often used when multiple parties and interests are present.

Fact finding. A process by which the facts relevant to a controversy are determined. A neutral fact finder may issue a recommended solution to the dispute, which the parties are free to accept or reject.

Final-offer arbitration. Arbitration in which each party submits a proposed award to the arbitrator. At the conclusion of the process, the arbitrator must choose one of the parties' proposals as is, without modification. *See also* Arbitration.

Impasse. A situation that results after the parties have exhausted all means available to them to resolve a dispute.

Interest dispute. A dispute that arises out of an effort by the parties in a relationship to negotiate a new contract or agreement.

Mandatory arbitration. *See* Compulsory arbitration.

Mediation. A voluntary and informal process in which the disputing parties select a neutral third party to assist them in reaching a negotiated settlement. Parties can use mediation as a result of a contract provision, by private agreement as disputes arise, or as part of a court-annexed program that diverts cases to mediation. The mediator has no power to impose a solution on the parties. There are three styles of mediators—facilitative, evaluative and transformative—and each uses a different approach to try to reach a settlement.

Mediation-arbitration. A process in which the parties agree to mediate a dispute, with the additional provision that should they not be able to negotiate a solution, the mediator will become an arbitrator for the issues that remain. Sometimes known as Med-Arb.

Minitrial. A structured process that provides disputing parties the opportunity to present their cases before a quasi-judge, sometimes with settlement authority.

Multistep process. A progressive series of dispute resolution procedures in which the disputing parties advance from one step to another if they continue to disagree.

Negotiation. Any direct interaction, implicit or explicit, in which parties who have opposing interests attempt to resolve their disagreement without the use of any third party.

Nonbinding arbitration. A process that works the same way as binding arbitration except that the arbitrator's decision is only advisory, not binding. The parties may agree in advance to use the advisory decision as a tool in resolving their dispute through negotiation.

Ombudsperson. A dispute resolution role within an organization. The ombudsperson is appointed by an organization and serves one or more of the following roles: investigating complaints, preventing disputes, or facilitating dispute resolution.

Rights dispute. A dispute that arises out of the administration, application, and interpretation of an existing contract or agreement.

Voluntary arbitration. Any form of arbitration in which the parties choose whether to submit a specific dispute to an arbitrator for resolution. Sometimes referred to as *postdispute arbitration. See also* Arbitration.

Notes

Preface

1. Ken Binmore, *Game Theory and the Social Contract*, Vol. 1: *Playing Fair*. Cambridge, Mass.: MIT Press, 1995, p. 6.
2. Hope Viner Samborn, "The Vanishing Trial," *ABA Journal* 88, Oct. 2002, pp. 26–27.
3. Samborn, 2002, p. 27.

Chapter One

1. Melanie Lewis, "Conflict Management System for Coca-Cola Enterprises," presentation at Resolving Conflict Conference, Baltimore, Md., May 24, 2001.
2. Interview with Jim Durham, PECO Energy, Philadelphia, Sept. 1999.
3. Interview with John Ryan, Len Timpone, and John Sander, Schering-Plough, Nov. 23, 1999.
4. Walter K. Olson, *The Litigation Explosion: What Happened When America Unleashed the Lawsuit*. New York: Truman Talley Books, 1991.
5. Harry C. Katz and Thomas Kochan, *An Introduction to Collective Bargaining and Industrial Relations*. New York: Irwin McGraw-Hill, 2000, Exhibit 6–1, p. 118.
6. Cathy A. Costantino and Christina Sickles Merchant, *Designing Conflict Management Systems*. San Francisco: Jossey-Bass, 1996.

7. Ann Gosline et al., *Designing Integrated Conflict Management Systems: Guidelines for Practitioners and Decision Makers in Organizations*. Ithaca, N.Y.: Institute on Conflict Resolution, 2001, p. 8.

8. For classic works on the systems concept, see, for example, Ludwig Von Bertalanffy, "General Systems Theory: A New Approach to the Unity of Science," *Human Biology* 23, Dec. 1951, pp. 302–361; and Kenneth E. Boulding, "General Systems—The Skeleton of Science," *Management Science* 2, Apr. 1956, pp. 197–208.

9. Gosline et al., 2001, pp. 35–36.

10. Gosline et al., 2001, pp. 9–16.

11. David B. Lipsky, Ronald L. Seeber, and Lavinia Hall, "An Uncertain Destination: On the Development of Conflict Management Systems in U.S. Corporations," in Samuel Estreicher and David Sherwyn (eds.), *Developments in Labor Law*. New York: Kluwer Law International, forthcoming.

12. Reynolds Holding, "AT&T's Arbitration System Ruled Illegal: Ban on Class Actions Condemned," *San Francisco Chronicle*, Jan. 17, 2002, p. A-1.

13. See *Gilmer v. Interstate/Johnson Corp.*, 500 U.S. 20 (1991), and *Circuit City Stores v. Saint Clair Adams*, 121 S. Ct. 1302 (2001).

14. DeLoitte Touche Tohmatsu International, *DeLoitte and Touche Litigation Services 1993 Survey of General and Outside Counsels: Alternative Dispute Resolution (ADR)*. New York: DeLoitte Touche Tohmatsu International, 1993.

15. David B. Lipsky and Ronald L. Seeber, *The Appropriate Resolution of Corporate Disputes: A Report on the Growing Use of ADR by U.S. Corporations*. Ithaca, N.Y.: Cornell/PERC Institute on Conflict Resolution, 1998a.

16. Michel Picher, Ronald L. Seeber, and David B. Lipsky, *The Arbitration Profession in Transition: A Survey of the National Academy of Arbitrators*. Ithaca, N.Y.: Cornell/PERC Institute on Conflict Resolution, 2000.

Chapter Two

1. Rudolph G. Penner, Isabel V. Sawhill, and Timothy Taylor, *Updating America's Social Contract: Economic Growth and Opportunity in the New Century*. New York: Norton, 2000, p. 16.
2. Penner, Sawhill, and Taylor, 2000, pp. 16–17.
3. Jeremy Rifkin, *The End of Work: The Decline of the Global Labor Force and the Dawn of the Post-Market Era*. New York: Tarcher/Putnam, 1995.
4. "Writing a New Social Contract," *Business Week*, Mar. 11, 1996.
5. "Social Contract," *Encyclopedia Britannica* [http://www.britannica.com/eb/article?eu=70216#cite]. Accessed Oct. 23, 2002.
6. "Social Contract," 2002. See also: Thomas Hobbes, *Leviathan* (1651), in William Molesworth (ed.), *The English Works of Thomas Hobbes*. London: John Bohn, 1839, Vol. 3. Jean-Jacques Rousseau, *The Social Contract*. London: Penguin Books, 1968 (originally published in 1762); John Locke, *Second Treatise of Government*. Indianapolis: Hackett, 1980 (originally published in 1690).
7. John Rawls, *A Theory of Justice* (rev. ed.). Cambridge, Mass.: Belknap Press, 1999. For a challenge to Rawls, see Robert Nozick, *Anarchy, State, and Utopia*. New York: Basic Books, 1974.
8. Thomas Donaldson and Thomas W. Dunfee, *Ties That Bind: A Social Contracts Approach to Business Ethics*. Boston: Harvard Business School Press, 1999, p. viii.
9. Hobbes, 1651.
10. Locke, 1690.
11. Rousseau, 1762.
12. See Rousseau, 1762, and Locke, 1690.
13. See Rawls, 1999, and Nozick, 1974.
14. John Dunlop, *Industrial Relations Systems*. New York: Holt, 1958. See also: Clark Kerr, John Dunlop, Frederick Harbison,

and Charles Myers, *Industrialism and Industrial Man*. Cambridge, Mass.: Harvard University Press, 1960. Clark Kerr and Abraham Siegel, "The Structuring of the Labor Force in Industrial Society: New Dimensions and New Questions." *Industrial and Labor Relations Review* 8, Jan. 1955, pp. 151–168. An account of the historical development of these concepts is contained in Bruce E. Kaufman, *The Origins and Evolution of the Field of Industrial Relations in the United States*. Ithaca, N.Y.: ILR Press, 1993, esp. pp. 87–102.

15. Sanford M. Jacoby, *Modern Manors: Welfare Capitalism Since the New Deal*. Princeton, N.J.: Princeton University Press, 1997, p. 15.

16. For a discussion of the work of Frederick Winslow Taylor, see Andrew J. DuBrin, R. Duane Ireland, and J. Clifton Williams, *Management and Organization*. Cincinnati, Ohio: Southwestern Publishing, 1989, pp. 32–38.

17. Robert M. MacDonald, *Collective Bargaining in the Automobile Industry*. New Haven, Conn.: Yale University Press, 1963, pp. 4–14.

18. David Halberstam, *The Reckoning*. New York: Morrow, 1986.

19. For an account of how regulation limited competition in the airline industry, see Peter Capelli, "Airlines," in David B. Lipsky and Clifford B. Donn (eds.), *Collective Bargaining in American Industry*, San Francisco: New Lexington Press, 1987, pp. 135–186.

20. U.S. Department of Labor, *Report on the American Workforce*. Washington, D.C.: U.S. Government Printing Office, 2001, pp. 3, 122, 134.

21. Harry C. Katz and David B. Lipsky, "The Collective Bargaining System in the United States: The Legacy and the Lessons," in Maurice F. Neufeld and Jean T. McKelvey (eds.), *Industrial Relations at the Dawn of the New Millennium*. Ithaca, N.Y.: New York State School of Industrial and Labor Relations, Cornell University, 1998,

pp. 146–147. See also *President's National Labor-Management Conference, November 5–20, 1945: Summary and Committee Reports: Bulletin No. 77*, Washington, D.C.: U.S. Government Printing Office, 1946, pp. 5–9.

22. Sumner H. Schlichter, James J. Healy, and E. Robert Livernash, *The Impact of Collective Bargaining on Management.* Washington, D.C.: Brookings Institution, 1960, pp. 746–747. See also: Philip Taft, *Organized Labor in American History.* New York: HarperCollins, 1964, pp. 565–566; Katz and Lipsky, 1998, p. 147.

23. Marlin M. Volz and Edward P. Goggin (eds.), *Elkouri and Elkouri: How Arbitration Works* (5th ed.). Washington, D.C.: Bureau of National Affairs, 1997, pp. 1–27. For a recent discussion, see Theodore W. Kheel, *The Keys to Conflict Resolution: Proven Methods of Settling Disputes Voluntarily.* New York: Four Walls Eight Windows, 1999, pp. 83–84.

24. *President's National Labor-Management Conference,* 1946, p. 5.

25. Charles Heckscher, *The New Unionism: Employee Involvement in the Changing Corporation.* New York: Basic Books, 1988, p. 50. See also: Katz and Lipsky, 1998, p. 147, and U.S. Department of Labor, *Report and Recommendations: The Commission on the Future of Worker-Management Relations.* Washington, D.C.: U.S. Government Printing Office, 1994.

26. *President's National Labor-Management Conference,* 1946, p. 52.

27. Daniel Bell, *The End of Ideology: On the Exhaustion of Political Ideas in the Fifties.* Cambridge, Mass.: Harvard University Press, 2000 (originally published in 1960).

28. *First National Maintenance Corp.* v. *NLRB,* 452 U.S. 666 (1981).

29. Katz and Lipsky, 1998, pp. 148–150. Neil W. Chamberlain and James W. Kuhn, *Collective Bargaining* (2nd ed.). New York: McGraw-Hill, 1965, pp. 110–114.

30. Volz and Goggin, 1997, pp. 884–894.

31. The Steelworkers' Trilogy consisted of the following cases: *Steelworkers* v. *American Manufacturing Co.,* 80 S. Ct. 1343

(1960); *Steelworkers v. Enterprise Wheel and Car Corp.*, 80 S. Ct. 1358 (1960); and *Steelworkers v. Warrior and Gulf Navigation*, 80 S. Ct. 1347 (1960). See also Volz and Goggin, 1997, pp. 28–47.

32. Picher, Seeber, and Lipsky, 2000. See also John T. Dunlop and Arnold M. Zack, *Mediation and Arbitration of Employment Disputes.* San Francisco: Jossey-Bass, 1997.

33. John F. Burton Jr. and Terry Thomason, "The Extent of Collective Bargaining in the Public Sector," in Benjamin Aaron, Joyce M. Najita, and James L. Stern (eds.), *Public-Sector Bargaining.* Washington, D.C.: Bureau of National Affairs, 1988, pp. 1–51.

34. Barry Bluestone and Bennett Harrison, *The Deindustrialization of America.* New York: Basic Books, 1982, pp. 25–81.

35. Cappelli, 1987, pp. 135–186.

36. Wallace E. Hendricks, "Telecommunications," in Lipsky and Donn, 1987, pp. 103–133.

37. Walter K. Olson, *The Litigation Explosion: What Happened When America Unleashed the Lawsuit.* New York: Dutton, 1991.

38. Terence Dunworth and Joel Rogers, "Corporations in Court: Big Business Litigation in U.S. Federal Courts, 1971–1991," *Law and Social Inquiry* 21, Summer 1996, pp. 497–592.

39. Patrick M. Garry, *A Nation of Adversaries: How the Litigation Explosion Is Reshaping America.* New York: Plenum Press, 1997, pp. 15–16.

40. Stephen Gold, "Step Ladders and Lawsuits," *Washington Times*, Nov. 21, 1997, reprinted in National Center for Policy Analysis, "Tort System Pays People to Hurt Themselves." [http://www.ncpa.org/pd/law/law1197c.html]. Accessed Mar. 24, 1999.

41. U.S. Department of Labor, 1994, pp. 25–33.

42. Marika F. X. Litras, *Civil Rights Complaints in U.S. District Courts, 1990–98.* Washington, D.C.: U.S. Department of Justice, Jan. 2000, pp. 1–13.

43. U.S. Department of Labor, 1994, p. 50.

44. U.S. Department of Labor, 1994, p. 50

45. Dunworth and Rogers, 1996, pp. 558–559.

46. Samuel Jan Brakel, "Using What We Know About Our Civil Litigation System: A Critique of 'Base-Rate' Analysis and Other Apologist Diversions," *Georgia Law Review*, 31, 1996, pp. 77–200. [http://www.lawsch.uga.edu/~galawrev/vol31/brakel.html]. Accessed Mar. 24, 1999.

47. Yesim Yilmaz, "Private Regulation: A Real Alternative for Regulatory Reform," *Policy Analysis*, Apr. 20, 1998, pp. 1–34.

48. Quoted in Randall S. Schuler, "Repositioning the Human Resource Function: Transformation or Demise," in Raymond A. Noe, John R. Hollenbeck, Barry Gerhart, and Patrick M. Wright (eds.), *Readings in Human Resource Management*. Burr Ridge, Ill.: Irwin, 1994, p. 10.

49. Randall S. Schuler, "Strategic Human Resources Management: Linking the People with the Strategic Needs of the Business," in Noe, Hollenbeck, Gerhart, and Wright, 1994, pp. 58–76.

50. Society for Human Resource Management, http://www.shrm.org/press/default.asp?page=history.html. Accessed Oct. 23, 2002.

51. U.S. Bureau of the Census, *Historical Statistics of the United States*. Washington, D.C.: U.S. Government Printing Office, 1970. U.S. Department of Labor, Bureau of Labor Statistics, *Employment and Earnings*. Washington, D.C.: U.S. Government Printing Office, Jan. 2001.

52. Robert Hutchens, David Lipsky, and Robert Stern, *Strikers and Subsidies: The Influence of Government Transfer Programs on Strike Activity*. Kalamazoo, Mich.: W. E. Upjohn Institute, 1989, pp. 59–68.

53. Barry Bluestone and Irving Bluestone, *Negotiating the Future: A Labor Perspective on American Business*. New York: Basic Books, 1992, p. 8.

54. Bluestone and Bluestone, 1992, pp. 8–9.
55. John J. Lawler, *Unionization and Deunionization: Strategy, Tactics and Outcomes*. Columbia: University of South Carolina Press, 1990, pp. 221–234. See also Richard B. Freeman and James L. Medoff, *What Do Unions Do?* New York: Basic Books, 1984, pp. 230–239.
56. Saul A. Rubinstein and Thomas A. Kochan, *Learning from Saturn: Possibilities for Corporate Governance and Employee Relations*. Ithaca, N.Y.: Cornell University Press, 2001.
57. Anil Verma, "Union and Nonunion Industrial Relations at the Plant Level," unpublished doctoral dissertation, Massachusetts Institute of Technology, 1983.
58. Thomas A. Kochan, Harry C. Katz, and Robert B. McKersie, *The Transformation of American Industrial Relations*. New York: Basic Books, 1986, p. 147.
59. Paul Osterman, "How Common Is Workplace Transformation and Who Adopts It?" *Industrial and Labor Relations Review* 47, Jan. 1994, pp. 173–188. Paul Osterman, "Work Reorganization in an Era of Restructuring: Trends in Diffusion and Effects on Employee Welfare," *Industrial and Labor Relations Review* 53, Jan. 2000, pp. 179–196.

Chapter Three

1. Leonard L. Riskin and James E. Westbrook, *Dispute Resolution and Lawyers*. St. Paul, Minn.: West Publishing Co., 1987, p. 215.
2. Warren Burger, "Agenda for 2000 A.D.," presentation at the Pound Conference on the Causes of Popular Dissatisfaction with the Administration of Justice, Apr. 1976. See also "Symposium on the Impact of Mediation: 25 Years After the Pound Conference," *Ohio State Journal on Dispute Resolution* 17, 2002.
3. David B. Lipsky and Ronald L. Seeber, "In Search of Control: The Corporate Embrace of ADR," *University of*

Pennsylvania Journal of Labor and Employment Law 1, Spring 1998b, p. 142.

4. Katherine Van Wezel Stone, "Mandatory Arbitration of Individual Employment Rights: The Yellow Dog Contract of the 1990s," *Denver University Law Review* 73, 1996, pp. 1017–1050.

5. Lisa B. Bingham, "On Repeat Players, Adhesive Contracts, and the Use of Statistics and Judicial Review of Arbitration Awards," *McGeorge Law Review* 29, 1998, pp. 222–260. See also Lisa B. Bingham and Denise R. Chachere, "Dispute Resolution in Employment: The Need for Research," in Adrienne E. Eaton and Jeffrey H. Keefe (eds.), *Employment Dispute Resolution and Worker Rights in the Changing Workplace.* Champaign, Ill.: Industrial Relations Research Association, 1999, pp. 95–135.

6. Stone, 1996, pp. 1036–1048. See also Jean R. Sternlight, "Mandatory Binding Arbitration and the Demise of the Seventh Amendment Right to a Jury Trial," *Ohio State Journal of Dispute Resolution* 16, 2001, pp. 669–733.

7. Lipsky and Seeber, 1998a, 1998b.

8. Probably the major survey of this type to date was DeLoitte and Touche, 1993. See also David W. Harwell and Michael E. Weinzierl, "Alternatives to Business Lawsuits," *Business and Economic Review*, Oct.-Dec. 1995, p. 40, for a discussion of the DeLoitte and Touche survey results. The U.S. General Accounting Office (GAO) surveyed two thousand businesses about their use of ADR in resolving discrimination complaints. See U.S. General Accounting Office, *Employment Discrimination: Most Private Sector Employers Use Alternative Dispute Resolution.* Washington, D.C.: U.S. Government Printing Office, 1995. The GAO found that 90 percent of the companies surveyed used one or more ADR methods for resolving discrimination complaints but few used arbitration. See also U.S. General Accounting Office, *Alternative Dispute Resolution:*

Employers' Experiences with ADR in the Workplace. Washington, D.C.: U.S. Government Printing Office, 1997.

9. Bingham and Chachere, 1999, p. 99.

10. The results pertain to corporate use of ADR in rights disputes, not interest disputes.

11. Wayne D. Brazil, "Institutionalizing ADR Programs in Courts," in Frank Sander (ed.), *Emerging ADR Issues in State and Federal Courts.* Chicago: ABA Litigation Section, 1991, pp. 52–165. Zev J. Eigen, "Voluntary Mediation in New York State," *Dispute Resolution Journal,* Summer 1997, pp. 58–66.

12. For a copy of the CPR Institute for Dispute Resolution Pledge, see the CPR website at http://www.cpradr.org/. Accessed Oct. 23, 2002.

13. Lipsky and Seeber, 1998a, p. 16.

14. For similar results, see John Lande, "Getting the Faith: Why Business Lawyers and Executives Believe in Mediation," *Harvard Negotiation Law Review* 5, Spring 2000, pp. 137–192.

15. Volz and Goggin, 1997, pp. 28–124.

Chapter Four

1. Gosline et al., 2001; Costantino and Merchant, 1996.

2. Richard E. Walton and Robert B. McKersie, *A Behavioral Theory of Labor Negotiations: An Analysis of a Social Interaction System* (2nd ed.). Ithaca, N.Y.: ILR Press, 1991 (originally published in 1965).

3. For nonprofit and public sector organizations, the analogue to the market factors is probably the condition of the organization's budget. We would hypothesize that public sector agencies that face budget constraints would be more likely to adopt ADR and conflict management strategies than agencies that do not face such constraints.

4. U.S. Department of Labor, 1994, p. 49.
5. The Federal Arbitration Act is found at 9 U.S. Code Sec. 1 (1994 and Suppl. 2000), and the National Labor Relations Act is found at 29 U.S. Code Sec. 157 (1994).
6. Susan FitzGibbon, "Appellate Settlement Conference Programs: A Case Study," in E. Wendy Trachte-Huber and Stephen K. Huber (eds.), *Alternative Dispute Resolution: Strategies for Law and Business*. Cincinnati, Ohio: Anderson Publishing Co., 1996, p. 977.
7. The RAND Corporation conducted an evaluation of ten pilot courts that adopted case management principles required by the Civil Justice Reform Act of 1990. It found that "some case management procedures—for example, certain types of alternative dispute resolution—have no major effects on cost and delay." See J. S. Kakalik et al., *Just, Speedy and Inexpensive? An Evaluation of Judicial Case Management Under the Civil Justice Reform Act*. Santa Monica, Calif.: RAND, 1996.
8. The ADR Act of 1998 gives federal district courts the authority to compel parties to participate in ADR processes such as mediation and early neutral evaluation. 28 U.S.C.A. Sec. 654 (West 1993 and Suppl. 2000).
9. See the U.S. Equal Employment Opportunity Commission's policy statement on alternative dispute resolution on July 10, 1997. See also Paul Steven Miller, "EEOC Adopts ADR Methods," *Dispute Resolution Journal*, Oct.-Dec. 1995, pp. 17, 87.
10. The Department of Labor made a grant to the Alliance for Education in Dispute Resolution to develop, manage, and evaluate this program. David B. Lipsky, Ronald L. Seeber, and Les Hough, "Developing a Mediation Program for the U.S. Department of Labor: An Interim Evaluation of a Pilot Program for Enforcement Cases," unpublished report, Aug. 2002.
11. Trachte-Huber and Huber, 1996, pp. 9–29.

12. David B. Lipsky and Ronald L. Seeber, "Resolving Workplace Disputes in the United States: The Growth of Alternative Dispute Resolution in Employment Relations," *Journal of Alternative Dispute Resolution in Employment* 2, Fall 2000, pp. 37–49.

13. Harrison M. Trice and Janice M. Beyer, *The Cultures of Work Organizations*, Upper Saddle River, N.J.: Prentice Hall, 1993, pp. 1–2.

14. See, for example, Terrence E. Deal and Allan A. Kennedy, *Corporate Cultures: The Rights and Rituals of Corporate Life.* Reading, Mass.: Addison-Wesley, 1982; Trice and Beyer, 1993, esp. pp. 33–76.

15. Trice and Beyer, 1993, pp. 66–67, 235–237.

16. Kochan, Katz, and McKersie, 1986; Bluestone and Bluestone, 1992.

17. Dave Ulrich, *Human Resource Champions: The Next Agenda for Adding Value and Delivering Results.* Boston: Harvard Business School Press, 1997, pp. 184–185.

18. Ulrich, 1997, pp. 184–188.

19. Gosline et al., 2001, p. 14. Gosline and her colleagues draw on the work of Alan F. Weston and Alfred G. Feliu, *Resolving Employment Disputes Without Litigation.* Washington, D.C.: Bureau of National Affairs, 1988.

20. Lipsky and Seeber, 1998a, pp. 24–25.

21. Ken Auletta reports that Gates was prepared to make some significant concessions, however, and that Posner came very close to mediating a settlement in the case. See Ken Auletta, *World War 3.0: Microsoft and Its Enemies.* New York: Random House, 2001.

22. See *Gilmer v. Interstate/Johnson Lane Corp.*, 500 U.S. 20 (1991), and *Circuit City Stores v. Saint Clair Adams*, 121 S. Ct. 1302 (2001).

23. See, for example, Ronald L. Seeber and Lois Gray, eds., *Under the Stars: Labor Relations in Arts and Entertainment*, Ithaca, N.Y.: ILR Press, 1996, esp. pp. 113–180.

24. See, for example: *San Francisco Chronicle*, Nov. 23, 1998, p. 7. *New Times of Los Angeles*, Dec. 9, 1999.

25. Michael Brick, "MGM Grand to Acquire Mirage Resorts for $4.4 Billion," *New York Times*, Mar. 6, 2000.

26. See, for example, Associated Press Newswires, Nov. 2, 1999, and Dow Jones Business News, Apr. 22, 1999.

27. F. Peter Phillips, *Employment Dispute Resolution Systems: An Empirical Survey and Tentative Conclusions*. New York: CPR Institute for Dispute Resolution, 2000. See also CPR Institute for Dispute Resolution, *How Companies Manage Employment Disputes: A Compendium of Leading Corporate Employment Programs*. New York: CPR Institute for Dispute Resolution, 2002.

28. Agis Salpukas, "PECO and Unicom to Merge in Big Bet on Nuclear Power," *New York Times*, Sept. 24, 1999, p. C5.

29. Coverage by the press of Prudential's troubles was extensive; see, for example, "Corporate Focus: Uncertainty Clouds Prudential's Settlement Process," *Wall Street Journal*, Dec. 11, 1998.

Chapter Five

1. Karl A. Slaikeu and Ralph H. Hasson, *Controlling the Costs of Conflict*. San Francisco: Jossey-Bass, 1996, Chaps. 4–5.

2. Costantino and Merchant, 1996, Chaps. 5–7.

3. Gosline et al., 2001, pp. 16–19.

4. U.S. Department of Labor, *Report and Recommendations: Commission on the Future of Worker-Management Relations* (Dunlop Commission). Washington, D.C. Government Printing Office, 1994.

5. *Circuit City Stores, Inc.* v. *Adams*, 121 S. Ct. 1302 (2001).

6. Slaikeu and Hasson, 1996, p. 59.

7. "In the News," *Corporate Counsel Journal*, Jan. 2002, p. 18.

8. Mary P. Rowe, "What Is It Like to Be an Organizational Ombudsman?" *Perspectives on Work*, 1997, p. 60. Also see reports of the Ombudsman Association, Dallas, Tex.

9. See reports of the Ombudsman Association, Dallas, Tex. Also see Slaikeu and Hasson, 1996, p. 136.
10. Ombudsman Association, *Code of Ethics*. Dallas, Tex.: Ombudsman Association, 1987.
11. When one of us (Fincher) was the vice president of human resources at an aerospace corporation with an unstaffed hot line, most of the telephone messages involved these issues. The hot line was required as part of a federal contract.
12. Lipsky and Seeber, 1998a, pp. 22–23.
13. Slaikeu and Hasson, 1996, pp. 60, 91, 101.
14. Slaikeu and Hasson, 1996, pp. 97–102.
15. Slaikeu and Hasson, 1996, p. 137.

Chapter Six

1. Mark Sherman, "Is There a Mediator in the House? Using In-House Neutrals," *Dispute Resolution Journal* 50, Apr. 1995, p. 48.
2. Edward J. Costello, Jr., *Controlling Conflict: ADR for Business*. Washington, D.C.: Commerce Clearinghouse, 1996.
3. Richard Faulkner, "Employment Arbitration; Advanced Dispute Resolution for the Global Economy," *Journal of Alternative Dispute Resolution in Employment*, June 1999, p. 57. Also see *Gilmer v. Interstate/Johnson Lane Corp.*, 500 U.S. 20 (1991).
4. *Circuit City Stores, Inc. v. Adams*, 121 S. Ct. 1302 (2001).
5. Lipsky and Seeber, 1998a, p. 28.
6. Slaikeu and Hasson, 1996, p. 139.
7. See *Ball v. SFX Broadcasting, Inc.*, 165 F. Supp. 230 (N.D.N.Y. 2001). A federal district court in New York has held that an arbitration policy administered under the fee-splitting rules of the American Arbitration Association does not provide an effective mechanism for the vindication of statutory rights. The court held that the focus should be on the likelihood of substantial arbitration costs, not on

the financial situation of the particular plaintiff. The imposition of such costs does not make arbitration a reasonable substitute for a judicial forum. Also see *Diaz* v. *Josephthal*, 1998 U.S. Dist. Lexis 22204 (SDNY 1998), where the court directed a securities firm to pay the arbitrator's fees in full because it was standard practice in that industry.

8. *Gilmer* v. *Interstate/Johnson Lane Corp.*, 500 U.S. 20 (1991).

9. *Circuit City Stores, Inc.* v. *Adams*, 121 S. Ct. 1302 (2001).

10. *EEOC* v. *Waffle House, Inc.*, 121 S. Ct. 1401 (2001).

11. *Duffield* v. *Robertson Stephens and Co.*, 144 F.3d 1181 (9th Cir. 1998).

12. See statements of the National Employment Lawyer Association, San Francisco, 2001. [http://www.nela.org]. Accessed Apr. 20, 2002.

13. See "EEOC Policy Statement on Mandatory Binding Arbitration," July 10, 1997, in *EEOC Compliance Manual*. Washington, D.C.: Bureau of National Affairs, 1997, pp. 3101–3106. Also see Equal Employment Opportunity Commission, *Corporate Counsel's Guide to Alternative Dispute Resolution in the Employment Context*. Chesterland, Ohio: Business Laws, 1998, p. 2501. Also see "EEOC Task Force Report on Alternative Dispute Resolution, Mar. 17, 1995," also found in *Corporate Counsel's Guide to Alternative Dispute Resolution in the Employment Context*, Chesterland, Ohio: Business Laws, 1998, p. 260.

14. Commission on the Future of Worker-Management Relations, *Fact Finding Report*, 1994. Department of Labor and U.S. Department of Commerce, May 1994. Also see John T. Dunlop, "Employment Litigation and Dispute Resolution: The Dunlop Report," in *1995 Proceedings of the National Academy of Arbitrators*. Washington, D.C.: Bureau of National Affairs, 1996, p. 124.

15. Dunlop and Zack, 1997, pp. 171–178.

16. See *First Options of Chicago Inc.* v. *Kaplan*, 514 U.S. 938, 944 (1995).

17. See *Quigley* v. *KPGM Peat Marwick LLP*, 749 A.2d. 405, 413 (N.J. Super. Ct. App. Div. 2000).

18. See *Morison* v. *Circuit City Stores Inc.*, 70 F. Supp. 2d, 815, 824 (S.D. Ohio 1999)

19. *Hooters of America Inc.* v. *Phillips*, 173 F.3d 933 (1999).

20. *Report of the Commission on Qualifications, SPIDR.* Washington, D.C.: SPIDR, 1989, and *Report No. 2*, 1995.

21. See various reports of the Association for Conflict Resolution. [http://www.acresolution.org].

22. Picher, Seeber, and Lipsky, 2000.

23. Picher, Seeber, and Lipsky, 2000, p. 5.

24. See "Guidelines on the Arbitration of Statutory Claims Under Employer-Promulgated Systems," in *1997 Proceedings of the National Academy of Arbitrators*. Washington, D.C.: Bureau of National Affairs, 1998, p. 313.

Chapter Seven

1. Costantino and Merchant, 1996, p. 69.

2. CPR Institute for Conflict Resolution, *How Companies Manage Employment Disputes: A Compendium of Leading Corporate Employment Programs* (New York: CPR Institute for Conflict Resolution, Jan. 2, 2002), p. 56.

3. Costantino and Merchant, 1996, p. 70.

4. Slaikeu and Hasson, 1998, p. 81.

5. Costantino and Merchant, 1996, p. 77.

6. Costantino and Merchant, 1996, p. 75.

7. Costantino and Merchant, 1996, pp. 105–111.

8. Costantino and Merchant, 1996, p. 69.

9. Gosline et al., 2001.

10. CPR Institute for Conflict Resolution, *ADR in Industries and Practice Areas*. New York: CPR Institute for Conflict Resolution, 1998.

11. *Corporate Counsel's Guide to Alternative Dispute Resolution in the Employment Context*. Chesterland, Ohio: Business

Laws, 1998, p. 18.008, establishing that there was not a floodgate of cases to arbitration after implementation of the system.

12. CPR Institute for Conflict Resolution, Dec. 19, 2001, p. 79.
13. *ADR in Industries and Practice Areas*, 1998, p. 41.
14. Costantino and Merchant, 1996, Chap. 3.
15. Costantino and Merchant, 1996, Chap. 9.
16. Slaikeu and Hasson, 1998, pp. 92–95. Also see Lipsky and Seeber, 1998a, pp. 22–23.
17. Costantino and Merchant, 1996, p. 135.
18. CPR Institute for Conflict Resolution, Jan. 3, 2001, p. 52.
19. Costantino and Merchant, 1996, Chap. 8.
20. Slaikeu and Hasson, 1998, p. 190.

Chapter Eight

1. Bingham and Chachere, 1999, pp. 95–135.
2. Shell RESOLVE, *Progress Report*, 1998.
3. Lisa B. Bingham and Charles R. Wise, "The Administrative Dispute Resolution Act of 1990: How Do We Evaluate Its Success?" *Journal of Public Administration Research and Theory* 6, 1996, pp. 383–414.
4. Bingham and Wise, 1996, p. 389.
5. Bingham and Wise, 1996, p. 388.
6. Ronald L. Seeber, Timothy B. Schmidle, and Robert S. Smith, *An Evaluation of the New York State Workers' Compensation Pilot Program for Alternative Dispute Resolution*. Albany: New York State Workers' Compensation Board, Dec. 2001.
7. Unified Court System of New York State, *The Mediation Alternative Pilot Program*. New York: Unified Court System of New York State, Jan. 2002.
8. Interview with Kathleen Aure, Dec. 14, 1999.
9. Chevron Corp., *Steps to Employee Problem Solution*. San Francisco: Chevron Corp., 1997.

10. William L. Bedman, "From Litigation to ADR: Brown & Root's Experience," *Dispute Resolution Journal* 50, Oct.–Dec. 1995, pp. 8–14.

11. Bingham and Chachere, 1999.

12. Jeanne M. Brett, Zoe I. Barsness, and Stephen B. Goldberg, "The Effectiveness of Mediation: An Independent Analysis of Cases Handled by Four Major Service Providers," *Negotiation Journal* 12, July 1996, pp. 259–269.

13. Seeber, Schmidle, and Smith, 2001, p. 8.

14. Karen E. Boroff, "Measuring the Perceptions of the Effectiveness of a Workplace Complaint Procedure," in Donna Sockell, David Lewin, and David B. Lipsky, eds., *Advances in Industrial and Labor Relations*, Vol. 5. Greenwich, Conn.: JAI Press, 1991, pp. 207–234.

15. Joshua L. Pascoe, "Management Effectiveness and Willingness to Grieve: The Search for Due Process in Employment Alternative Dispute Resolution Procedures," unpublished master's thesis, School of Industrial and Labor Relations, Cornell University, 2000.

16. *Hooters of America, Inc.* v. *Annette R. Phillips*, U.S. Court of Appeals, Fourth Circuit, No. 98–1459, Apr. 8, 1999.

17. Rosemary Batt, Alexander J. S. Colvin, and Jeffrey Keefe, "Employee Voice, Human Resource Practices, and Quit Rates: Evidence from the Telecommunications Industry," *Industrial and Labor Relations Review* 55, July 2002, pp. 573–594.

18. Alexander James Colvin, "Citizens and Citadels: Dispute Resolution and the Governance of Employment Relations," unpublished doctoral dissertation, School of Industrial and Labor Relations, Cornell University, 1999.

19. Seeber, Schmidle, and Smith. 2001, See pp. 5–11 for a summary of the results.

20. Seeber, Schmidle, and Smith, 2001, pp. 35–40.

21. Richard Gannon, *The Construction Carveout Program: A Report of Activities in Calendar Year 1999*. San Francisco: California Division of Workers' Compensation, Jan. 2001.

22. Thomas A. Kochan, Brenda A. Lautsch, and Corinne Bendersky, "An Evaluation of the Massachusetts Commission Against Discrimination Alternative Dispute Resolution Program," *Harvard Negotiation Law Review* 5, Spring 2002, pp. 233–278.

23. Lipsky and Seeber, 1998a.

24. Lipsky, Seeber, and Hough, 2002.

25. Lisa B. Bingham et al., *Mediation at Work: The Report of the National REDRESS Evaluation Project of the United States Postal Service*, Bloomington: Indiana Conflict Resolution Institute, 2001.

26. For a much more complete explanation, see the original source on the subject: Robert A. Baruch Bush and Joseph P. Folger, *The Promise of Mediation: Responding to Conflict Through Empowerment and Recognition*. San Francisco: Jossey-Bass, 1994.

27. E. Patrick McDermott, Ruth Obar, Anita Jose, and Mollie Bowers, *An Evaluation of the Equal Employment Opportunity Commission Mediation Program*. 2000. [http://www.eeoc.gov/mediate/report/index/html]. Accessed Dec. 20, 2002.

28. Craig McEwen, "Managing Corporate Disputing: Overcoming Barriers to the Effective Use of Mediation for Reducing the Cost and Time of Litigation," *Ohio State Journal of Dispute Resolution* 14, 1998, pp. 1–28.

29. McDermott, Obar, Jose, and Bowers, 2000.

Chapter Nine

1. Bingham and Chachere, 1999, p. 101.

2. U.S. Department of Labor, *Working Together for Public Service: Report of the U.S. Secretary of Labor's Task Force on Excellence in State and Local Government through Labor-Management Cooperation*. Washington, D.C.: U.S. Government Printing Office, 1996, p. 81.

3. Bingham and Chachere, 1999, p. 102.

4. Jill Kriesky, "Trends in Dispute Resolution in the Public Sector," in Eaton and Keefe, 1999, p. 250.
5. Dunlop and Zack, 1997.
6. Picher, Seeber, and Lipsky, 2000, pp. 7–8.
7. Osterman, 2000.
8. See Lipsky and Seeber, 1998a.

Chapter Ten

1. Peter M. Senge, *The Fifth Discipline: The Art and Practice of the Learning Organization*. New York: Doubleday/Currency, 1990.
2. Malcolm Gladwell, *The Tipping Point*. New York: Little, Brown, 2000.
3. Gladwell, 2000, p. 132.
4. Costantino and Merchant, 1996.

References

ADR Act of 1998. 28 U.S.C.A. Sec. 654 (West 1993 & Supp. 2000).

Association for Conflict Resolution. [http://www.acresolution.org]. Accessed Oct. 23, 2002.

Auletta, Ken. *World War 3.0: Microsoft and Its Enemies.* New York: Random House, 2001.

Ball v. SFX Broadcasting, Inc., 165 F. Supp. 230 (N.D. N.Y. 2001).

Batt, Rosemary, Colvin, Alexander J. S., and Keefe, Jeffrey. "Employee Voice, Human Resource Practices, and Quit Rates: Evidence from the Telecommunications Industry," *Industrial and Labor Relations Review* 55, July 2002, 573–594.

Bedman, William L. "From Litigation to ADR: Brown & Root's Experience," *Dispute Resolution Journal* 50, Oct.-Dec. 1995, 8–14.

Bell, Daniel. *The End of Ideology: On the Exhaustion of Political Ideas in the Fifties.* Cambridge, Mass.: Harvard University Press, 2000. (Originally published in 1960.)

Bingham, Lisa B. "On Repeat Players, Adhesive Contracts, and the Use of Statistics and Judicial Review of Arbitration Awards," *McGeorge Law Review* 29, 1998, 222–260.

Bingham, Lisa B., and Chachere, Denise R. "Dispute Resolution in Employment: The Need for Research." In Adrienne E. Eaton and Jeffrey H. Keefe (eds.), *Employment Dispute Resolution and Worker Rights in the Changing Workplace.* Champaign, Ill.: Industrial Relations Research Association, 1999, pp. 95–135.

Bingham, Lisa B., and Wise, Charles R. "The Administrative Dispute Resolution Act of 1990: How Do We Evaluate Its Success?" *Journal of Public Administration Research and Theory* 6, 1996, 383–414.

Bingham, Lisa B., et al. *Mediation at Work: The Report of the National REDRESS Evaluation Project of the United States Postal Service.* Bloomington: Indiana Conflict Resolution Institute, 2001.

Binmore, Ken. *Game Theory and the Social Contract,* Vol. 1: *Playing Fair.* Cambridge, Mass.: MIT Press, 1995.

Bluestone, Barry, and Bluestone, Irving. *Negotiating the Future: A Labor Perspective on American Business*. New York: Basic Books, 1992.

Bluestone, Barry, and Harrison, Bennett. *The Deindustrialization of America*. New York: Basic Books, 1982.

Boroff, Karen E. "Measuring the Perceptions of the Effectiveness of a Workplace Complaint Procedure." In Donna Sockell, David Lewin, and David B. Lipsky, eds., *Advances in Industrial and Labor Relations*, Vol. 5. Greenwich, Conn.: JAI Press, 1991, pp. 207–234.

Boulding, Kenneth E. "General Systems—The Skeleton of Science." *Management Science* 2, Apr. 1956, 197–208.

Brakel, Samuel Jan. "Using What We Know About Our Civil Litigation System: A Critique of 'Base-Rate' Analysis and Other Apologist Diversions." *Georgia Law Review* 31, 1996, 77–200. [http://www.lawsch.uga.edu/~galawrev/vol31/brakel.html]. Accessed Mar. 24, 1999.

Brazil, Wayne D. "Institutionalizing ADR Programs in Courts." In Frank Sander (ed.), *Emerging ADR Issues in State and Federal Courts*. Chicago: ABA Litigation Section, 1991, pp. 52–165.

Brett, Jeanne M., Barsness, Zoe I., and Goldberg, Stephen B. "The Effectiveness of Mediation: An Independent Analysis of Cases Handled by Four Major Service Providers." *Negotiation Journal* 12, July 1996, 259–269.

Brick, Michael. "MGM Grand to Acquire Mirage Resorts for $4.4 Billion." *New York Times*, Mar. 6, 2000.

Burger, Warren. "Agenda for 2000 A.D." Presentation at the Pound Conference on the Causes of Popular Dissatisfaction with the Administration of Justice, Apr. 1976.

Burton, Jr., John F., and Thomason, Terry. "The Extent of Collective Bargaining in the Public Sector." In Benjamin Aaron, Joyce M. Najita, and James L. Stern (eds.), *Public-Sector Bargaining*. Washington, D.C.: Bureau of National Affairs, 1988, pp. 1–51.

Bush, Robert A. Baruch, and Folger, Joseph P. *The Promise of Mediation: Responding to Conflict Through Empowerment and Recognition*. San Francisco: Jossey-Bass, 1994.

Capelli, Peter. "Airlines." In David B. Lipsky and Clifford B. Donn (eds.), *Collective Bargaining in American Industry*. San Francisco: New Lexington Press, 1987, pp. 135–186.

Chamberlain, Neil W., and Kuhn, James W. *Collective Bargaining*, 2nd ed. New York: McGraw-Hill, 1965.

Chevron Corp. *Steps to Employee Problem Solution*. San Francisco: Chevron Corp., 1997.

Circuit City Stores v. Saint Clair Adams. 121 S. Ct. 1302 (2001).

Colvin, Alexander James. "Citizens and Citadels: Dispute Resolution and the Governance of Employment Relations." Unpublished Ph.D. dissertation, Cornell University, 1999.

"Corporate Focus: Uncertainty Clouds Prudential's Settlement Process." *Wall Street Journal*, Dec. 11, 1998.

Costantino, Cathy A., and Merchant, Christina Sickles. *Designing Conflict Management Systems*. San Francisco: Jossey-Bass, 1996.

Costello, Edward J., Jr. *Controlling Conflict: ADR for Business*. Washington, D.C.: Commerce Clearinghouse, 1996.

CPR Institute for Dispute Resolution. *ADR in Industries and Practice Areas*. New York: CPR Institute for Dispute Resolution, 1998. CPR Web site found at [http://www.cpradr.org/] on October 23, 2002.

CPR Institute for Dispute Resolution. *How Companies Manage Employment Disputes: A Compendium of Leading Corporate Employment Programs*. New York: CPR Institute for Dispute Resolution, 2002.

Deal, Terrence E., and Kennedy, Allan A. *Corporate Cultures: The Rights and Rituals of Corporate Life*. Reading, Mass.: Addison-Wesley, 1982.

DeLoitte Touche Tohmatsu International. *DeLoitte and Touche Litigation Services 1993 Survey of General and Outside Counsels: Alternative Dispute Resolution (ADR)*. New York: DeLoitte Touche Tohmatsu International, 1993.

Diaz v. Josephthal, 1998 U.S. Dist. Lexis 22204 (S.D.N.Y. 1998).

Donaldson, Thomas, and Dunfee, Thomas W. *Ties That Bind: A Social Contracts Approach to Business Ethics*. Boston: Harvard Business School Press, 1999.

DuBrin, Andrew J., Ireland, R. Duane, and Williams, J. Clifton. *Management and Organization*. Cincinnati, Ohio: Southwestern Publishing Co., 1989.

Duffield v. Robertson Stephens and Co. 144 F.3d 1181 (9th Cir. 1998).

Dunlop, John. *Industrial Relations Systems*. New York: Holt, 1958.

Dunlop, John T. "Employment Litigation and Dispute Resolution: The Dunlop Report." In *1995 Proceedings of the National Academy of Arbitrators*. Washington, D.C.: Bureau of National Affairs, 1996.

Dunlop, John T., and Zack, Arnold M. *Mediation and Arbitration of Employment Disputes*. San Francisco: Jossey-Bass, 1997.

Dunworth, Terence, and Rogers, Joel. "Corporations in Court: Big Business Litigation in U.S. Federal Courts, 1971–1991." *Law and Social Inquiry* 21, Summer 1996, 498.

Eaton, Adrienne E., and Keefe, Jeffrey H. *Employment Dispute Resolution and Worker Rights in the Changing Workplace*. Champaign, Ill.: Industrial Relations Research Association, 1999.

EEOC v. Waffle House, Inc. 121 S. Ct. 1401 (2001).

Eigen, Zev J. "Voluntary Mediation in New York State." *Dispute Resolution Journal*, Summer 1997, 58–66.

Equal Employment Opportunity Commission. *EEOC Task Force Report on Alternative Dispute Resolution*. Washington, D.C.: U.S. Government Printing Office, Mar. 17, 1995.

Equal Employment Opportunity Commission. "EEOC Policy Statement on Mandatory Binding Arbitration." In *EEOC Compliance Manual*. Washington, D.C.: Bureau of National Affairs, 1997, pp. 3101–3106.

Equal Employment Opportunity Commission. *Corporate Counsel's Guide to Alternative Dispute Resolution in the Employment Context*. Chesterland, Ohio: Business Laws, 1998.

Faulkner, Richard. "Employment Arbitration; Advanced Dispute Resolution for the Global Economy." *Journal of Alternative Dispute Resolution in Employment*, June 1999, 57.

Federal Arbitration Act. 9 U.S.C. Sec. 1 (1994 and Supp. 2000).

First National Maintenance Corp. v. *NLRB*. 452 U.S. 666 (1981).

First Options of Chicago Inc. v. *Kaplan*. 514 U.S. 938, 944 (1995).

FitzGibbon, Susan. "Appellate Settlement Conference Programs: A Case Study." In E. Wendy Trachte-Huber and Stephen K. Huber (eds.), *Alternative Dispute Resolution: Strategies for Law and Business*. Cincinnati, Ohio: Anderson Publishing Co., 1996.

Freeman, Richard B., and Medoff, James L. *What Do Unions Do?* New York: Basic Books, 1984.

Gannon, Richard. *The Construction Carveout Program: A Report of Activities in Calendar Year 1999*. San Francisco: California Division of Workers' Compensation, Jan. 2001.

Garry, Patrick M. *A Nation of Adversaries: How the Litigation Explosion Is Reshaping America*. New York: Plenum Press, 1997.

Gilmer v. *Interstate/Johnson Lane Corp*. 500 U.S. 20 (1991).

Gladwell, Malcolm. *The Tipping Point*. New York: Little, Brown, 2000.

Gold, Stephen. "Step Ladders and Lawsuits." *Washington Times*, Nov. 21, 1997.

Gosline, Ann, et al. *Designing Integrated Conflict Management Systems: Guidelines for Practitioners and Decision Makers in Organizations*. Ithaca, N.Y.: Institute on Conflict Resolution, 2001.

Halberstam, David. *The Reckoning*. New York: Morrow, 1986.

Harwell, David W., and Weinzierl, Michael E. "Alternatives to Business Lawsuits." *Business and Economic Review*, Oct.-Dec. 1995, 40.

Heckscher, Charles. *The New Unionism: Employee Involvement in the Changing Corporation*. New York: Basic Books, 1988.

Hendricks, Wallace E. "Telecommunications." In David B. Lipsky and Clifford B. Donn (eds.), *Collective Bargaining in American Industry*. San Francisco: New Lexington Press, 1987, pp. 103–133.

Hobbes, Thomas. *Leviathan*. In William Molesworth (ed.), *The English Works of Thomas Hobbes*. London: John Bohn, 1839, Vol. 3. (Originally published in 1651.)

Hooters of America Inc. v. *Phillips*. 173 F.3d 933 (1999).

Hutchens, Robert, Lipsky, David, and Stern, Robert. *Strikers and Subsidies: The Influence of Government Transfer Programs on Strike Activity*. Kalamazoo, Mich.: W. E. Upjohn Institute, 1989.

"In the News." *Corporate Counsel Journal*, Jan. 2002, p. 18.

Jacoby, Sanford M. *Modern Manors: Welfare Capitalism Since the New Deal.* Princeton, N.J.: Princeton University Press, 1997.

Kakalik, J. S., et al. *Just, Speedy and Inexpensive? An Evaluation of Judicial Case Management Under the Civil Justice Reform Act.* Santa Monica, Calif.: Rand, 1996.

Katz, Harry C., and Kochan, Thomas A. *An Introduction to Collective Bargaining and Industrial Relations.* New York: Irwin McGraw-Hill, 2000.

Katz, Harry C., and Lipsky, David B. "The Collective Bargaining System in the United States: The Legacy and the Lessons." In Maurice F. Neufeld and Jean T. McKelvey (eds.), *Industrial Relations at the Dawn of the New Millennium.* Ithaca, N.Y.: New York State School of Industrial and Labor Relations, Cornell University, 1998.

Kaufman, Bruce E. *The Origins and Evolution of the Field of Industrial Relations in the United States.* Ithaca, N.Y.: ILR Press, 1993.

Kerr, Clark, Dunlop, John, Harbison, Frederick, and Myers, Charles. *Industrialism and Industrial Man.* Cambridge, Mass.: Harvard University Press, 1960.

Kerr, Clark, and Siegel, Abraham. "The Structuring of the Labor Force in Industrial Society: New Dimensions and New Questions." *Industrial and Labor Relations Review* 8, Jan. 1955, 151–168.

Kheel, Theodore W. *The Keys to Conflict Resolution: Proven Methods of Settling Disputes Voluntarily.* New York: Four Walls Eight Windows, 1999.

Kochan, Thomas A., Katz, Harry C., and McKersie, Robert B. *The Transformation of American Industrial Relations.* New York: Basic Books, 1986.

Kochan, Thomas A., Lautsch, Brenda A., and Bendersky, Corinne. "An Evaluation of the Massachusetts Commission Against Discrimination Alternative Dispute Resolution Program." *Harvard Negotiation Law Review* 5, Spring 2002, 233–278.

Kriesky, Jill. "Trends in Dispute Resolution in the Public Sector." In Adrienne E. Eaton and Jeffrey H. Keefe (eds.), *Employment Dispute Resolution and Worker Rights in the Changing Workplace.* Champaign, Ill.: Industrial Relations Research Association, 1999.

Lande, John. "Getting the Faith: Why Business Lawyers and Executives Believe in Mediation." *Harvard Negotiation Law Review* 5, Spring 2000, 137–192.

Lawler, John J. *Unionization and Deunionization: Strategy, Tactics and Outcomes.* Columbia: University of South Carolina Press, 1990.

Lewis, Melanie. "Conflict Management System for Coca-Cola Enterprises." Presentation at Resolving Conflict Conference, Baltimore, May 24, 2001.

Lipsky, David B., and Seeber, Ronald L. *The Appropriate Resolution of Corporate Disputes: A Report on the Growing Use of ADR by U.S. Corporations.* Ithaca, N.Y.: Cornell/PERC Institute on Conflict Resolution, 1998a.

Lipsky, David B., and Seeber, Ronald L. "In Search of Control: The Corporate Embrace of ADR." *University of Pennsylvania Journal of Labor and Employment Law* 1, Spring 1998b, 133–157.

Lipsky, David B., and Seeber, Ronald L. "Resolving Workplace Disputes in the United States: The Growth of Alternative Dispute Resolution in Employment Relations." *Journal of Alternative Dispute Resolution in Employment* 2, Fall 2000, 37–49.

Lipsky, David B., Seeber, Ronald L., and Hall, Lavinia. "An Uncertain Destination: On the Development of Conflict Management Systems in U.S. Corporations." In Samuel Estreicher and David Sherwyn (eds.), *Developments in Labor Law*. New York: Kluwer Law International, forthcoming.

Lipsky, David B., Seeber, Ronald L., and Hough, Les. "Developing a Mediation Program for the U.S. Department of Labor: An Interim Evaluation of a Pilot Program for Enforcement Cases." Unpublished report, Aug. 2002.

Litras, Marika F. X. *Civil Rights Complaints in U.S. District Courts, 1990–98*. Washington, D.C.: U.S. Department of Justice, Jan. 2000.

Locke, John. *Second Treatise of Government*. Indianapolis: Hackett, 1980. (Originally published in 1690.)

MacDonald, Robert M. *Collective Bargaining in the Automobile Industry*. New Haven, Conn.: Yale University Press, 1963.

McDermott, E. Patrick, Obar, Ruth, Jose, Anita, and Bowers, Mollie. *An Evaluation of the Equal Employment Opportunity Commission Mediation Program*. 2000. [http://www.eeoc.gov/mediate/report/index/html]. Accessed Dec. 20, 2002.

McEwen, Craig. "Managing Corporate Disputing: Overcoming Barriers to the Effective Use of Mediation for Reducing the Cost and Time of Litigation." *Ohio State Journal of Dispute Resolution* 14, 1998, 1–28.

Miller, Paul Steven. "EEOC Adopts ADR Methods." *Dispute Resolution Journal*, Oct.-Dec. 1995, pp. 17, 87.

Molesworth, William (ed.). *The English Works of Thomas Hobbes*. London: John Bohn, 1839.

Morison v. Circuit City Stores Inc. 70 F. Supp. 2nd 815, 824 (S.D. Ohio 1999).

National Academy of Arbitrators. "Guidelines on the Arbitration of Statutory Claims Under Employer-Promulgated Systems." In *1997 Proceedings of the National Academy of Arbitrators*. Washington, D.C.: Bureau of National Affairs, 1998.

National Center for Policy Analysis. "Tort System Pays People to Hurt Themselves." [http://www.ncpa.org/pd/law/law1197c.html]. Accessed Mar. 24, 1999.

National Employment Lawyers Association (NELA), San Francisco, California. [http://www.nela.org]. Accessed Oct. 22, 2002.

National Labor Relations Act. 29 U.S.C. Sec. 157 (1994).

Neufeld, Maurice F., and McKelvey, Jean T. (eds.). *Industrial Relations at the Dawn of the New Millennium*. Ithaca, N.Y.: New York State School of Industrial and Labor Relations, Cornell University, 1998.

Noe, Raymond A., Hollenbeck, John R., Gerhart, Barry, and Wright, Patrick M. (eds.). *Readings in Human Resource Management*. Burr Ridge, Ill.: Irwin, 1994.

Nozick, Robert. *Anarchy, State, and Utopia*. New York: Basic Books, 1974.

Olson, Walter K. *The Litigation Explosion: What Happened When America Unleashed the Lawsuit*. New York: Truman Talley Books, 1991.

Ombudsman Association. *Code of Ethics*. Dallas: Ombudsman Association, 1987.

Osterman, Paul. "How Common Is Workplace Transformation and Who Adopts It?" *Industrial and Labor Relations Review* 47, Jan. 1994, 173–188.

Osterman, Paul. "Work Reorganization in an Era of Restructuring: Trends in Diffusion and Effects on Employee Welfare." *Industrial and Labor Relations Review* 53, Jan. 2000, 179–196.

Pascoe, Joshua L. "Management Effectiveness and Willingness to Grieve: The Search for Due Process in Employment Alternative Dispute Resolution Procedures." Unpublished master's thesis, Cornell University, 2000.

Penner, Rudolph G., Sawhill, Isabel V., and Taylor, Timothy. *Updating America's Social Contract: Economic Growth and Opportunity in the New Century*. New York: Norton, 2000.

Phillips, F. Peter. *Employment Dispute Resolution Systems: An Empirical Survey and Tentative Conclusions*. New York: CPR Institute for Conflict Resolution, 2000.

Picher, Michel, Seeber, Ronald L., and Lipsky, David B. *The Arbitration Profession in Transition: A Survey of the National Academy of Arbitrators*. Ithaca, N.Y.: Cornell/PERC Institute on Conflict Resolution, 2000.

President's National Labor-Management Conference, November 5–20, 1945: Summary and Committee Reports. Washington, D.C.: U.S. Government Printing Office, 1946.

Quigley v. KPMG Peat Marwick LLP, 749 A.2d. 405, 413 (N.J. Super. Ct. App. Div. 2000).

Rawls, John. *A Theory of Justice* (rev. ed.). Cambridge, Mass.: Belknap Press, 1999.

Report of the Commission on Qualifications, SPIDR. Washington, D.C.: Society for Professionals in Dispute Resolution, 1989.

Rifkin, Jeremy. *The End of Work: The Decline of the Global Labor Force and the Dawn of the Post-Market Era*. New York: Tarcher/Putnam, 1995.

Riskin, Leonard L., and Westbrook, James E. *Dispute Resolution and Lawyers*. St. Paul, Minn.: West Publishing, 1987.

Rousseau, Jean-Jacques. *The Social Contract*. London: Penguin Books, 1968. (Originally published in 1762.)

Rowe, Mary P. "What Is It Like to Be an Organizational Ombudsman?" *Perspectives on Work*, 1997, 60.

Rubinstein, Saul A., and Kochan, Thomas A. *Learning from Saturn: Possibilities for Corporate Governance and Employee Relations*. Ithaca, N.Y.: Cornell University Press, 2001.

Salpukas, Agis. "PECO and Unicom to Merge in Big Bet on Nuclear Power." *New York Times*, Sept. 24, 1999, p. C5.

Samborn, Hope Viner. "The Vanishing Trial." *ABA Journal*, Oct. 2002, 88.

Sander, Frank (ed.). *Emerging ADR Issues in State and Federal Courts*. Chicago: ABA Litigation Section, 1991.

Schlichter, Sumner H., Healy, James J., and Livernash, E. Robert. *The Impact of Collective Bargaining on Management*. Washington, D.C.: Brookings Institution, 1960.

Schuler, Randall S. "Repositioning the Human Resource Function: Transformation or Demise." In Raymond A. Noe, John R. Hollenbeck, Barry Gerhart, and Patrick M. Wright (eds.), *Readings in Human Resource Management*. Burr Ridge, Ill.: Irwin, 1994.

Schuler, Randall S. "Strategic Human Resources Management: Linking the People with the Strategic Needs of the Business." In Raymond A. Noe, John R. Hollenbeck, Barry Gerhart, and Patrick M. Wright (eds.), *Readings in Human Resource Management*. Burr Ridge, Ill.: Irwin, 1994.

Seeber, Ronald L., and Gray, Lois (eds.). *Under the Stars: Labor Relations in Arts and Entertainment*. Ithaca, N.Y.: ILR Press, 1996.

Seeber, Ronald L., Schmidle, Timothy B., and Smith, Robert S. *An Evaluation of the New York State Workers' Compensation Pilot Program for Alternative Dispute Resolution*. Albany: New York State Workers' Compensation Board, Dec. 2001.

Senge, Peter M. *The Fifth Discipline: The Art and Practice of the Learning Organization*. New York: Doubleday/Currency, 1990.

Shell Oil Corp. *Shell RESOLVE, Progress Report*. Houston, Tex.: Shell Oil Corp., 1998.

Sherman, Mark. "Is There a Mediator in the House? Using In-House Neutrals," *Dispute Resolution Journal* 50, Apr. 1995, 48.

Slaikeu, Karl A., and Hasson, Ralph H. *Controlling the Costs of Conflict*. San Francisco: Jossey-Bass, 1996.

"Social Contract," *Encyclopedia Britannica*. [http://www.britannica.com/eb/article?eu=70216#cite]. Accessed on Oct. 22, 2002.

Society for Human Resource Management. [http://www.shrm.org/press/default.asp?page=history.html]. Accessed Oct. 23, 2002.

Sockell, Donna, Lewin, David, and Lipsky, David B. (eds.). *Advances in Industrial and Labor Relations*, Vol. 5. Greenwich, Conn.: JAI Press, 1991.

Steelworkers v. American Manufacturing Co. 80 S. Ct. 1343 (1960).

Steelworkers v. Enterprise Wheel and Car Corp. 80 S. Ct. 1358 (1960).

Steelworkers v. Warrior and Gulf Navigation. 80 S. Ct. 1347 (1960).

Sternlight, Jean R. "Mandatory Binding Arbitration and the Demise of the Seventh Amendment Right to a Jury Trial." *Ohio State Journal of Dispute Resolution* 16, 2001, 669–733.

Stone, Katherine Van Wezel. "Mandatory Arbitration of Individual Employment Rights: The Yellow Dog Contract of the 1990s." *Denver University Law Review* 73, 1996, 1017–1050.

"Symposium on the Impact of Mediation: 25 Years After the Pound Conference." *Ohio State Journal on Dispute Resolution* 17, 2002.

Taft, Philip. *Organized Labor in American History*. New York: HarperCollins, 1964.

Trachte-Huber, E. Wendy, and Huber, Stephen K. (eds.). *Alternative Dispute Resolution: Strategies for Law and Business*. Cincinnati: Anderson Publishing Co., 1996.

Trice, Harrison M., and Beyer, Janice M. *The Cultures of Work Organizations*. Upper Saddle River, N.J.: Prentice Hall, 1993.

Ulrich, Dave. *Human Resource Champions: The Next Agenda for Adding Value and Delivering Results*. Boston: Harvard Business School Press, 1997.

Unified Court System of New York. *The Mediation Alternative Pilot Program*. New York: Unified Court System of New York State, Jan. 2002.

U.S. Bureau of the Census. *Historical Statistics of the United States*. Washington, D.C.: U.S. Government Printing Office, 1970.

U.S. Department of Labor. *Report and Recommendations: The Commission on the Future of Worker-Management Relations*. Washington, D.C.: U.S. Government Printing Office, 1994.

U.S. Department of Labor. *Working Together for Public Service: Report of the U.S. Secretary of Labor's Task Force on Excellence in State and Local Government Through Labor-Management Cooperation*. Washington, D.C.: U.S. Government Printing Office, 1996.

U.S. Department of Labor. *Report on the American Workforce*. Washington, D.C.: U.S. Government Printing Office, 2001.

U.S. Department of Labor. Bureau of Labor Statistics. *Employment and Earnings*. Washington, D.C.: U.S. Government Printing Office, Jan. 2001.

U.S. Equal Employment Opportunity Commission. Policy statement on alternative dispute resolution on July 10, 1997.

U.S. General Accounting Office. *Employment Discrimination: Most Private Sector Employers Use Alternative Dispute Resolution*. Washington, D.C.: U.S. Government Printing Office, 1995.

U.S. General Accounting Office. *Alternative Dispute Resolution: Employers' Experiences with ADR in the Workplace*. Washington, D.C.: U.S. Government Printing Office, 1997.

Verma, Anil. "Union and Nonunion Industrial Relations at the Plant Level." Unpublished Ph.D. dissertation, Massachusetts Institute of Technology, 1983.

Volz, Marlin M., and Goggin, Edward P. (eds.). *Elkouri and Elkouri: How Arbitration Works* (5th ed.). Washington, D.C.: Bureau of National Affairs, 1997.

Von Bertalanffy, Ludwig. "General Systems Theory: A New Approach to the Unity of Science." *Human Biology* 23, Dec. 1951, 302–361.

Walton, Richard E., and McKersie, Robert B. *A Behavioral Theory of Labor Negotiations: An Analysis of a Social Interaction System* (2nd ed.). Ithaca, N.Y.: ILR Press, 1991. (Originally published in 1965.)

Weston, Alan F., and Feliu, Alfred G. *Resolving Employment Disputes Without Litigation*. Washington, D.C.: Bureau of National Affairs, 1988.

"Writing a New Social Contract." *Business Week*, Mar. 11, 1996.

Yilmaz, Yesim. "Private Regulation: A Real Alternative for Regulatory Reform." *Policy Analysis*, Apr. 20, 1998, 1–34.

About the Authors

DAVID B. LIPSKY is professor of industrial and labor relations and director of the Institute on Conflict Resolution at Cornell University. He also serves as director of educational planning and review for eCornell, Cornell University's distance learning subsidiary. The Institute on Conflict Resolution engages in teaching, research, and outreach programs in the field of alternative dispute resolution. It also serves as the lead organization of the Alliance for Education in Dispute Resolution, a nationwide consortium consisting of eighteen universities and professional organizations in the dispute resolution field.

Lipsky served as dean of the School of Industrial and Labor Relations from 1988 until 1997. Between 1997 and 1999, he established and served as the first director of Cornell's Office of Distance Learning, the predecessor organization of eCornell. He has been a member of the Cornell University faculty since 1969. He received his B.S. degree in 1961 from the School of Industrial and Labor Relations at Cornell and his Ph.D. degree in economics in 1967 from M.I.T. In his research and teaching activities, he primarily focuses on negotiation, conflict resolution, and collective bargaining.

Lipsky is the author of over forty-five articles and the author or editor of seventeen books and monographs, including *Collective Bargaining in American Industry: Contemporary Perspectives and Future Directions* (1987), *Strikers and Subsidies: The Influence of Government Transfer Programs on Strike Activity* (1989), *The Appropriate*

Resolution of Corporate Disputes: A Report on the Growing Use of ADR in U.S. Corporations (1998, with Ronald L. Seeber), and *The Arbitration Profession in Transition: A Survey of the National Academy of Arbitrators* (2000, with Michel Picher). His latest book is *Negotiations and Change: From the Workplace to Society* (2003, coedited with Thomas A. Kochan).

RONALD L. SEEBER is executive director of the Institute on Conflict Resolution. He is also associate professor and associate dean at the School of Industrial and Labor Relations at Cornell University. Seeber's research activities have covered a wide range of topics in the field of labor-management relations that reflect his interest in union and management strategies in the workplace and their connection to collective bargaining in the United States.

Seeber has been an active participant in the professional meetings of the Academy of Management, the Industrial Relations Research Association (IRRA), and the University and College Labor Education Association. Seeber has published extensively in scholarly academic journals. He has authored or edited six books on labor relations topics, including *Under the Stars: Essays on Labor Relations in Arts and Entertainment* (1995). He also is the coeditor of *Research in the Sociology of Organizations: Unions and Labor Relations* (1993) and *Restoring the Promise of American Labor Law* (1994). Most recently, he has been involved in several studies of alternative dispute resolution in the United States: the use of ADR by American corporations, a pilot project on ADR in Workers' Compensation in New York, and a multiyear project on the use of mediation by the U.S. Department of Labor.

RICHARD D. FINCHER is managing partner of Workplace Conflict Resolutions (WCR), a full-service ADR consulting practice. His business provides mediation and arbitration services to litigants, workplace dispute systems services, ADR training, and class action services.

As a full-time mediator and arbitrator, Fincher serves on the Commercial, Mass Claims, and Employment Panels of the American Arbitration Association and on the Employment Panel of the CPR Institute for Dispute Resolution. The scope of his caseload includes commercial and employment litigation. Prior to establishing his neutral practice, Fincher served as a senior executive in law and human resources with three Fortune 50 corporations. A nationally known expert on workplace conflict resolution, he frequently lectures on design, implementation, and assessment of workplace systems.

Fincher is a faculty member of the College of Business at Arizona State University, where he teaches dispute resolution. His is a national co-chair of the Workplace Section of the Association of Conflict Resolution (ACR). He received his undergraduate degree in industrial relations from Cornell University and his law degree from DePaul University College of Law. He lives and works in Phoenix, Arizona.

Index